RESEARCHING
RACISM

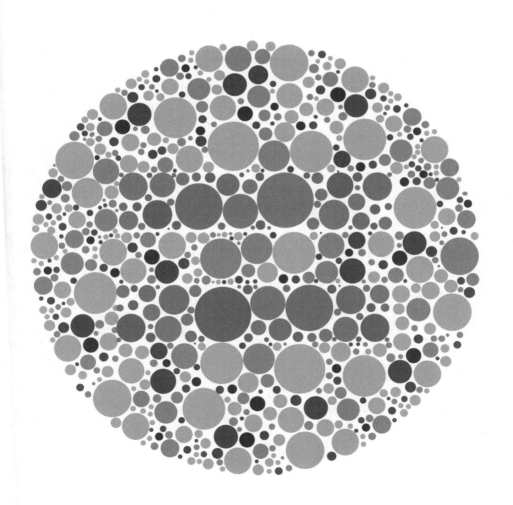

For Yasmine, Ibrahim, Zayd and Iyla
For Elke

MUZAMMIL QURAISHI & ROB PHILBURN

RESEARCHING
RACISM

A **GUIDE BOOK** *for* **ACADEMICS & PROFESSIONAL INVESTIGATORS**

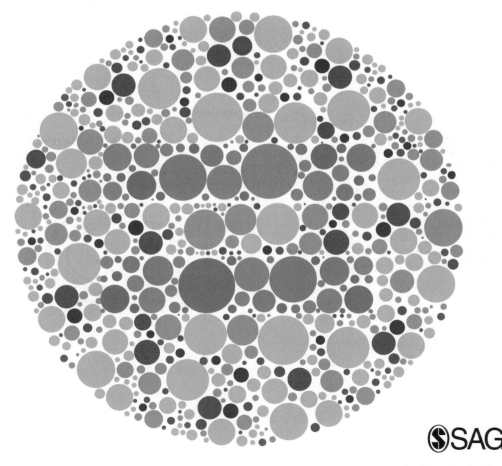

⑤SAGE

Los Angeles | London | New Delhi
Singapore | Washington DC

Los Angeles | London | New Delhi
Singapore | Washington DC

SAGE Publications Ltd
1 Oliver's Yard
55 City Road
London EC1Y 1SP

SAGE Publications Inc.
2455 Teller Road
Thousand Oaks, California 91320

SAGE Publications India Pvt Ltd
B 1/I 1 Mohan Cooperative Industrial Area
Mathura Road
New Delhi 110 044

SAGE Publications Asia-Pacific Pte Ltd
3 Church Street
#10-04 Samsung Hub
Singapore 049483

Editor: Chris Rojek
Assistant editor: Gemma Shields
Production editor: Katherine Haw
Copyeditor: Jane Fricker
Proofreader: Christine Bitten
Marketing manager: Michael Ainsley
Cover design: Francis Kenney
Typeset by: C&M Digitals (P) Ltd, Chennai, India
Printed in Great Britain by Henry Ling Limited at
    The Dorset Press, Dorchester, DT1 1HD

Library of Congress Control Number: 2014954627

British Library Cataloguing in Publication data

A catalogue record for this book is available from
the British Library

ISBN 978-1-84787-533-4
ISBN 978-1-84787-534-1 (pbk)

At SAGE we take sustainability seriously. Most of our products are printed in the UK using FSC papers and boards.
When we print overseas we ensure sustainable papers are used as measured by the Egmont grading system.
We undertake an annual audit to monitor our sustainability.

CONTENTS

LIST OF BOXES AND CASE STUDIES

Boxes

Case Studies

ABOUT THE AUTHORS

Muzammil Quraishi is a Senior Lecturer in Criminology and Criminal Justice at the University of Salford. He is author of numerous texts on Muslim populations with regards to offending and victimisation. His research interests include Islamic jurisprudence, religion/ethnicity in prison, colonialism and comparative criminology. His methodological leanings are towards qualitative ethnographic research informed by the critical race theory perspective.

His latest work involves collaborative criminological research in Malaysia examining, *inter alia,* crimes of apostasy, rehabilitation detention centres and the treatment of sexual offenders. He convenes and teaches on a number of postgraduate and undergraduate modules covering topics such as criminal justice and human rights, intersectionality and crime, ethnicity and race and criminological theory.

Rob Philburn is a lecturer in Sociology at the University of Salford. His research interests and previous publications centre upon social interaction, the sociological analysis of conversational interaction, ethnography and the sociology of Erving Goffman. He also has interests in face-work and politeness studies; social stigma; youth and criminal gangs. He convenes sociological modules including topics of symbolic interactionism, research methods and theoretical sociology.

ACKNOWLEDGEMENTS

This text has had a considerably long gestation period throughout which we have been extremely grateful for the patience, professionalism and guidance from our editorial and support team at SAGE. We would like to thank Jai Seaman, Martine Jonsrud, Gemma Shields and Chris Rojek in particular.

Thanks are also due to our colleagues at the University of Salford for their kind support, input and reflection along the way, particularly Tina Patel for permitting us to share a current working project with the readers.

Muzammil Quraishi and Rob Philburn

INTRODUCTION

The title on the front of this text has two meanings, and reflects two intentions on our part. First, we aim to equip you, whatever your stage as a researcher or practitioner, with a body of background knowledge and conceptual awareness that will enable you to confidently conduct your own research into racism. Second, we want to recount our own research, presenting this to you in a meaningful and illustrative way. This text does not provide an encyclopaedic reference source of race and racism, nor does it constitute a traditional 'methods' book as such. Rather, the text seeks to bring together these two aspects of the book in a meaningful and manageable way. In this sense, the text is, and should be read and used as, a guidebook rather than a manual. To that extent, the text seeks to illuminate and direct, rather than prescribe and instruct.

Three key guiding principles of the text are to seek clarity, coherence and contextualisation of an understandably complex phenomenon. These concerns have very much guided the content and organisation of the material presented here. For example, the first three chapters of the book are devoted to outlining origins, conceptualisation, and legislative and policy frameworks of race and racism. This focus on historical, conceptual and legislative context may seem at first unconventional for a text that has 'researching' as part of the title. However, we feel that our discussion in the early chapters of the text is not only instructive, but essential for all researchers of race and racism in contemporary society.

Two obvious frameworks running through the text are the temporal and spatial contexts of researching race and racism in contemporary society. In terms of the former, although we begin with, and return to, the historical context of race and racism, our emphasis is very much on contemporary society. The relationship between the historical and the contemporary is a recurrent theme, and one which we urge you not to underplay or neglect. In terms of the latter, our focus is very much on a particular spatial context – that of the UK. Having said that, we hope to show that our discussion throughout has a wider, global relevance. Indeed, we recognise that any discussion of racism, even at a local level, must be couched in a global context. Part of the reason we have chosen to focus in large part on a particular contemporary context – that of the UK – is to clearly and coherently articulate the relationship between the historical and the contemporary, the global and the local.

Whilst recognising the complexity of racism in academia we also illustrate that governments and policy makers, nevertheless, have to make sense of the phenomenon and convert it into statutes, policies and procedures which recognise its abhorrence and the political struggles to counter it. Furthermore, the text illustrates why a sociological or criminological lens is an appropriate means for researching racism given it resides in institutions, arises out of interactions and informs the ascription and claiming of identities. We argue it is through the contributions from sociological theory and research that scholars are equipped with the tools and means to make sense of racism in contemporary society.

These links and points of coherence and contradiction, the possibilities and problems that they manifest, are revealed and examined in three case studies which provide a qualitative examination of quite specific racial identities, particular to UK society. From a purely research perspective, the case studies illustrate the use of some of the research methods discussed in the chapters that precede them, the sort of data these can generate, and the depth and richness that these data provide. Each of these case studies also reflects a criminological approach to understanding race and racism in contemporary society. We recognise that this is just one way in which the notion of race can be sociologically examined but we are eager to emphasise two points. The first is that racism often constitutes a 'crime', in both the moral and legal senses, with consequences for both victims and perpetrators. The second is to uncover the intimate relationship between prevailing notions of such things as deviance, threat and criminality, and racial characteristics attached and attributed to certain groups or persons. We will illustrate how such thought both has a long history and continues to be manifest in a number of ways in contemporary society.

The case studies map onto a chronology in social science research in terms of the stages researchers typically go through from planning to the full execution of a project. The first case study (Rationalising Racist Attacks, see pages 79–90) presents a project which is currently being undertaken as we go to print and usefully demonstrates, *inter alia*, the challenges of addressing ethical considerations whilst negotiating access to a research field. The second case study (Transnationality in the Lives of Muslim Ex-offenders, see pages 90–103) is an example of a pilot study, typically undertaken by researchers as a prelude to a more substantial project. The final case study (The Construction of Racial 'No-Go' Zones, see pages 102–112) illustrates a full qualitative project and an example of an academic output or research paper.

The approach explained above has been adopted to some extent at the cost of a broader and less contextualised overview of research methods, However, as we have noted, this text should not be regarded as a 'how to do' manual of research.

In terms of our research position, as will become quickly evident, our emphasis is on qualitative methodology. As we shall discuss at various points in the text, we recognise the uses and sometimes usefulness of quantitative research. However, we argue and illustrate that a qualitative approach is better suited to solve the puzzles and address the complexities of issues in race and racism in contemporary society, from particular personal experiences to broader institutional organisations.

There is also a personal dimension to the text. At one level, this refers to the emphasis we put on race and racism as 'experienced' phenomena. Our emphasis on the personal side of race and racism is evident in our discussion of research methods. At another level, the discussion throughout and the materials we present are very much based on our personal experience of researching race and racism, as much as on our professional expertise.

Finally, in choosing to write such a book as a monograph, rather than as, for example, an edited collection of chapters on particular aspects of researching race and racism or traditional research methods text, we hope not only to reflect researching as an activity we have carried out, but also to generate some coherence across successive chapters, and the text as a whole.

In Chapter 1 we begin by providing an historical overview of the notion of race. We focus in particular on the period known as the Enlightenment, and the practices and processes of racialisation that marked this period. In contexts such as scientific classification, political discourse and militaristic expansion, we show how notions of race were at the core of much Enlightenment thinking. In particular, we focus on the British context. We do this for a number of reasons, none more so than British colonialism that had notions of and discourses about race as one of its key components, but also because we focus throughout on the British context, and ultimately present two case studies that reveal particularities about race and racism in contemporary Britain. Although largely historical in nature, the chapter moves on to understand how a racialised historical legacy of the Enlightenment can be found in contemporary society, located within populist representations and debates about race, criminality and deviance.

In Chapter 2 we examine more closely the concept of race, and in doing so reveal the sheer complexity of conceptualising race and of defining racism. Our emphasis in this chapter is not on how race points to some external objective category – as seen in much Enlightenment thought discussed in the previous chapter – but on how notions of race, and indeed definitions of racism, are the outcome of social processes through which persons become defined as such. In this chapter we discuss in some detail a range of potentially racist behaviours which run through contemporary society. One point of emphasis in the chapter is on how racist behaviour can operate at both an institutional and individual level and, as we shall show in Chapter 6, at the intersection between the institutional and the individual. However, we also draw attention to the myriad of cultural contexts and social situations that mark contemporary everyday life – and the social interaction that occurs in and constitutes them, in which persons might find themselves – and find race is in some way an, or at, issue. The implication here, and one that we shall focus on in Chapter 4, is the importance of understanding race and racism as part of everyday life, in the communities and groups that form the backdrop of everyday life. In this latter context, what we draw attention to is what we shall refer to in Chapter 4 as 'institutionalised racism'. Alongside alerting the reader to what racism is in contemporary society, a key aim in this chapter is to warn against essentialist arguments surrounding race. The former will be dealt with to some extent in our discussions of the meaning attributed to any given social action in Chapter 4; the latter in our discussion of sociological approaches to understanding experience, meaning and action in Chapter 4, and the development of the notion of intersectionality we discuss in Chapter 7. These discussions also point us in the direction of how notions of race can, and are, used in contemporary society in the processes of identity construction, including in attempts to both exert and claim power. Finally, as in Chapter 1, we focus on the particular context of the UK, with particular reference to issues surrounding Islamophobia and notions of Asian (Muslim) folk devils developed in the UK media (an issue that will in large part inform the case studies we present in Chapter 6).

In Chapter 3 we outline anti-racist and anti-discriminatory policy and legislation as both the reflection of understandings of race and racisms and the context in which particular actions and behaviours are understood (including a range of criminal offences). As in Chapters 1 and 2, we provide an historical grounding to the discussion, but point also to contemporary society, including contemporary forms of media and communication which have been the focus of recent legislation against racist and discriminatory practice. We focus on a European and more specifically a UK context in our discussion, but try to point also to wider, more international and global concerns with racist and discriminatory practice. The civil and criminal legal options and individual redress in incidents of racial discrimination are argued to be dependent upon a wide range of extra-legal factors and, although various legislation exists to counter racism, we suggest that the figures on race hate crime in the UK are a sober indicator of the ineffectiveness of such law to prevent significant acts of discrimination and racial violence from escalating in the UK and Europe. Part of the rationale for including the discussion in this chapter is to point to potential documentary sources for further examination in your research into race and racism (something we shall take up in more detail in Chapter 5).

In Chapter 4 we extend our focus on contemporary society with a closer examination of race and racism as part of everyday life. Consolidating much of our discussion in Chapters 1–3, the chapter suggests ways in which the researcher into race and racism can start to examine a range of contemporary sites, settings and contexts. Our focus here, and in subsequent chapters, is on the ways in which race and racism is experienced, defined and given meaning in any given social or cultural context, and in the way it is present in institutions, informs interaction and forms the basis of identities. In preparation for the following chapter, we discuss more explicitly the ontological and epistemological issues that have been implicitly touched on in Chapters 1–3, and outline a series of theoretical approaches to understanding everyday life that allow for an examination of some of the issues mentioned above. One central argument we advance is the need to conduct qualitative research if one is to fully appreciate and understand race and racism, and avoid some of the pitfalls mentioned in previous chapters. Finally, we draw the reader's attention to what we refer to as the personal side of researching race and racism. This is particularly important to us, as we have found, and will illustrate in the discussion of our case studies in Chapter 6, that researcher biography is something that is omnipresent in research.

In Chapter 5, although attempting to contextualise our discussion, our focus turns quite deliberately to qualitative research methods. The chapter does not constitute a 'catch-all' of qualitative research methods, which would be beyond the scope of a single chapter (or even a volume of this size), but rather aims to present for the reader an introductory set of comments on qualitative research methods and methodology.

We begin by examining documentary sources, several of which have been pointed to in earlier chapters. Following this we examine the centrality of language to everyday life, interaction, and to some extent, identities. The bulk of the chapter examines ethnographic work and the various contingencies that can arise when exposing oneself to and immersing oneself in the lifeworld of those persons and groups in naturally occurring sites, settings and contexts. The chapter concludes by examining ways in which analysis of qualitative data might be carried out.

Whereas Chapter 5 examines qualitative research methods, and touches on issues discussed in preceding chapters, in something of an abstract manner, Chapter 6 is noticeably concrete. In the chapter we present three case studies which illustrate many of the issues we discuss in the preceding chapter: the historical roots and legacy of race and racialisation; the legislative context; conceptual debates; the legacy in contemporary society; issues surrounding identity and belonging; and the qualitative approach to research practice. Nevertheless, the chapter is not simply illustrative in nature, but builds on and develops a set of very particular issues and concerns that we ultimately argue, in the following chapter, are essential for research into race and racisms in contemporary society. Each of the studies presented outlines particular substantive issues pertaining to notions of race. In the first of the three case studies, we engage with victims' perspective of racism to examine how they make sense of racial attacks. In the second case study (pages 90–103) our focus is on the social construction of public urban places and spaces, with an emphasis on how places and spaces can come to be defined and experienced along racial lines. In the third case study (pages 103–113) we look at a quite different context – that of the 'total institution' of the prison – and examine more closely the notions of how race – along with other variables such as faith, class, age and gender – inform identities. Although three quite different institutional – and institutionalised – contexts are examined, each study reflects the focus in the preceding chapters by being historically and culturally grounded in each piece of research, combining an historical background with a contemporary research focus, and highlighting the cultural and social contexts, along with prevailing political and popular discourses, in which each study was carried out. In addition, each study illustrates how a range of different methods outlined in the previous chapter have been applied, how conceptual and theoretical understanding has been pointed to, and how some of the issues we point to in previous chapters (access, sampling, biography, ethical issues) have been managed by the researcher. The nature of the data presented in this chapter reflects the focus on accessing meaning and experience from a first-person perspective, and to that end, is quite personal and candid in nature. However, what we also seek to demonstrate in this chapter is the uses to which quantitative data are put by various institutions and agencies, as well as the uses to which they may be put by you as a researcher of race and racism. As we noted in the previous chapter, although our focus will be on qualitative methodology, we recognise the importance of quantitative data, particularly for providing contextualisation, as illustrated in this chapter. Although the focus is partly on the experience of British Asians, again, in using case studies taken from a particular social, cultural, political and historical context, we also try to expand our discussion to more global issues pertinent to race and racism, and the practice of research into these phenomena.

In Chapter 7 we return to the issue of intersectionality introduced earlier in the text. Extending the discussion that ran through the preceding chapter, we argue that the concept has travelled significantly from its roots in Black feminist legal scholarship but that it also presents some significant conceptual and methodological challenges for research on racism. This chapter outlines both the complexity of the concept as well as suggestions and methodological frameworks through which intersectional research may provide a useful lens for the study of racism.

Finally we have included an Appendix of what we feel are useful materials pertaining to many of the issues we deal with in preceding chapters.

Together, these chapters provide a clear, coherent and contextualised set of inroads into conducting race and racism research in contemporary society.

We have tried to gear our discussion to appeal to a range of researchers into race and racism in contemporary society – professionals and practitioners working in a range of contexts and settings, academics working in the field of race and racism, and students at both undergraduate and postgraduate level. However, we would also hope that those with a broader interest in race and racism will find the material and discussion over the following pages useful and illuminating.

We would not try to prescribe 'how to read this book', however, our suggestion is that, rather than 'dip in and out of' the text (as might be done with a manual), you read the text as it is presented, chapter by chapter. We feel this is important as any research into race and racism in contemporary society must take into account the wider contextual issues we discuss in the earlier chapters, and we have designed the book with this specifically in mind.

Finally, in terms of what we hope you get out of this book, we would hope that the discussion brings you to greater awareness, comprehension and appreciation of the origins and roots of racism. In one sense, we hope that this provides something not only of an introduction to, but of a pathway into researching race and racism in contemporary society. Alongside our efforts to make this text informative, equally – and perhaps more so – we have striven to make the material presented and discussions in and across the chapters both relevant and useful. We hope that this relevance and usefulness bears fruit in your future research into race and racism.

THE HISTORY OF RACE

Keywords: *history, Antiquity, Enlightenment, Social Darwinism, eugenics, 'science of race'*

The phenomenon of racism occupies a controversial and powerful position in contemporary societies; it has become embedded in discussions of inequality, oppression and discrimination. The purpose of this chapter is to elucidate the historical concept of 'race' upon which modern racism is founded.

The questions raised are:

- How are such historical events related to our contemporary understanding of race?
- How does the former treatment of colonial subjects influence their current socio-economic positions?
- Are the origins and vocabulary of contemporary racial discrimination traceable to the not so distant past?

Racism and the History of 'Race'

Academics are far from united in their approach regarding how racism is defined; whilst some consider it a reflection of class inequalities in a capitalist society (Miles, 1989), others emphasise a need to evaluate the multiple ways in which racisms have been historically constructed (Goldberg, 1993). Furthermore, for some the focus should be on understanding the concept of 'racialisation', i.e. how some groups of people become socially constructed as 'races' which are biologically or culturally inferior (Back and Solomos, 2000). In order to fully comprehend how such divergent approaches have arisen we must explore the very origins of the modern concept of 'race' itself.

Earliest Notions of 'Race' and Racial Difference

Some scholars have asserted that the roots of racism pre-date the science of race which emerged during the nineteenth century. It has been noted that in Antiquity the Babylonian Talmud construed humankind as descendants of the three sons of Noah. According to certain religious narratives and mythology some of those descended from Ham were 'cursed' by being black. Some of those descended from Ham were cursed by being black (El-Hamel, 2002; Garner, 2010). Furthermore, the Greek philosopher Aristotle, whilst not discussing specific 'races', distinguished between Greeks being free by nature but barbarians being slaves by nature (Lewis, 2003). Scholars have also highlighted the common use of black slaves amongst early Jewish, Christian and Islamic societies despite the absence of any theologically sanctioned differentiation of black people amongst these Abrahamic faiths (Byron, 2003; Schwartz, 1997). Furthermore, the expulsion of Muslim and Jewish populations from Spain as part of the violent *Reconquista* of the fifteenth century was built upon the *cleanliness of blood doctrine* which sought to establish a firm demarcation between those within white Christian Europe and barbarians outside its fold (Lacey, 1983).

Such conceptions of the world had a profound impact upon European expansion, colonisation and the consequent subjugation and indeed destruction of native peoples in Africa, Asia, Australasia and the Americas.

It is important to recall these historical contexts for they arguably shape the discourse about race which permeated the subsequent eras. However, the modern concept of race can be traced to the European Enlightenment, although as discussed below, distinctions must be drawn between pre-Enlightenment prejudice, the universal commonality of humankind principles of early Enlightenment thinkers and the subsequent overturning of this position following the expansion of European capitalism.

The European Enlightenment and 'Race'

Jurists applaud the intellectual inroads made by Enlightenment thinkers such as Locke, Beccaria and Rousseau with regard to checking the vagaries and harshness of European legal systems of the time. However, there are other less explored consequences of Enlightenment scholarship which arguably compounded discriminatory beliefs of this period. The scholar Emmanuel Chukwudi Eze asserts that the modern concept of 'race' can be traced to the Enlightenment during the late eighteenth and early nineteenth centuries (Eze, 1997). The assertion made by Eze, and others such as Said (1978) and Gilroy (1993), is that the Enlightenment scholars, including Hume, Kant and Voltaire, blended populist and early scientific notions of 'race' to articulate an 'Age of Reason' which was essentially racially constructed. Whilst humankind was free to use reason, this reason was the preserve of white Europeans within the fold of a civilised Europe; those lands outside Europe were deemed void of reason and consequently marked by savagery and barbarism (Eze, 1997).

A closer examination of Enlightenment scholarship, however, reveals a series of complex intellectual developments which confirms that early thinkers such as Rousseau, Locke and Degerando conceived a common humanity devoid of racial hierarchical divisions between Europeans and non-Europeans. Whilst some Enlightenment thinkers did espouse what could be deemed racist views, it is important not to wholly judge their writings with twenty-first-century eyes. For example, assertions of racism in Hume's work may be contested since his work contains both a footnote to a text which ranks white Europeans above black people but also a subsequent text which is diametrically opposed to this ranking. Similarly, Buffon accepted the existence of distinct races of humans and slavery but also claimed that human differences were determined by environmental and cultural factors (Malik, 1996).

A clear distinction can be made between the universality of humankind principles articulated by the first architects of the Enlightenment such as Rousseau, Locke and Degerando and the racialised discourse and thoughts of others inspired by Enlightenment thinkers one hundred years later such as Thomas Huxley in Britain. Kenan Malik asserts that '*belief in reason, espousal of the scientific method and a universalist conviction do not of themselves imply a racial viewpoint*' (Malik, 1996: 41). According to Malik, the Enlightenment is a useful starting point for understanding racism but '*not because Enlightenment discourse was imbricated with the concept of race, but because through Enlightenment philosophy humanity had for the first time a concept of a human universality that could transcend perceived differences. Before the modern concept of race could develop, the modern concepts of equality and humanity had to develop too*' (Malik, 1996: 42).

The assertion, therefore, that the modern concept of race is simply a continuation of age-old prejudices is contested. The early common humanity view, espoused by thinkers such as Locke, was overturned with the arrival of capitalism. An expanding bourgeoisie in Europe were emboldened by the equality principles of the Enlightenment aiming to dismantle the feudal system and ultimately culminating in the French Revolution. However, the social and political upheaval also gave vent to a backlash against the Enlightenment amongst some sections of the bourgeoisie. A particular contradiction arose amongst thinkers about equality and more particularly towards the ownership of property. How could the belief in equality be reconciled with defending the inequality of private property? Rousseau had argued that there were differences between natural and artificial inequality, the '*modern concept of race arises from the attempt to attribute to nature the inequality that Rousseau rightly regards as the product of the moral or political domain*' (Malik, 1996: 60).

The 'Science of Race'

In the mid-eighteenth century the discipline of biology was making significant progress in terms of classifying the natural world. Carl Linne (Linneaus) established a classification system for plants before establishing a racial taxonomy for his 'homo sapiens' construed within an hierarchy based upon skin colour with white humans on top (Eze, 1997). Linne described the white race as:

... 'inventive, full of ingenuity, orderly and governed by laws' whereas 'negroes were endowed with all the negative qualities which made them a counterfoil for the superior race; they were regarded as lazy, devious and unable to govern themselves'. (Mosse, 1978: 20)

In 1775, Johann Fredrich Blumenbach developed his physical anthropology and the most widely accepted racial taxonomies of the period originating from skull measurements. He divided humanity into five types based on geographical factors and representing gradations: I. Caucasian, II. Mongolian, III. Ethiopian, IV. Malay and V. American (Blumenbach, 1969 [1775, 1795]). It is worth noting that Blumenbach did not assert any physical hierarchy or ranking amongst humans although he did erroneously claim that the earliest humans were most likely to be white rather than black. Blumenbach established humans were a distinct species (monogeny) and that there was no evidence of cross-species of humans as a result of breeding with animals. Perhaps most importantly, Blumenbach recognised heterogeneity amongst populations living in one geographical location; the classifications represented gradations rather than distinct races (Bhopal, 2007).

The early 'scientific' view of races as fixed and determined buttressed the birth of racist ideology with the writings of Joseph Arthur Gobineau in his essay of 1853 entitled 'The Inequality of Human Races' (Gobineau, 1853). Gobineau is often attributed with the infamous title of 'father of racist ideology' since his work asserted a belief that the decline of civilisation was due to the disease of 'degeneration' of 'racially superior' stock which was 'inbreeding with inferior stock' (Bowling and Phillips, 2002: 2). This work was subsequently translated into German and English providing fuel for the development of white supremacist ideologies in Europe and America.

The absurdity of some early genetics research is particularly well demonstrated by the proponents of polygenesis which asserted that the varied 'races' of man reflected their origins in different animal species. The work of Nott and Gliddon in 1854 entitled *Types of Mankind* included elaborate pictorial examples of how, according to the theorists, contemporary racial attributes could be traced to their distinct evolutionary paths. The theory of polygenesis, therefore, enabled theorists to assert that one race may have originated from bison, whilst another could be traced to the giraffe or ox (Nott and Gliddon, 1854).

Although economic utility rather than racial ideology has been asserted as underpinning slavery (see Malik, 1996), perceptions of humankind divided biologically were instrumental in the expansion and perpetuation of the Atlantic slave trade as well as in the eradication of native peoples in the Americas, Australasia and South Africa during European colonial expansion. This was made possible in part by the ability of white Europeans to view such expansion as part of the natural order of events whereby racially superior races superseded those deemed racially inferior (Fryer, 1984). Similarly, such reasoning was expanded to include beliefs that white Europeans were empowered via divine guidance and endorsement to civilise the world and this eventually led to the development of moral trusteeship and paternalism towards colonial subjects (Bowling and Phillips, 2002).

It was the psychologist and son-in-law of Charles Darwin, Francis Galton, who asserted his objections to the existence of natural equality among humans. In his text of 1869 entitled *Hereditary Genius* Galton developed his theory of 'racial hygiene', which essentially founded the eugenics movement. Galton also founded the use of intelligence testing and in the same text asserts, '*The mistake that the Negroes made in their own matters were so childish, stupid and simpleton-like, as frequently to make me ashamed of my own species*' (Galton, 1869: 339). Galton influenced the birth of psychometry, which was particularly popular during World War II in Britain initially for military recruits and subsequently in the sphere of education. The reduction of human behaviour into testable units was reflective of the essentially anti-democratic nature of the Galton paradigm, centred upon determining why certain people in society should be excluded from decision making (Daniels and Hougton, 1972).

More profound was the development of the eugenics movement which was essentially founded upon Social Darwinian ideology. Advocates for eugenics believed that the state should actively encourage certain populations to breed whilst others should be restricted from doing so, policies extended to the taking of lives if society as a whole would benefit. Such concepts of racial hygiene were actualised most destructively during Nazi rule in Germany from 1933 to 1945. The Nazis resurrected the fictional notion of a superior Aryan race and legislated for the preservation of an assumed German racial purity via the Law for the Protection of German Blood and Honour (1935). This law, *inter alia*, prohibited persons deemed to have German or kindred blood from marrying Jews on the basis that such prohibition would safeguard the future of the German nation. The Nazi racial purification programme included research, experimentation and sterilisation of people designated racially impure, criminals, homosexuals and 'mixed-offspring' of German women and French North African troops based in the Rhineland (Bowling and Phillips, 2002).

Manipulating Racial Identity: Historical Examples

Indentured Labour

Taking into consideration the preceding overview, the following examples demonstrate how notions of race have been socially constructive for 'political' purposes at key moments in the nineteenth century. History has presented many examples from which to demonstrate the creation, maintenance and utilisation of constructions about race; for the purposes of this text the examples are largely, though not exclusively, from British rule in India.

The Emancipation Act of 1833, whilst abolishing slavery, had created the need for the cost-effective provision of labour on plantations. One of the solutions came in the form of indentured labour as part of the nineteenth-century coolie system of Indian and Chinese labour. Between 1834 and 1927, 30 million Indians left India as part of this global division of labour (Davis, 1951). The indentured labourers went to colonies which were governed by Europeans to work on plantations, railroads, canals and in mines. The coolie system was a hybrid system somewhere between slavery and free-waged labour (Banaji, 1933). Scholars have identified evidence, for example in correspondence between plantation owners and British recruitment agents as well as Parliamentary and Royal reports, which illustrates the construction of racial stereotypes by Europeans to entice and govern indentured labourers from Asia (Mahmud, 1997). Indian recruits were deemed useful in disciplining and controlling black labourers who had been labelled as 'lazy, unreliable and dishonest' (Mahmud, 1997: 644). In contrast, an initial stereotype emerged of Indians who were praised for their industriousness, loyalty and respect for authority. The latter shifted once indentured labourers experienced the harsh conditions in plantations and construction sites in the Caribbean, Kenya and East Africa. As resistance and self-preservation movements developed amongst them, the indentured Indians were to become labelled as 'avaricious, jealous, dishonest, idolatrous and filthy' (Mahmud, 1997: 644). Such dissatisfaction with Indian labourers prompted plantation owners to shift their strategies to the Chinese, who for a short time at least were viewed in a positive light.

Martial Races Theory

A further example of racial identity formation and manipulation during European colonial rule is found within the policies and practices of recruitment for the Indian colonial army and the promotion of the martial races theory by the British following the uprisings of 1857. Martial races theory asserts that certain races and people are inherently more martial than others. Martial in this sense was to imply a capacity for warfare, not in a barbaric sense but rather as possession of a military instinct. White Europeans, including the British, were deemed to be martial but this was not extended to all 'races' in India. Until the Indian Mutiny of 1857, the Indian colonial army relied heavily upon soldiers from Bengal who had been compared to the finest Prussian soldiers (Heathcote, 1974). Following the Mutiny the British prohibited recruitment from Bengal and instead developed an elaborate recruitment strategy based on the notion that races in the north of India and from the Punjab were more martial. Simultaneously, Bengalis were now construed as feeble, effeminate and lacking constitution (Mahmud, 1997).

The British went to considerable lengths to identify, document and photograph the ideal and most martial army recruits. Caste and tribal affiliations were often equated to race; Rajputs for example were praised for preservation of their Aryan racial purity through strict adherence to caste. It was not without design that most of the new recruits were from rural peasant populations whilst the Bengalis had included members of the emerging urban middle classes more likely to challenge imperial rule. The legacy of such practices should not be understated since they have arguably influenced not only the current ethnic composition of the Pakistani and Indian military but also reflect the origin of certain stereotypes about contemporary populations in the Indian sub-continent (Cohen, 1971; Quraishi, 2005).

Box 1.1   **The British Obsession with Martial Races**

Recruitment to the Indian army in the late nineteenth and early twentieth centuries was restricted largely to the following groups:

'Pathans from the NW Frontier districts and the independent tribal regions;
Baluchis and Brahuis from Kalat and British Baluchistan;
Sikhs, Jats, Dogras and Muslims from the Punjab;
Garhwalis, Kumaonis and Gurkhas from the Himalayan regions;
Rajputs, Brahmans and Muslims from the Delhi and Hindustan regions;
Rajputs, Jats, Mers and Muslims from Rajastan and central India;
Marathas and Deccani Muslims from Western India;
Christians, Untouchables, Tamils and Muslims from Southern India.'

(Heathcote, 1974: 94)

Criminal Tribes

In addition to the examples above, the British in India also passed specific legislation which deemed sections of Indian society criminal by birth. The legislation had been preceded by a lengthy campaign against 'thagi' or 'thugs' by the Thagi and Dakaiti Department from the 1830s to the 1840s. The thagi campaign reflected ideas about hereditary criminality amongst groups considered hierarchically subordinate to the British both in terms of morality and physiology (Brown, 2001). The British passed the Criminal Tribes Act (Act XXVII) in 1871, in part influenced by the emergence of determinist biological theories about crime in Europe during this period. Under this Act, the colonial authorities in India designated approximately 13 million people as belonging to a criminal tribe (Yang, 1985). Once a local government had designated a group of people as members of a criminal tribe they were subject to registration, surveillance and control which required compulsory reporting at identified police stations as part of a complex pass system. There was no right of appeal to being defined as belonging to a criminal tribe and local officials were empowered to resettle tribes or remove them to a reformatory. Furthermore, it was assumed that criminal genes could be transmitted between criminal tribe members and so inter-marriage within a criminal tribe was prohibited. It was not uncommon for children to be separated from their parents and kept in custody. Breaches of the pass system were met by punitive measures including imprisonment, fines and whipping. It has been argued that a key motivation for the legislation was the control and reclamation of nomadic communities who were deemed unproductive within a colonial economic agenda (Mahmud, 1999; Nigam, 1990).

Ethnographic Showcases

Between 1851 and 1930, European colonial powers were keen to display their advances in industry, agriculture, science and culture via large exhibitions including the Great Exhibition 1851, Colonial and Indian Exhibition 1886, World's Colombian Exposition 1893, Greater Britain Exhibition 1899, Paris World Fair 1878 and Imperial International Exhibition 1909. These events were typically very large affairs and provided opportunities for ritualised competition amongst the social and economic elites of the period. They also reflected an obsession amongst colonial powers with the identification, classification and 'displaying' of 'savage' native tribes and people who had been 'tamed' and subjugated by the white coloniser (Corbey, 1995). The Paris World Fair of 1878 marks the first event where people from non-western cultures were exhibited. Four hundred natives from the French colonies of Indochina, Senegal and Tahiti were displayed in elaborate village sets. The tribes on 'display' were often presented as brutal savages who had been 'tamed' triumphantly by civilising white Europeans. Once more, scholars have argued that these practices reflect the origins of contemporary notions of racial hierarchies and white supremacy (Corbey, 1995; Mahmud, 1997).

The first question you may have of approaching the topics explored above is to ask how do these historical contexts help my understanding about race in the twenty-first century? Surely, are not such misdeeds and outmoded ways of thinking about humans confined to dusty history? Whilst this would be an admirable approach, it would fail to acknowledge the complex legacy that such practices and history have left in their wake. The practices outlined above are simply a fraction of the exchanges between the powerful and powerless over the centuries. They represent the ways in which human populations have been classified and categorised in pseudo-scientific ways based on unsustainable biological categories of race. Any cursory examination of an official form (passport or driver's licence application, crime report, marketing questionnaire) will demonstrate that classifying difference is still very much on the agenda of governments and agencies around the globe. We will now demonstrate some of the ways in which the history discussed above has impacted upon how ethnic minorities in Britain have become criminalised.

Impact of History upon the Contemporary: The Policing of Ethnic Minorities in Britain

The legacy of the events outlined above should not be underestimated and we seek to demonstrate the pervasiveness and impact of the early notions or scientific concepts of race upon contemporary practices. No discussion about racism in contemporary society would be complete without engagement with the ways in which ethnic minorities have become criminalised and over-represented in official criminal statistics. The following discussion outlines the history of conflict in Britain between visible ethnic minorities and the police which perpetuates the myth about racial differences and negative traits being attributed to non-white populations.

The ethnicity and crime debate is based upon the largely consistent over-representation of black and minority ethnic (BME) populations in each stage of the criminal justice system of England and Wales. Simply put, this means that more BME people are stopped and searched, arrested, charged, convicted and sentenced to prison, than is proportionate to their percentage representation within the whole British population as recorded by the Census (Ministry of Justice, 2013a).

The first public concerns aired regarding immigrant populations and crime followed significant in-migration from Britain's former Commonwealth nations following the postwar re-building efforts in the 1950s. Initial migrants were encouraged to come to Britain from the West Indies and Indian sub-continent. Prompted by public concerns about immigration and crime levels, a Parliamentary Select Committee of 1973 concluded that incidents of crime amongst the immigrant population were lower than amongst the white population. However, this initial conformist representation shifted to one of suspect populations following a series of exchanges between black populations and the police during the 1970s and 1980s (Bowling and Phillips, 2002).

The work of Hunte in 1966 demonstrated that black people had become the subject of over-policing within the urban locations where they had tended to settle following the demand for employment and affordable housing (Hunte, 1966). By the 1970s in Birmingham, for example, one report concluded that black people were over-policed by a police force amongst which racist views were widespread (All Faiths for One Race, 1978).

Reports of this period by the Royal Commission on Criminal Procedure 1979 and the Institute for Race Relations 1987 concluded that there was little regard from the police for the human rights of black people. Black people were targeted, repeatedly stopped and searched, the subject of hostile and racially insulting language and often subject to violence upon arrest (IRR, 1987). The character of policing minorities in the inner cities of the UK during the 1970s and 1980s is best described as militaristic, with the deployment of mass stop and search, raids, riot squads and continuous surveillance. The tensions between the police and the black communities during the 1980s is marked by the eruption of public disorder in the predominantly black residential areas of cities across England which included Liverpool, Manchester, Birmingham and London (Bowling and Phillips, 2002).

The policing of criminal offences coincided with the policing of the immigration status of black suspects coupled with the misrepresentation about the extent of drug-related and violent crimes attributed to black males (Gilroy, 2002; Gutzmore, 1983; Hood, 1992). The concept of mugging as a socially constructed moral panic best illustrates exaggerated fears amongst the white British population of violent crime committed by black males (Hall et al., 1978). Academics studying this period point towards the confluence of a number of factors which created a myth around black criminality. Black males were being brought into the criminal justice system by proactive policing methods which targeted symbolic inner-city locations buttressed by myths perpetuated in the media about inherent criminal and anti-authoritarian traits amongst the black population (Gilroy, 2002; Hall et al., 1978).

Therefore, the black community came to know the police and criminal justice system as oppressive forces, whereas the police viewed black neighbourhoods as suspect populations.[1] Research about attitudes held by the police during this period reveals that officers thought black people were 'behaving like animals' or 'bestial' and therefore 'should be shot' (Gilroy, 2002: 132). This rhetoric, in jest or otherwise, is reflective of the dehumanisation of black people and an echo of the colonial discourse outlined at the start of this chapter. Whilst widespread explicit racism amongst the police has now passed, incidents in each decade since the 1980s are clear reflections of the corrupting legacy of the categorisation of humans into distinct races and attribution of deviant traits to visible minorities.

Whilst the over-representation of black people in the criminal justice system has persisted, since the 1990s a new discourse around Asian and more recently Muslim criminals has emerged. Certainly Muslim populations were a constituent part of the black communities targeted during the 1980s, but the trajectory of the discourse about them has taken a distinctly different path whilst illustrating the intersection of identities of faith and ethnicity (Quraishi, 2005).

The construction of Muslim populations as deviant and criminal pre-dates the attacks in the USA on 11 September 2001, although the terrorist events certainly acted as a catalyst for formal surveillance of Muslim populations. Scholars of Islamophobia note that Muslim populations have been depicted in disparaging terms for many centuries, as fundamentalists, book-burners or wife-beaters (Runnymede, 1997). In terms of the criminal justice system, the discourse has emerged as a result of a rising British Muslim prisoner population as well as perceived threats from amongst indigenous Muslims following terrorist offences in London in July 2005. As with black populations before them, British Muslims are presently the subject of disproportionate surveillance by the police and military intelligence pursuant to counter-terrorism measures (Fekete, 2009; Patel and Tyrer, 2011). It brings with it media and political debates about the loyalty of Muslims to Britain against a projected clash of civilisations between Islam and both British secular and Christian values (Kundnani, 2007).

In both of the sample populations discussed above, 'black' people and 'Muslims', the categorisation may give the mistaken impression of distinct homogeneous populations. As we will see later in this text, the formal categorisation of human beings into such groups tends to deny the true diversity within any given group as well as any intersection between them. The historic processes of categorisation, division and dehumanisation have served to perpetuate myths of difference between 'races' rather than emphasise the complexity within and commonalities between what are actually socially, rather than biologically, constructed categories.

Summary

In summary then, in Europe, the historical period known as the Enlightenment initiated various processes of racialisation. These sought to categorise and typify particular races. This was underpinned by scientific aspirations and political dogmas. We focused in large part on the British context, in particular as part of colonialism. However, again, by looking at the UK in particular, we showed how such activities continue in contemporary society, in the way races and racial types are both policed and how popular discourses are constructed around notions of racial types and racial identities. We drew attention to the way the media has fuelled negative stereotyping of racial groups, and a particular point we emphasised was the 'criminalisation' of particular racial groups. Two particular examples we gave in the UK context were the moral panic surrounding Black African, Black Caribbean males in the 1970s, and more recently with the notion of Islamophobia that has developed in the last decade or so. Fundamentally, we have argued that the notion of race is socially constructed. This is something we want to focus on more closely in the following chapter.

Note

1 For a parallel discussion in the USA see Bolton and Feagin (2004).

DEFINING AND CONCEPTUALISING RACISM

Keywords: *racialisation, ethnicity, discrimination, institutional racism, anti-Semitism, Islamophobia*

The main questions or areas for reflection raised by this chapter are:

- How do academics define complex concepts such as ethnicity and racism?
- What are the associated attributes of racism and racialisation?
- How are notions of intersectionality, white governmentality, xeno-racism and religious discrimination relevant to contemporary debates on racism?

The discussion in the previous chapter demonstrated that race is socially constructed rather than biologically determined. Certainly, there are external differences in the way humans appear with regard to skin tone, eye shape and hair colour. However, any attempt to scientifically categorise humans into distinct races based upon these rather arbitrary indicators has been unsustainable since all humans share a common biological origin. This common origin, although questioned by some palaeontologists, has been substantiated by molecular geneticists analysing mitochondrial DNA which links all humans to an African ancestry 200,000 years ago (Cann et al., 1987; Cavalli-Sforza, 2001; Wilson and Cann, 1992).

The common root of racism is to equate superficial external appearances as descriptors of distinct races and then to classify these in terms of superiority or inferiority. The categorisation of humans in this way leads to the emergence of a taxonomy and ranking of populations based on notions of mental, physical and social capacities. This chapter will highlight how we have largely departed from crude notions of race in biological terms and moved towards cultural constructions of race.

Conceptualising Racism

Racialisation

Racialisation is aptly defined by Robert Miles as '*a process of delineation of group boundaries and of allocation of persons within those boundaries by primary reference to (supposedly) inherent and/or biological (usually phenotypical) characteristics*' (Miles, 1982: 157). Therefore, racialisation refers to the social processes through which people become defined as a group with reference to their biological and or cultural characteristics and these are then reproduced and compounded by individuals and institutions. Further interpretations of racialisation emphasise its dehumanising role (Fanon, 1967), or a reaction by white Europeans to colonial subjects (Banton, 1977). A key aspect of the concept is the interplay of power relations within exchanges between different groups of people through which negative and detrimental constructions about particular people are created and maintained. Racialisation depicts a constantly evolving process of social relations, intertwined with sociological concepts of class and labour, not simply about biological or phenotypical categorisation (Miles, 1982). Steve Garner prudently contests the notion that all practices which come under the label of racialisation may be negative by stating:

> ... *the door should be left open to the idea that racialisation may also be a reflexive act initiated towards an emancipatory end – as a form of group solidarity.* (2010: 22)

Examples of such emancipation are found in the politicised resistance of minority populations via movements such as Black Power in the USA and South Asian grass-roots organisations in the UK.

Racialisation may also become combined with criminalisation, which is the process by which some groups in society are more likely to encounter the suspicion of the police and enter the criminal justice system because of an ascription of criminal characteristics (Webster, 2007). The combining of these concepts leads to the racial loading of certain terms such as 'crime' or 'riot'.

Ethnicity

Steve Fenton argues there are many arguments for discrediting the science of race approach. These include acknowledging that it is impossible to sustain a classificatory system of races because the '*degree of variation within postulated races came to be recognised as greater than the variation between them*'; sociological and anthropological observations asserted that historical and cultural difference accounted for differences between people more satisfactorily than race; finally, that the science of racial difference had been '*allied to the denial of dignity and the very right to life of "races" perceived lower and dispensable*' (Fenton, 1999: 5).

Given the discredited scientific notion of 'race' some scholars have advocated the use of the arguably less controversial analytical term 'ethnicity'. Ethnicity usually refers to a group of people having common origins and sharing beliefs, culture or language; it is more pluralistic and fragmented than the concept of race.

Box 2.1	**A Basic Anthropological Model of Ethnicity**

a)   ethnicity is about cultural differentiation, but identity is always a dialectic between similarity and difference;

b)   ethnicity is centrally concerned with culture but it is also rooted in, and to a considerable extent the outcome of, social interaction;

c)   ethnicity is no more fixed or unchanging than the culture of which it is a component or the situation in which it is produced and reproduced;

d)   ethnicity as a social identity is collective and individual, externalised in social interaction and internalised in personal self-identification

(Jenkins, 1997:18).

Although the concept of ethnicity is in some respects less problematic than 'race' there is the possibility that it comes to represent an homogeneous and self-reproducing group which in turn is in fact treated as a distinct race. Furthermore, addressing ethnic differences may become a coded way of speaking about race (Webster, 2007). Scholars have made a distinction between definitions of ethnicity as a form of 'primordialism' based upon certain people sharing a collective memory of the past and situational interpretations which enable '*multi-dimensional ethno-cultural identities*' (Ratcliffe, 2004: 28). Situational interpretations of ethnicity describe the ways in which different social contexts provide arenas for alternate aspects of an individual's identity to surface. An example of this could be a South Asian Pakistani speaking Urdu or Punjabi at home and wearing traditional dress whilst adopting an Anglo–Asian persona or identity and speaking English when attending work, college, school or university (Ratcliffe, 2004).

In the USA the ethnicity paradigm has arguably shifted through three stages. The first stage may be considered the pre-1930s era where the emphasis was upon challenging the biology of race. The second stage was between the 1930s and 1965 where the two recurrent themes of 'assimilation' and 'cultural pluralism' became defined; whilst the third stage represents the post-1965 era of neo-conservatism which expressed opposition to the emerging affirmative anti-discrimination policies (Omi and Winant, 1994).

Definitions of Racism and Associated Concepts

It is more prudent to speak of racisms rather than racism. The distinction emphasises the variety and diversity of behaviours which may fall within the scope of racist actions. This section will include discussion of sociological concepts of racism whilst exploration of the legal definitions and anti-discriminatory strategies will be reserved for the following chapter. It is important to note that the behaviours and practices discussed below are not mutually exclusive categories, for example the 'scientific' racism explored in Chapter 1 may also be understood as a form of direct discrimination; whilst some Islamophobic behaviour can also be seen as a xenophobic or xeno-racist response. The complex layers to racism are comprehensively illustrated by the research of Philomena Essed and her analyses of the everyday experiences of racism of black women in the USA and the Netherlands (Essed, 1991; see Box 2.2).

The scholar David Mason asserts that social scientists risk dilution of the term 'racism' by extending it beyond ideas and beliefs to social structures and practices. For Mason, the difficulty arises when attempting to evaluate whether a particular pattern of discrimination has arisen owing to racism or some other factor such as class. Furthermore, the ambiguity over the meaning of the term for different parties to a debate may limit its usefulness as an analytical concept (Mason, 2000).

It is clear that racism is a very difficult concept to define since it has been used to describe a great variety of behaviours and practices across many centuries and within multiple contexts. Steve Garner, in his text *Racisms* helpfully summarises what he feels are the three basic elements to any definition of racism:

1. **An historical power relationship** in which, over time, groups are *racialised* (that is treated as if specific characteristics were natural and innate to each member of the group).
2. **A set of ideas** [*ideology*] in which the human race is divisible into distinct 'races', each with specific natural characteristics.
3. **Forms of discrimination** flowing from this [*practices*] ranging from denial of access to resources through to mass murder (Garner, 2010: 11).

Box 2.2	Experiences of Racism Reported by Rosa N.

Biological denigration
Overvaluation of white skin colour
To attribute sexual permissiveness [a]

Biological/cultural denigration
To define as overly fertile
Underestimation
Cultural denigration
To pathologise [b]

(Continued)

(Continued)

Personal denigration
Attributing oversensitivity

Cognitive detachment

Neglect/indifference about race relations

Tolerating without accepting

Euro/whitecentrism

Obstacles impeding equal participation

Barring
Avoiding or withdrawal from social contact
Not acknowledging
Contribution/qualification

Denial of conflict

Reluctance to deal with racism
Anger against blacks who point out racism [c]

Management of ethnic difference

Failing to take a stand against racism
Overemphasising difference
Cultural non-recognition
Rejection of 'ethnic' behaviour

Pacification
Patronising behaviour

Denial of dignity
Humiliation/disrespect
Intimidation

Disregard for feelings (racist talk)
Rudeness
Physical violence
Sexual harassment

a.   Includes insinuations about prostitution.
b.   Includes pathologising of culture and personality Rosa N. discusses.
c.   Includes counteractions Rosa N. discusses such as incrimination and other retali-
     ation against blacks who oppose racism.

(Essed, 1991: 183)

It is worth bearing these elements in mind as we progress through this text, particularly when discussing legal attempts to prevent and prosecute racist behaviour as well as when planning research projects on racism.

Prejudice

As with racism, there is no universal definition of prejudice. However, a clear way of conceptualising prejudice is to reflect upon the way you think about other people who are different to you and whether your attitude and behaviour towards them are justified. An important aspect of prejudice is the action of prejudgement: making your mind up about someone or group before any personal experiences or facts are known about them (Clements and Spinks, 2009). Although not all prejudicial thoughts will be vented in discriminatory action it may be viewed as an aspect of the internal thought process which fuels discrimination and racism.

Stereotyping

Stereotyping describes the attribution of essential character traits to members of a visible group. Although the roots of stereotyping may be found in lived experiences it represents a distortion of that reality and an extension of usually negative attributes to a particular group of people. Depictions of minority groups in popular fiction, humour and the visual arts may further work to compound stereotypes and myths such as the belief that black people are more aggressive, more criminal or less intelligent than white people (Back and Solomos, 2000; Gilroy, 2002; Miles and Brown, 2003).

Discrimination

Discrimination is borne of prejudicial views about groups of people, often defined on the basis of their racial or ethnic categorisation. For Clements and Spinks, discrimination and prejudice share common causes which include *ignorance*; *power*; *vulnerability*; *upbringing*; and *conformity* (Clements and Spinks, 2009). Ignorance describes a lack of knowledge about how and why certain people behave the way they do. In the absence of specific knowledge about cultural and religious practices, dress, customs and beliefs there is a possibility that people will rely upon stereotypes and politically constructed information to form their views about others. Within this process there is a danger that 'difference' will become equated with 'threat'.

We have already indicated that an important aspect of racism is the complex interplay and outcome of power relationships. In addition to institutional power, it is useful to consider how individuals may wield power. For example, when evaluating human rights abuses by state officials in countries including India, South Africa, Costa Rica and Palestine, researchers were able to demonstrate the existence of complex power relationships between citizens and junior staff not immediately considered as especially empowered (Jefferson and Jensen, 2009).

For Clements and Spinks, vulnerability describes the sentiments of individuals who fear newcomers that challenge a way of life or access to basic provisions such as jobs, housing and social services (Clements and Spinks, 2009). Another way of interpreting such vulnerability is to view it as a feeling of threat from another way of life, or thinking or practice. Prejudging people who are different from the majority provides a coping mechanism to perceived threat.

Upbringing relates to the processes of socialisation in terms of how individuals are influenced in their attitudes, ideals, morals and world views by their immediate family, friends and social circles. Conformity refers to a willingness to maintain the *status quo*. By way of illustration, research examining racially motivated violence towards BME people in the UK has asserted that a key part of the perpetuation of such behaviour was the inaction and unwillingness to intervene from white community members who arguably shared a degree of empathy with the perpetrators (Hesse et al., 1992; Sibbitt, 1997).

Discrimination may be direct and indirect, the latter is more difficult to ascertain since it is often unintentional. A clear example would be the timetabling of inter-wing football matches in prison on Friday lunchtimes since this is the weekly opportunity for congregational prayers for Muslims. Another would be the setting of minimum height standards for entry into the armed forces or police since it could indirectly discriminate against minority populations with lower than average height.

Institutional Racism

The term 'institutional racism' emerged during the 1960s in the USA (Carmichael and Hamilton, 1968). During the early 1980s a number of cities in England including London, Manchester, Liverpool and Bristol witnessed race riots. The official inquiry into the causes of the disruption in South London was led by Lord Scarman who published his findings in 1981. Lord Scarman had acknowledged that racism could be an outcome of actions despite the absence of an intention to commit racist behaviour. By construing institutional racism as an outcome Scarman was able to assist the legal definition of the concept which required tangible consequences for litigation (Scarman, 1981, 1986). A key aspect of his definition was to emphasise the 'unwitting' nature of institutional racism, removing the focus from the individual towards broader collective practices which could serve to compound discriminatory action.

A definition from the 1980s claims it is when racist actions are *'built into the policy or mode of operation of institutions irrespective of the attitudes of the individuals who carry out the activities of the institutions*' (Lea, 1987: 148). In 1996, the sociologist Ellis Cashmore claimed institutional racism was when '*Institutions can operate along racist lines without acknowledging or even recognising this and how such operations can persist in the face of official policies geared to the removal of discrimination*' (Cashmore, 1996: 172).

The most prominent definition of the concept in the UK, post Scarman (1981, 1986), arose from the publication of the Macpherson Inquiry Report in 1999 following the racist murder of the black London teenager Stephen Lawrence in 1993. According to Lord Macpherson institutional racism represents the:

> ... *collective failure of an organisation to provide an appropriate and professional service to people because of their colour, culture and ethnic origin. It can be seen or detected in processes, attitudes and behaviour which amount to discrimination through unwitting prejudice, ignorance, thoughtlessness and racist stereotypical behaviour.* (Macpherson, 1999: para. 0.34)

Macpherson provides a comprehensive definition of institutional racism which acknowledges that racism can be individual, collective and cumulative. Institutional racism can also involve omission or neglect rather than simply proactive racist behaviour. Although the context of this definition was prompted by an examination of the practices of the London Metropolitan Police the scope and application of the concept extends to the spheres of housing, education, employment, health and social services.

It is worth noting the recommendations made by the researcher Marian FitzGerald in her advice to the Royal Commission on Criminal Justice 1993 on how to limit discrimination within an organisation. According to FitzGerald, discrimination is more likely to occur in an organisation or institution when:

- there are no clear guidelines about the criteria on which decisions should be taken;
- decisions depend on subjective judgements rather than (or in addition to) objective criteria;
- there is considerable scope for the exercise of individual discretion;
- there is no requirement to record or monitor the reasons for decisions;
- local and organisational cultural norms (rather than the requirements of service delivery) strongly influence decision making (FitzGerald, 1993).

The concept of institutionalised racism is not without its critics. Indeed Marian FitzGerald, having provided the guidance above, argues that the concept simply describes police racism rather than explaining it whilst denying individual responsibility and potentially fostering impotence and resentment (FitzGerald, 2001). Colin Webster, whilst reflecting the views of a number of scholars, argues that the resolution for police racism lies in power and community relationships between the police and politically powerless groups, '*including those within the white population-groups towards whose demands the police have little incentive to respond, who are most likely to be disproportionately stopped and searched and who are as likely to be discriminated against because of their social class and area of residence as because of their ethnicity – a crucial factor ignored by Macpherson*' (Webster, 2007: 79).

Anti-Semitism

Jewish people have endured discriminatory treatment for many centuries and anti-Semitism describes behaviour which conceives Jews as a treacherous, undesirable and hostile population. Contemporary anti-Semitism has been borne out of the creation and maintenance of myths about Jews as belonging to a distinct 'race'. These myths include the 'blood libel' which conceives Jews as perpetrators of ritual murders of Christian children and fantasies concerning a universal Jewish-power conspiracy (Mosse, 2000).

Scholars of political history in Britain are keen to emphasise incidents of anti-Jewish sentiment and prejudice during the late part of the nineteenth century and early twentieth century. Anti-alien or anti-immigrant issues were used by Conservative candidates in the East End of London (where Jewish migrants had settled) between 1892 and 1906 during election campaigns (Garrard, 1993). According to Garrard:

> ... *the Jewish aspect of the problem seems to have exercised as strong an influence over the anti-alien public consciousness as it did over that of agitators and the pro-aliens.* (Garrard, 1993: 379)

The resurfacing of anti-Semitism in Europe during the 1930s unleashed historical prejudices against Jews and provided a focus and scapegoat for social deprivation which was politically mobilised by the Nazis (McMaster, 2001; Žižek, 1989). During Nazi rule in Germany Jewish people were the subject of a systematic genocide (holocaust) and the application of a racial hygiene agenda which included torture, medical experimentation, forced sterilisation, forced labour and extermination in concentration camps (Burleigh and Wipperman, 2008; Goldhagen, 1996).

Contemporary forms of anti-Semitism include the denial and trivialisation of the Jewish holocaust whilst the intensity of anti-Semitic incidents tends to be influenced by ongoing political unrest in the Middle East (Bell, 2008). According to the FBI Uniform Crime Reporting Hate Crime Statistics for 2008, of 1606 reported hate crimes in the USA motivated by religious bias, 65.7% were anti-Jewish (FBI, 2008).

Islamophobia

As with anti-Semitism, Islamophobia has an established history. In the UK, the Runnymede Trust published a report in 1997 which detailed the historic and contemporary nature of Islamophobia which was defined as a '*dread or hatred of Islam and therefore, to the fear and dislike of all Muslims*' (Runnymede, 1997: 1). It is worth noting that some scholars challenge this definition of Islamophobia: most notably Fred Halliday suggests a more accurate term would be 'anti-Muslimism' since the focus of contemporary attacks is Muslim people and that the term 'Islamophobia' tends to reproduce the distortion of a monolithic Islam whilst '*indulging conformism and authority within Muslim communities*' (Halliday, 1999: 899).

Academics have pointed towards the role of the media in constructing, projecting and maintaining stereotypical and discriminatory images and perceptions of Islam and Muslim populations. Muslims are typically construed as an homogeneous, antagonistic and fanatical population (Alexander, 2000; Sayyid and Abdoolkarim, 2010; Spalek, 2002; Webster, 1997a).

It is worth noting that in Britain, the criminological discourse about Muslims has moved through three distinct phases. During the early 1980s the few criminological studies undertaken in this field had to rely upon statistics about 'Asian' crime rates. Within this period Asians were deemed conformist and not considered a crime problem (Mawby and Batta, 1980). This conformist image shifted to one of Asian deviant or 'folk devil' following high profile public disorder in predominantly Pakistani and Bangladeshi communities in key towns and cities in north western England during the 1990s (Webster, 1997b). Following the terrorist attacks in the USA on 11 September 2001 and incidents in London in July 2005, there has been a clear shift from discourse about Asian deviance to a focus upon the Muslim 'folk devil' (Quraishi, 2005). This latest construction is predicated upon a conspiratorial myth involving the perceived Islamisation of Britain (Marranci, 2009).

Following the terrorist attacks in the USA on 11 September 2001, anti-Muslim sentiment and assaults upon Muslims in Europe intensified in all 15 member states of the European Union (EUMC, 2001). Incidents against Muslims included arson attacks against a Muslim school in the Netherlands, Nazi graffiti on Muslim business premises in Sweden and arson attacks on mosques in the UK (EUMC, 2001). There is evidence to suggest Islamophobia is more widespread and prevalent in the USA than in the period immediately following 9/11, as concluded by a *Washington Post-ABC News* poll on 9 March 2006 (Goldenberg, 2006). Although most hate crime remains unreported, the official statistics for 2008 suggest anti-Islamic hate crimes motivated by religious bias amounted to 7.7% of 1606 incidents in the USA (FBI, 2008). The recent controversy around the development of Park 51, an Islamic cultural centre in New York, illustrates politicised and media sustained hostility towards American Muslims.

Since the Runnymede Trust report in 1997, the concept of Islamophobia has been the focus of considerable scholarship across many fields including education, politics, media, criminology and sociology, which reflects the pervasiveness of the phenomenon (see Allen and Nielsen, 2002; Ansari and Farid, 2012; Helbling, 2012; Klug, 2012; Kumar, 2012; Morey and Amina, 2011; Morgan and Poynting, 2012; Petley and Richardson, 2011; Poole, 2002; Poole and Richardson, 2006; Sayyid and Abdoolkarim, 2010; Shaik, 2011).

Xenophobia and Xeno-racism

Whilst xenophobia depicts the fear or dread of foreigners often categorised by their skin colour, xeno-racism represents a more recent and nuanced concept articulated in the UK by writers associated with the Institute of Race Relations (IRR) such as Ambalavaner Sivanandan, Liz Fekete and Arun Kundnani. According to Sivanandan, xeno-racism describes racism directed at newer white migrants who have been displaced or dispossessed, particularly from Eastern to Western Europe. This racism is articulated as a fear of foreigners rather than of people with different skin colours and it becomes enmeshed with political debates about economic migration which attempt to mask its parallels with traditional racism (Sivanandan, 1992). According to Liz Fekete, the New Labour administration in the UK from 1998 made deterrence rather than human rights a guiding principle of its political asylum policy, which, she argues, has cultural acceptability for racism towards asylum seekers in the UK (Fekete, 2009).

Essentialism

Although the origin of essentialism lies with the writings of Plato and philosophy the concept has relevance to scholars of biology, gender and identity politics. When speaking of race or ethnicity, essentialism describes the belief that certain groups are distillable to a core set of common fixed traits, cultural values or identities whilst any variation across the group is considered secondary. The opposition to such a position is occupied by social constructionists who claim phenomena are dependent upon ongoing human action in social contexts (see Berger and Luckmann, 1966; Fuchs, 2001; Harris, 1990; Modood, 1998).

Eurocentrism

Eurocentrism is an implied or explicit world view from a European perspective. Although the roots of the behaviour the term describes may be traced to the European Renaissance, colonial and imperial expansion during the sixteenth and eighteenth centuries compounded its influence whilst the term itself became popular during the processes of decolonisation in the late twentieth century. As illustrated in Chapter 1, the essence of this concept is a belief in the triumph of a superior European civilisation over what are deemed primitive and barbaric nations and cultures – stages the Europeans believe they have overcome in their not too distant past. The legacy of European global influence can be seen in the export of international standards of measurement, Latin symbols, language and geographical centrality such as the setting of global world times from Greenwich in the UK (see Lambropoulos, 1993; Sardar, 1999; Sayyid, 2004).

Whiteness and White Governmentality

In the same way that we have come to acknowledge that assertions and attributions to black and minority 'races' are the product of social constructions, so too we must realise that 'white' and 'whiteness' are the output of multiple discourses and contexts about what it means to be a member of the white 'race'. As discussed in Chapter 1, racial taxonomies sought to classify humans within a hierarchy of biologically distinct racial groups with white Europeans, as colonisers of 'subordinate' races, exerting claims of superiority bound by a fictional notion of an homogenous 'white' race.

Defining whiteness and the white 'race' is a very complex affair and some scholars assert it is probably easier to define what being white is not. Whiteness may be constituted against an assessment of who is not allowed within its fold but also upon how categories of 'race' work alongside other aspects of identity such as gender, class, religion and nationality. According to Haney Lopez, '*Being White is not a monolithic or homogenous experience, either in terms of race or other social identities, space or time. Instead, Whiteness is contingent, changeable, partial, inconstant, and ultimately social. As a descriptor and as an experience, "White" takes on highly variegated nuances across the range of social axes and individual lives*' (Haney Lopez, 2006: xxi).

Deciding who is and is not 'white' has been the subject of legal construction, most notably in the USA as embodied in the historical 'one drop rule' or rule of hypo-descent which asserted that any person with non–white ancestry could not claim membership of the white 'race' and was thus disenfranchised from political, social and economic capital. Various manifestations of this ideology are evidenced by the experiences of people defined under 'mixed–race' categories in a wide number of geographical contexts including Latin America, the Caribbean, Canada and South Africa (Garner, 2010).

The British and American academic literature on 'whiteness' share some common strands. The overlapping themes include '*invisibility/visibility; the roles of cultural capital and shared values in making "White" meaningful vis-à-vis others; and the contingent class and ethnic hierarchies within the White group*' (Garner, 2010: 123). The concept of invisibility involves viewing 'white' as the norm and explains the experiences of white people who claim that they do not possess racial identities since race was a non–issue in their upbringing. Another aspect of the concept of invisibility is the ability of dominant groups to make individual black and minority people 'invisible'. Such invisibility is to think of individual BME people against labels and traits (such as deviant and criminal) ascribed to the whole group.

Cultural capital describes non-economic forms of wealth which are unevenly distributed throughout society. Those possessing cultural capital, such as knowledge of the high arts or access to particular forms of education, are cushioned from the rigours of economic disadvantage. White people are construed to have benefited from a social contract to maintain a racial hierarchy; although not all are signatories to this contract all white people do benefit by it, albeit unequally. The tacit contract also provides a mechanism through which criticism of racism can occur without the fundamental inequality being overturned (Mills, 1997).

Racialisation also produces contingent hierarchies of 'whiteness' whereby certain 'white' populations are treated as inferior and flawed. Certain white Europeans such as Italians, Jews, Romany and Irish have been the subject of centuries of discourse which characterises them as defective, deviant and dysfunctional (Panayi, 1996). Although this is a centuries-old phenomenon, it also connects and describes more contemporary practices under the lens of 'new racisms' such as xenophobia and xeno-racism.

Intersectionality

Intersectionality acknowledges that the concept of race does not operate independently but rather it interacts with other aspects of a person's identity such as their class, gender, age and faith, as will be more fully explored in Chapters 6 and 7. As a methodological concept, intersectionality was borne out of feminist sociology but also via the writings of critical race theorists (Crenshaw, 1991).

The key aspect of the perspective is to understand how socially constructed categories of identity interact to produce marginalisation and discrimination. In other words, racism is shaped by sexism, homophobia and other forms of oppression. The outcome of this approach is to acknowledge that social life is complex and irreducible to homogeneous categories. This presents particular challenges to researchers of race, who have to deconstruct, redefine or abandon official categories of race and ethnicity which are popular in a particular society. The methodological challenges to studying intersectionality are prudently summarised in Box 2.3. This discussion will also be explored in Chapter 5 when discussing qualitative methods for researching racism.

Box 2.3	**Three Different Approaches to Studying Intersectionality (adapted from McHall, 2005)**

1. Anti-categorical Complexity

This approach acknowledges that social categories are arbitrary constructions of history and language. They play little part in how people actually experience life. However, inequalities and oppression are connected to relationships which are defined by race, class, sexuality and gender. Therefore, the only way to truly eradicate oppression is to dismantle the categories currently deployed to define complex populations. Such categorisation leads to demarcation which in turn leads to exclusion and then inequality. Since society is comprised of individuals with complex and varied identities any attempt to boil down such complexity into limited categories leads ultimately to oppression.

2. Inter-categorical Complexity

This approach acknowledges that inequality exists in society but the focus for researchers should be the relationships among and between social groups and how these are changing over time. Here the existing categories for classifying populations are retained.

3. Intra-categorical Complexity

This approach represents a half-way between 1 and 2 above. The shortcomings of existing categories of defining populations are acknowledged whilst questioning how boundaries are drawn. The importance of categories is not completely rejected, however, and instead the focus in this approach is upon people who cross the boundaries of constructed categories. There is an acknowledgement that some social categories represent robust relationships whilst others do not.

McCall has attempted to address the methodological challenges of using intersectionality in empirical research by conceptualising the ways researchers may interpret existing categorisations of race and ethnicity. We explore the precise ways in which such categories are conceptualised in Chapter 7 where we discuss McCall's anti-categorical, inter-categorical and intra-categorical complexities.

Summary

This chapter illustrates the sheer complexity of defining racism whilst representing a very small proportion of the scholarship addressing this issue. As has been demonstrated, there is no consensus amongst scholars about precisely how racism is to be defined, nevertheless we can identify the range of behaviour which the concept includes as well as the processes which perpetuate and maintain racial discrimination.

Our emphasis in this chapter has been on how notions of race are the outcome of social processes through which persons become defined as such. We drew attention to the way power can be exerted by one group in defining race to the detriment of another, but also pointed to the way in which notions of race can be employed by particular groups as a source of solidarity, empowerment and identity construction/affirmation.

We also noted that the reproduction of such notions operates at both an institutional and individual level. In terms of the former, we discussed notions of institutional racism; in terms of the latter we focus more on particular cultural contexts and social situations – and the social interaction that occurs in and constitutes them, in which persons might find themselves — and find race is in some way an, or at, issue. The implication here, and one that we will focus on in Chapter 4, is the importance of understanding race and racism as part of everyday life, in the communities and groups that form the backdrop of everyday life. In this latter context, what we drew attention to was what we shall refer to in Chapter 4 as 'institutionalised racism'.

One problematic aspect of understanding racism we pointed to was the array of behaviours that can themselves, through a process of classification and typification, be regarded as such. A second was the complexity of the notion of race, and problems with essentialist arguments. The former will be dealt with to some extent in our dis-cussions of the meaning attributed to any given social action in Chapter 4; the latter in our discussion of sociological approaches to understanding experience, meaning and action in Chapter 4, and in the development of the notion of intersectionality we introduced here in Chapter 7.

Finally, as in the previous chapter, we focused on the particular context of the UK, with particular reference to issues surrounding Islamophobia and notions of Asian folk devils developed in the UK media (an issue that will in large part inform the case studies we present in Chapter 6).

Governments have conceived working definitions of racist behaviour in order to establish anti-racist policies and legislation, which are the focus of the following chapter.

3

ANTI-RACISM: LAW AND POLICIES

Keywords: *European Convention of Human Rights, Race Relations Acts, criminal offences, hate crime*

This chapter raises the following questions and points for reflection:

- How does legislation define racism and discrimination and how does this differ or coalesce with academic definitions and interpretations?
- How have historic and more recent formal policies interpreted and codified racism and anti-racism?
- How are some of the themes and concepts explored in the previous chapter manifested in legislation, polices and formal documents challenging racism and hate crime?

Despite academic uncertainty about what racism constitutes, governments have been tasked to address working definitions of racial discrimination for many decades. This chapter will provide an overview of some of the key forms of anti-racist policies and laws. Again, the discussion will relate chiefly to European and British contexts, although some of the overarching principles clearly pertain to the global arena and international law. Furthermore, the chapter is not an evaluation of the various anti-racist movements and grassroots struggles in the UK.[1]

Before discussing particular legislation it is worth exploring some of the approaches adopted by anti-racist policies. Anti-racist policies themselves are also often inseparable from broader anti-discrimination or equality initiatives. One of the first perspectives to address inequality has become known as the 'equal treatment approach'. This approach acknowledges that discrimination exists but in order to address it one must treat everybody the same via a sense of formal equality. The logic pursued here is '*If I treat everybody the same, irrespective of their ethnicity, race, religion, gender, et cetera, then surely I cannot be accused of discrimination?*' This approach may also be termed the 'colour-blind approach' and can be criticised since it denies the differences which exist between different sections of the population as a result of centuries of discrimination as well as the qualitatively different resource needs for different sections of a community.

Another relevant policy perspective may be termed the 'level playing fields' or 'equal opportunities' approach. In this perspective, cultural differences are acknowledged and it is accepted that discrimination has created patterns of inequality for minorities over time. It acknowledges that barriers to attainment have been established for minorities in a wide range of positions in society. The approach seeks to address the obstacles which have prevented BME groups from competing fairly for various social positions such as employment, housing, education and public office. The practice of affirmative action in the USA and positive discrimination in Europe are examples of policies reflecting the equal opportunities approach. In 1999, the Amsterdam Treaty inserted Article 119(4) to the European Community Treaty (now known as the Treaty on the Functioning of the European Union, TFEU) allowing member states to permit positive discrimination on the grounds of gender.

Another useful policy perspective to be aware of is the 'equal outcome approach'. This perspective tends to focus upon the end results of policies or programmes seeking to address discrimination. A key application of this approach is demonstrated in the ethnicity and crime debate where monitoring of official criminal statistics may reveal disproportionate targeting or treatment of minorities at key stages of the criminal justice process.

Historic Anti-discrimination Legislation

In international law, principles of equality are well established. Article 1 of the 1945 Charter of the United Nations acknowledges a global aim in '*promoting and encouraging respect for human rights and for fundamental freedoms for all without distinction as to race, sex, language, or religion*' (United Nations, 2010). Furthermore, Article 7 of the 1948 Universal Declaration of Human Rights established a global principle that all are equal before the law and are entitled without any discrimination to equal protection of the law (United Nations, 1948). By 1950, Article 14 of the European Convention for the Protection of Human Rights and Fundamental Freedoms sought to ensure that human rights were to be secured '*without discrimination on any grounds such as sex, race, colour, language, religion, political or other opinion, national or social origin, association with a national minority, property, birth or other social status*' (ECHR, 1950).

In March 1966, the United Nations also introduced the International Convention on the Elimination of All Forms of Racial Discrimination, which required governments to review national and local policies and to amend, rescind or nullify any laws or regulations which had the effect of creating or perpetuating discrimination. The Convention prompted a duty on signatories to promote tolerance and equality of opportunity.

It is worth noting however, despite these historic treaties and conventions, racial discrimination was still commonplace and in fact institutionalised amongst many of the nation-states who were signatories to the agreements at the time. Black people in the Southern states of the USA endured the Jim Crow Laws whilst many thousands of marginalised people experienced bonded labour in the Soviet gulags (Ignatieff, 2002).

European Legislation

In 1997, the European Union decided to take a proactive position on its role in formulating anti-discrimination policies across Europe. The founding Treaties were amended to enable the EU *'to take appropriate action to combat discrimination based on sex, racial or ethnic origin, religion or belief, disability, age or sexual orientation'* (EC Treaty, Art. 13). The EU Treaty was also amended to emphasise combating racism and xenophobia as a core objective with the Council of Ministers adopting Directive 2000/43 in June 2000 which implemented the principle of equal treatment between persons irrespective of racial or ethnic origin (Bell, 2008).

The Directive marks simply one aspect of a very broad policy agenda for the EU on combating racism. Initiatives include the establishment of the European Council's Consultative Committee on Racism and Xenophobia and the Commission's 'Action Plan Against Racism' in 1998 with a long-term objective of mainstreaming anti-discrimination in all aspects of EU law and policy (Bell, 2008).

The UK, in an attempt to comply with the EC Framework Directives, introduced a draft of regulations including the Race Relations Act 1976 (Amendment) Regulations 2003; the Employment Equality (Sexual Orientation) Regulations 2003; the Employment Equality (Religion or Belief) Regulations 2003; and the Employment Equality (Age) Regulations 2006. These provisions have met with extensive criticism, including the fact that they unduly complicate the existing anti-discriminatory legislative provision and fail to address how individuals not falling within defined protected groups or those straddling multiple protected groups are to be dealt with (Milner, 2010).

UK[2] Anti-discrimination Law

The first piece of legislation to specifically address racial discrimination in England and Wales was the Race Relations Act of 1965. The 1965 Act enabled civil rather than criminal sanctions to be applied to individuals refusing to serve a person, unreasonable delay in serving someone or overcharging on the grounds of colour, race or ethnic or national origins. The Act did not include Northern Ireland and excluded shops or private boarding houses; therefore its impact upon curbing racial discrimination was very limited. The Act was subsequently amended by the second Race Relations Act in 1968, which extended the scope of the legislation to include the spheres of housing and employment. Both of these early pieces of law were limited to incidents of individual direct discrimination.

The 1968 Act was repealed by the Race Relations Act of 1976, which extended the definition of racial discrimination to include 'indirect discrimination'. Racial discrimination, in English law, became defined as treating someone less favourably than you would treat other people, on racial grounds. The question to be asked is not whether the person's treatment was good or bad, fair or unfair, but simply whether it would have been different but for his or her racial background. Importantly, the 1976 Act (§16) brought the police within the remit of accountability for racial discrimination. The Act also established the Commission for Racial Equality (CRE). This was a body comprising 14 members appointed by the Home Secretary but independent of the government. The CRE had investigatory powers and the power to issue notices requiring compliance where there was reasonable suspicion that acts of discrimination had occurred. The CRE was formally dissolved by the Equality Act 2006 which established the Equalities and Human Rights Commission.

In 2000 the government introduced the Race Relations (Amendment Act) (RRA 2000) which imposed an enforceable race equality duty on all public authorities. As with previous race relations legislation, the Act conferred civil remedies for compensation rather than criminal penalties. An important aspect of this Act was its inclusion of incidents when a white person may be discriminated against because of their association with people belonging to an ethnic minority group. The 2000 Act defines three types of unlawful discrimination: direct, indirect and victimisation. The last means treating a person less favourably than other persons because the person has complained of discrimination. Behaviour will not constitute victimisation if the allegation of discrimination was false and not made in good faith. The remit for the RRA 2000 includes employment, conferring qualifications for a trade or profession, vocational training, trade union membership or professional association, partnerships, education, housing, planning control, provision of goods, facilities or services and membership of clubs and associations.

The RRA 2000 also extended the scope of activity to include the carrying out of public functions such as policing, running prisons, detention centres, collecting taxes, detaining mental patients, local authority enforcement, immigration control (with some exceptions) and customs and excise. Therefore, the Act represented a more robust means for civil redress against criminal justice agencies for discrimination as well as placing a statutory obligation on public bodies to promote racial equality. It was not necessary to prove that the discriminator intended to discriminate, merely that either direct, indirect discrimination or victimisation had occurred. There was also an onus upon public bodies to demonstrate that their means of preventing racial discrimination were effective.

The 2005 Labour Party manifesto included an aim to consolidate and clarify equality and discrimination legislation in the UK via a single Equality Act. The current Coalition government inherited this policy via the introduction of the Equality Act in 2010 (EA 2010). The EA 2010 repeals a number of previous Acts such as the Equal

Pay Act 1970, Sex Discrimination Act 1975 and Disability Discrimination Act 1995. It also consolidates a number of regulations prompted by the EU Directives on discrimination such as the Employment Equality (Religion and Belief) Regulation 2003 and the Employment Equality (Sexual Orientation) Regulation 2003. There are two main consequences of the EA 2010. First, the Act has created a set of protected characteristics and prohibited actions, with some minor exceptions, which apply across the board. Second, there is a duty which applies to all public authorities across all the main equality strands. There are nine equality strands or protected characteristics: sex, race, disability, sexual orientation, religion or belief, age, marriage and civil partnership, gender and reassignment, and pregnancy and maternity. The Act also reflects the previous law by standardising definitions of prohibited conduct which may be constituted as direct discrimination, indirect discrimination, victimisation and harassment. For disability, there are two additional forms of prohibited conduct: discrimination arising from disability and a failure to make reasonable adjustments (Government Equalities Office, 2010).

The EA 2010 also places an onus upon public sector organisations to adopt an equality duty prompting them to establish equality objectives as well as retaining the use of positive action to promote the interests of people falling within a protected group.

Criminal Offences

The 1965 Race Relations Act had introduced 'inciting racial hatred' as an unlawful act and this was included in the subsequent Race Relations Acts of 1968 and 1976. The crime of racial hatred became part of the Public Order Act 1986 Part III and constituted six separate offences. The key elements of the offence relate to words or behaviour or material in any form that is threatening, abusive or insulting and that, by their actions, the person intends to stir up racial hatred or in all the circumstances racial hatred is likely to be stirred up. Racial hatred constitutes hatred against a group of persons in Great Britain defined by reference to colour, race, nationality (including citizenship) or ethnic or national origins (§17). The offences in Part III include using words or behaviour or displaying written material (§18); publishing or distributing written material (§19); presenting or directing a public performance (§20); distributing, showing or playing a film, video, sound recording (§21); broadcasting a programme including abusive or insulting images or sound; possessing written material or film, video or sound recording which is threatening, abusive or insulting or a recording with a view to displaying, publishing or distributing or broadcasting the material (§23) (Public Disorder Act 1986, Part III).

The proceedings required the consent of the Attorney General who is the main legal adviser of the government responsible for major domestic and international litigation involving the administration in power. The sentencing powers attached to offences committed under the Public Disorder Act 1986 included up to two years' custodial sentence and/or a fine in the Crown Court and a custodial sentence of up to six months in the Magistrates Court and/or a fine.

The Public Disorder Act 1986 became subject to a number of amendments as well as being buttressed by subsequent legislation. The most notable legal development pertaining to race was the introduction of the Racial and Religious Hatred Act in 2006. The 2006 Act made it an offence for a person to use threatening words or behaviour, or display any written material which is threatening '*if he intends thereby to stir up religious hatred*'. The 2006 Act also extended the meaning of 'religious hatred' to include those with a lack of religious belief following opposition to the original Bill, both from sections of the public and in the House of Lords (Goodhall, 2007).

Since 1991, it has been an offence in the UK to engage or take part in chanting of an '*indecent or racialist nature at a designated football match*' by virtue of §3 of the Football Offences Act 1991. This Act acknowledges a social reality whereby both fans and players belonging to an ethnic minority group have been subject to racist verbal and physical abuse whilst attending football matches in the UK (Back et al., 2001). The Act defines 'chanting' as repeated uttering of any words or sounds, whether alone or with others (§3(2)(a)). The term 'racialist nature' means '*consisting of or including matter which is threatening, abusive or insulting to a person by reason of his colour, race, nationality (including citizenship) or ethnic or national origins*' (§3(2)(b)). The offence can be committed two hours before and one hour after a football match. The maximum sentence for somebody convicted under this Act is a fine.

In 1998, the Crime and Disorder Act (CDA 1998) introduced new categories of racially aggravated offences which supplemented previously existing laws on violent and abusive behaviour. The CDA 1998 introduced two alternative tests to ascertain whether an action could constitute a racially aggravated offence. The first test prompts an evaluation of whether at the '*time of committing the offence, or immediately before or after doing so, the offender demonstrates towards the victim hostility based on the victim's membership (or presumed membership) of a racial or religious group*' (CDA 1998, §28(1)(a)). The second test enquires whether the offence was '*motivated (wholly or partly) by hostility towards members of a racial or religious group based on their membership of that group*' (CDA 1998, §28(1)(b)). The offences which may be committed with racially aggravated factors include malicious wounding or grievous bodily harm (under the Offences Against the Person Act 1861), common assault, criminal damage (pursuant to §1 of the Criminal Damage Act 1971), public disorder offences and harassment (under the Protection from Harassment Act 1997). Furthermore, §2 of the CDA 1998 imposes a duty on a court sentencing for any other offence that is racially aggravated to treat that as a factor that increases the seriousness of the offence.

Another controversial area of the CDA 1998 was the introduction of Anti-social Behaviour Orders (ASBOs). Although an ASBO may be imposed upon anyone over 10 years of age on a civil burden of proof (on a balance of probabilities), breach of the same can mean imprisonment of up to five years. These orders may be used to curb some forms of racist behaviour since the implication is that certain conduct is likely to constitute harassment, alarm or distress. The orders, however, tend to involve low level incivility rather than serious crime. Furthermore, the orders have been criticised for the criminalisation of trivial behaviour as well as granting a very broad discretion to local authorities and magistrates with regard to what constitutes anti-social behaviour (Ashworth, 2004). The government is currently reviewing the law around ASBOs and proposing to replace them with a Crime Prevention Injunction and Criminal Behaviour Order, although critics have claimed there are little material differences between these new orders and what they will be replacing (Ireland, 2011).

Another way in which people experience racist behaviour is through malicious communications. This is an increasing challenge, given the pervasiveness of new media such as e-mail, social networking sites, blogs and the like. The Malicious Communication Act of 1988 made it an offence to send race hate mail, punishable by a limited fine. The original Act of 1988 referred to a telecommunications system. However, to incorporate technological advances such as the Internet, the Act was amended by the Malicious Communications Act 2003, which introduced the concept of an electronic communications network. Similarly, it is an offence, pursuant to §43 of the Telecommunications Act 1988, to send a grossly offensive, indecent, obscene or menacing message by telephone.

Hate Crime

Hate crimes are those committed against someone because of their disability, gender-identity, race, religion or belief, or sexual orientation and can include threatening behaviour, assault, robbery, damage to property, inciting others to commit hate crime and harassment. The approach in England and Wales has been to deal with hate crimes as a distinct strand of policing and local authority policy.

The definition of hate crime differs across countries and between academics. There is no agreed definition but what they tend to have in common is their assertion that hate crime must involve a criminal offence (Perry, 2001). The definition of hate crime is necessarily complex since, like race, it is a socially constructed concept which is relative to cultural and political contexts (Grattet and Jenness, 2014;[3] Hall, 2013). Wolfe and Copeland assert that hate crime comprises '*violence directed towards groups of people who generally are not valued by the majority society, who suffer discrimination in other arenas and who do not have full access to remedy social, political and economic injustice*' (Wolfe and Copeland, 1994: 201). Whilst Perry suggests, '*hate crime involves acts of violence and intimidation, usually directed towards already stigmatised and marginalised groups. As such it is a mechanism of power oppression, intended to reaffirm the precarious hierarchies that characterise a given social order. It attempts to re-create simultaneously the theoretical (real or imagined) hegemony of the perpetrators' group and the "appropriate" subordinate identity of the victims' group*' (Perry, 2001: 10). For Nathan Hall, defining hate crime has more to do with prejudice, hostility or bias than hate *per se*. Hate crime is about criminal behaviour which is motivated by prejudice '*of which hate is just one small but extreme part*' (Hall, 2013: 9). For Hall, it is more useful to concentrate upon 'prejudices', which provide for a broader spectrum of behaviour to be examined. Determining which prejudices are to be included as hate crimes, however, involves a very complex task of establishing boundaries or characteristics which require subsequent protection (Hall, 2013).

Such academic definitions, whilst useful to conceptualise hate crime, serve policy makers and legislators less well owing to their rather broad and often contested nature. It is worth noting that the 43 police forces of England and Wales are guided by the definition provided by the Association of Chief Police Officers (ACPO). Following the Stephen Lawrence Inquiry, the police have adopted and refined the definition by Sir William Macpherson: '*a racist incident is any incident which is perceived to be racist by the victim or any other person*' (Macpherson, 1999). ACPO's latest definition is therefore '*any hate incident, which constitutes a criminal offence, perceived by the victim or any other person, as being motivated by hostility or prejudice. Prejudice or hate may be based on characteristics including disability, race, religion, sexual orientation and transgender*' (College of Policing, 2014; see Resource 11 in the Appendix for fuller details).

However, the ACPO guidelines differ from legislative definitions and the fluidity of defining hate crime has recently been demonstrated by a prudent policy adopted in April 2013 by the Greater Manchester Police in creating an additional strand of recording hate crimes by those perpetrated against an 'alternative subcultural' group. This follows a campaign by the family of a murdered teenager, Sophie Lancaster, who was the victim of lethal violence owing to her membership of a 'Goth' subcultural group. The trial judge in her case asserted that the incident was a hate crime which prompted campaigners to push for 'alternative subcultures' or 'lifestyle and dress-code' to be included as equal strands for recording and monitoring alongside the categories of race, religion, disability, homophobia and transgender (Sophie Lancaster Foundation, 2014).

However, although laws may be passed to prohibit hate crimes, prosecutions brought pursuant to them are often not forthcoming as illustrated by the introduction of the Racial and Religious Hatred Act 2006.

This somewhat controversial Act came into law in England and Wales in October 2007 and added to the existing Public Order Act 1986. The 2006 Act defined religious hatred as '*against a group of persons defined by reference to religious belief or lack of religious belief*' (§29(a)). Pursuant to §29(b) '*a person who uses threatening words or behaviour, or displays any written material which is threatening, is guilty of an offence if he intends thereby to stir up religious hatred*'. Opponents of this Act were concerned it would criminalise holy texts as well as make satirists vulnerable to prosecution.

However, the success of this law could be questioned when examining successful prosecution of offenders charged with offences pursuant to the Act. The Ministry of Justice, when prompted by a freedom of information request, revealed only six persons had been convicted under this Act between 2007 and 2011, whilst a lower figure of just one conviction up to 2011 had been cited in a brief to the Attorney General as recorded by Hansard (Ministry of Justice, 2012).

Summary

In this chapter we have outlined anti-racist and anti-discriminatory policy and legislation as both the reflection of understandings of race and racisms and the context in which particular actions and behaviours are understood (including a range of criminal offences). The legal options outlined here constitute both civil (between individuals) and criminal (between the state and individuals) liabilities in England and Wales for racial discrimination. They are part of the methods through which individuals may find redress but success is dependent upon a wide range of extra-legal factors including the presumption of confidence amongst victims of racial abuse and violence to report it in the first instance. As in Chapters 1 and 2, we have focused on a European and more specifically a UK context in our discussion, but have tried to point to wider, more international and global concerns about racist and discriminatory practices. Our discussion has been critical in addition to descriptive and we have suggested that, although various legislation exists to counter racism, the figures on race hate crime in the UK are a sober indicator of the ineffectiveness of such law to prevent significant acts of discrimination and racial violence from escalating in the UK and Europe (Athwal et al., 2010).

Again, we have provided some historical commentary to our discussion, which, as we have argued in previous chapters, is essential in contextualising and understanding more contemporary practice. We have also pointed to more contemporary forms of behaviour, including a range of media and new forms of everyday communication, such as e-mails, networking and social media. Part of the rationale for including the discussion in this chapter is to point to potential documentary sources for further examination in your research into race and racism (something we shall take up in more detail in Chapter 5).

Notes

1 For a discussion of the theoretical struggles in anti-racism, see Anthias and Lloyd (2002).
2 Please note that Scotland has a distinct legal system. Although some key legislation extends to Scotland the discussion here refers largely to the law applicable in England, Wales and with some exceptions, Northern Ireland.
3 See recent analysis by Ryken Grattet and Valerie Jenness (2014) of characteristics of hate crime policies in the USA.

RACE, RACISM AND EVERYDAY LIFE

Keywords: *contemporary society, everyday life, experience, meaning, identities and interactions, practice, language, research problematics, sociological theory*

Introduction

Up to now we have presented overviews of the historical context of race and racism (Chapter 1), definitions and conceptualisations of racism (Chapter 2) and legislative issues (Chapter 3). In this chapter we want to do three things. First, we shall draw together some of the key themes and central issues outlined in Chapters 1–3 that we feel are important to bear in mind before setting about your research into race and racism. Second, we want to look at how these issues may manifest themselves in and as part of *everyday contemporary society*. Third, we want to point to some fundamental research considerations that may have to be taken into account when researching race and racism in everyday contemporary society. We also want to briefly outline some fundamental 'problems' that you will need to take into account before embarking on your research project. This chapter also provides something of a backdrop to the following chapter, in which we will outline specific aspects of qualitative research methods, practice and experience that we feel are particularly important and will enable you to proceed along your research route in an informed, sensitive and ethical manner, before moving on in Chapter 6 to show how the issues dealt with here and in the following chapter inform and play out in the reality of actual research practice and experience.

Specifically, the questions raised in this chapter are:

- To what extent is the legacy of race, racialisation and racism evident in contemporary society?
- What are the 'institutional' and 'institutionalised' features of race and racism?

- How do issues of race and racism manifest themselves as part of 'everyday life'?
- What are the roles of 'identities' and 'interactions' in the construction of race and practices of racism?
- What are some of the 'personal' aspects of researching race and racism that you might need to take into account in your work?
- What fundamental 'problems' might race and racism researchers need to consider in light of the above?
- What key sociological 'perspectives' allow us to investigate experience, meaning, practice and everyday language?

The Relevance of Race and Racism

Historical Legacy and Contemporary Society

As we outlined in Chapter 1, notions of race, practices of racialisation and instances of racism have a long history. Across eras and through generations, notions of race have been used in the typification, categorisation and classification of individuals, groups and communities. These practices of racialisation have been carried out for particular purposes (e.g. scientific, political, legal) by particular bodies and particular persons, at particular periods in world, European and British history. Although we have critiqued this set of processes and practices, and the discourse that surrounded them, and shown how the ontological and epistemological claims that underpinned them are largely unsubstantiated and indefensible, some of this historical legacy is evident in the processes, practices – and experiences - of racialisation that pervade contemporary society.

Much of what we have discussed so far in this volume has pointed to quite formal examples of racialisation, in a range of state, political, institutional, organisational and legislative policies and practices. In contemporary society, the notion of institutional racism that these examples point to (see Chapter 2), that is, '*collective failure*', evident in '*processes, attitudes and behaviours which amount to discrimination ... which disadvantages minority ethnic people*' (Macpherson, 1999, cited in Mason, 2000: 9; see also e.g. Bhavnani and Davis, 2000), is one with which most of us are, at least in a general sense, familiar. The notion of institutional racism is still an actively debated one, with various organisations – often those in some way part of or affiliated to the criminal justice system (see Chapter 7) – being targeted as exemplars of such practice (Phillips, 2005; Runnymede, 2012). However, the legacy of race and racism is not restricted to institutional or organisational practice. The simplification and generalisation that underpinned some Enlightenment thought and the science of race, and the racially charged discourses and dogmas that allowed these processes to be articulated (see Chapter 1), can often be seen in their most basic, and perhaps most insidious, form in the racial and ethnic stereotypes and generalisations that run through contemporary society at a cultural level.

One oft-cited example of the use of racial stereotypes (and stereotyping *per se*) has been the news media, and we have already touched on this in respect of Hall et al.'s (1978) analysis of race and the mugging crisis in the UK (see Chapter 1). Such accusations are not without foundation, as there have been many examples of racial stereotypes being promulgated in the contemporary tabloid press (including those that present 'threat' and fuel 'moral panic') (Cohen, 2011; Thompson, 1998). A body of sociological work has analysed how issues, images and identities of race and ethnicity have been reported and constructed over several decades and beyond (see e.g. Pearson's [1983] work on Victorian racial and class-based moral panics). In contemporary British society, for example, the most glaring example in recent years of media manipulation of racial stereotyping has been seen in the representation of British Asian (Muslim) youth as potential 'home-grown' terrorists, prompting a highly charged securitisation and criminalised discourse (Kundnani, 2007; Morey and Amina, 2011; Sayyid and Abdoolkarim, 2010). This has both been informed by and further fuels popular discourse about race.

The invocation of racial stereotypes in contemporary society can be seen to operate on a much wider basis though, evident at a cultural level in many forms, from popular culture to quite mundane practices. As we shall discuss further below (see Chapter 5), this has led to race and racism weaving themselves into how we experience contemporary society, from the (sometimes unthinking, often uncritical) consumption of notions of race to the (sometimes routine, often mundane) construction of race.

Critical Awareness, Proactive Anti-racisms and Race as an 'Issue'

Such suggestions should not imply however a contemporary world that engages in practices analogous to those outlined in Chapter 1. As we discussed in the preceding chapter, over recent years, and following a series of racially aggravated incidents (such as, in the UK, the Stephen Lawrence and Zahed Mubarak incidents), we have become more sensitive to and politically aware of racism. We would, of course, like to think that we have (all) 'advanced' since the 'bad old days'. Indeed, with the aim of 'stamping out' practices and policies that smack of racism, contemporary western society has seen a noticeable moral, political, legal, legislative shift towards tolerance, equality and fairness, manifest in a range of legislation over the last two decades or so (see Chapter 3). Racially related issues have been addressed and countered via a range of formal and informal dictates, legislation, campaigns and strategies to prevent and sanction discriminatory practice and behaviour as well as to provide education and encourage understanding (Bonnett, 2000).[1]

Such measures have undoubtedly moved us forward and improved society no end. However, for many, race can still be an 'issue'. It is in many spheres still something that is regarded as a salient and relevant basis for difference and discrimination, not simply in terms of racial 'features' but more widely in terms of more *fundamental* differences between persons, groups, nations or cultures. In the context of the sort of advances noted above, this can sometimes manifest itself as indicative of some sort of underlying and unspoken – 'unspeakable' – strain. For example, as we suggested earlier, a potential, and negative, backlash of tackling the issue of racism is the perception of political correctness (gone mad), positive discrimination (see the film *Falling Down*) and 'cultural naivety' (we recently heard a right-wing politician claim the UK needed a 'wake-up' call to what was 'really happening' with UK-based Muslims, although this politician has since performed a significant U-turn [*The Guardian*, 11 October 2013]). This may in no small part be exploiting perceptions of what Clements and Spinks (2009) see as the sometimes 'confrontational' and 'accusatory' edge of attempts to tackle race and racism. Our discussion in Chapter 7 suggests how some of these tensions can be resolved, and notions underpinning them problematised.

Everyday Life

When we talk of 'everyday life' we refer to a range of *places, spaces, persons, relationships, institutions, contexts, settings and encounters* that form what is, in effect, the 'experiential backdrop' of contemporary society. There is no one single 'everyday' for all – even any - of course, but as we go about what the sociologist Erving Goffman (1961) called our 'daily round' we move through various places, interact with various persons and perform some or the other role in collaboration with a range of 'others'. Thus, the train to work, the workplace itself and the leisure sites we use as 'escape' from the world of work (see Cohen and Taylor, 1992) all form part of our daily rounds, as do those others persons whom we encounter. However, less explicit contexts also help constitute our everyday daily rounds – the chat round the photocopier, the fleeting joke we may enjoy with friends, even daydreams we may have (Schutz, 1945).

A key point here is that there is, in effect, nothing 'spectacular' about everyday life. When looked at in this sense, then, everyday life may display no signs or evidence of race or the kind of racism or processes of racialisation discussed above. We have already employed the term 'institutional' to point to organisational practices. When we consider race – and processes and practices of racialisation – in this myriad of everyday encounters we might speak of 'institutionalised' racism, that is, the '*systematic, structural character of racism that ha[s] its roots in the organization of societies*' (Mason, 2000: 9) but in a less formal sense. This is what we refer to when we speak of the 'everyday' of racism, that is, '*systematic, recurrent, familiar practices*' (Essed, 1991: 3).[2] Alongside focusing on institutional issues noted above, these often *mundane taken-for-granted* and routine aspects and manifestations of racism should be something you want to examine – or at least be sensitive to – in your research. Indeed, the two do not exist as separate realms of activity, experience and practice, but are inextricably linked, and to some extent work to co-construct each other. For example, sociological studies have shown how 'common-sense' reasoning in everyday life feeds its way into and helps constitute institutional practices, sometimes in highly formal and consequential settings and contexts (see e.g. Atkinson, 1978). As we shall discuss in the following chapter, there are many ways in which everyday race and racism can be *revealed* in our mundane, routine practices, and particular research approaches that are geared towards exposing and analysing these.

One prime example of the type of thing we are talking about is in the way we are prepared to 'talk about' the social world (from formalised speech, through research interviews, to the most idle of chit-chat), which can reveal evidence of *prevailing* notions and pragmatic uses of race and a range of racisms. The philosopher Alfred Schutz described everyday language as the '*typifying medium par excellence*' (Schutz, 1973), and the role of language – of linguistic classification and typification – cannot be stressed enough, particularly when one considers mundane and routine articulations of race and racism. When considering race and the everyday, what we are suggesting then is that notions of race, and the way these understandings are, in the above example, 'talked about',[3] are not restricted to particular discourse domains and 'higher' power bases, as we have alluded to in previous chapters (e.g. the discourse of politics or science[4]). As we shall see below, the way language is used in and as part of everyday activity – including in and as part of *research activity* – is central to its social construction.

Finding Race, Racism and Racialisation in Everyday Life

Race, Space and Place

Everyday life in contemporary society – and all social phenomena, indeed, all action, meaning and experience – must be, and generally is, understood in context. Today, of course, as has been intimated in previous chapters, we live in a global context. Indeed, in contemporary society, what might be perceived as the local has become increasingly impacted by the global (Gunaratnam, 2003; Miles and Brown, 2003). The world is often described as a 'small place', and recent advances in communications and media technologies have led to an ever shrinking idea of the global and an increasing relevance of global issues. Quite often, whenever persons speak of global issues, they couch them in terms of what these *mean*, or the consequences these have for them locally, or even personally. This assertion is perhaps no more clearly illustrated than when we consider global events over the last 10 years, and how occurrences or behaviours in one place can impact processes and practices of racialisation in others far removed. The events of 9/11, for example, have impacted almost all parts of human society; the burning of religious texts in Middle America can have effects on the streets of Accrington, Lancashire (Maney, 2011; Watkinson, 2010).

This is not, however, to imply that experiences and practices of racism across cultural boundaries are one and the same. Indeed, as we shall see in Chapter 6 (see Case

Study 3), there is much to be gained in conducting comparative research of race and racisms across cultural contexts (see Liamputtong, 2010).

Of course, there have been for decades, migration and diasporas that have moved various racial and ethnic groups around the globe, resulting in many 'locales' characterised by multiculturalism in many contemporary societies (Barry, 2011; Modood, 2013). In the context of our focus here, much of the everyday nevertheless 'takes place' in – and is experienced as – local context, that is activity in particular places, at particular times, for particular purposes, with particular others.

One primary way of conceptualising the local as part of contemporary everyday life is in the notion of 'neighbourhood', along with the related notion of 'community'. Indeed, this has been one that has been used in numerous studies of race and racism in various contexts (Morris, 1999; Owens and Randhawa, 2004; Ray and Reed, 2005; Ray and Smith, 2004; Ray et al., 1997; Williams et al., 2002). As far back as the early twentieth century, neighbourhoods, communities and contemporary urbanity in general have been subject to mapping, often involving racial and ethnic criteria (Ellis et al., 2004). The work of the Chicago School, for example, often included reference to mapped areas or zones of the city (see Park and Burgess, 1925). However, such racially informed mapping can be seen to operate at a more informal level as part of everyday practice as we go about racially constructing spaces and places. The notions of 'ghettos' and 'no-go zones', and, conversely, 'patches' and 'safe areas', point to the sort of thing we are talking about here – and persons and groups in everyday life themselves routinely talk about – areas often classed as such because of the racial make-up of the demographics of particular areas (see Chapter 6).

What this points us to is the fact that sites, settings and contexts are not simply physical in nature, but are often characterised by certain values, beliefs, attitudes and morals of their members. Indeed, these may be predominant in both the immediacy of encounters and interactions (passed on, for example through association [see Sutherland, 1947]) and across time, as, passed down via processes of what sociologists refer to as 'cultural transmission' (see Shaw, 1966). In this sense, both everyday life and institutional domains are highly regulated by moral and behavioural norms, expectations, codes and sanctions (see e.g. Wieder [1974] for a discussion of this in the context of the prison, another of the sites that will receive our attention in Chapter 6).

From Primitives to Pilots: Groups and Affiliations

The sociologist Erving Goffman once wrote that '*any group of persons – prisoners, primitives, pilots or patients – develop a life of their own that becomes meaningful, reasonable, and normal **once you get close to it**'* (Goffman, 1961: 7; emphasis added). A little later on we examine just how you will 'get close' to various groups in and through the use of research methods. However, the point we want to make here is that the social world – and everyday life – often consists of groups and their *affiliations* and *disaffiliations* – be it by virtue of birth, actively pursued out of volition, or unwillingly ascribed. There are many bases for such affiliation and disaffiliations, an obvious one being our main concern in this book, race. Indeed, several of these can 'intersect' to make us who we are (and are not). An important dimension to this is the pragmatic nature of such affiliations and disaffiliations, that is, deliberate and purposeful affiliation with (or disaffiliation from) particular persons or groups, for particular purposes. We shall discuss some of these issues in Chapter 7.

Racially based affiliations and disaffiliations are sometimes quite explicit (e.g. segregation in the years of Apartheid) (Wolpe, 1990). Others may be more mundane and implicit (e.g. choosing who and who not to sit with in the works canteen). When affiliations extend beyond the immediacy of any particular (local) site, setting or context we might start to think of communities in a wider sense, that is, persons who share some affiliation but may not necessarily ever come into one's immediate co-presence. Such possibilities take us back to see how the local can be impacted by the global, and how affiliations with 'like' others need not ever involve real, but often 'virtual' communities (something that has been facilitated by the increase in communications, media and information technologies in recent times).

As we have suggested in the previous chapters, racial categorisation and typification of 'otherness' has often been synonymous with disempowerment. The possibilities afforded by affiliation via reflexive acts of self-directed self-racialisation (especially with racially or ethnically similar others) can conversely form the basis for emancipation and empowerment. Vernacular expressions such as 'strength in numbers' and 'brothers'/'sisters' are everyday ways of pointing to this affiliation and solidarity with 'like' others. Moreover, such affiliations can allow persons to lay claim to cherished or 'revered' racial or ethnic identities, which can be used as a basis for empowerment, or at least attempts to self-empower. A range of classic studies have shown how this affiliation with 'similar' others can be used to carve out some power, and serve as a basis for the definition (often pejoratively) of others and otherness (see Becker, 1963; Goffman, 1961), and the power of affiliation has been pointed to in texts focusing specifically on race (Gilroy, 2002; Hall et al., 1978).

Identities and Interactions

The issue of identities should not be underemphasised in your research into race and racism. Indeed, certain identities in everyday life can reach the level of what sociologist C. Everett Hughes, in his examination of the dilemmas faced by black medical doctors, called 'master status' (Hughes, 1945). The charge levelled at such racial stereotypes and the racially charged discourses they index is one of simplification and generalisation, based on indefensible premises. However, as we have noted, and will demonstrate later in this book, notions of whom a person is to him/herself and others as a 'social category' is complex, changing and often contradictory. In addition, racial 'identity' may be argued to be inherently unstable (Blee, 2000), and in your research you yourself should avoid invoking (or even reifying) 'essentialist' categories of race and ethnicity (Gallagher, 2000; Gunaratnam, 2003; Islam, 2000). Having said that, as we have suggested, and shall examine in more detail in Chapter 6, 'cherished' racial identities can be invoked at particular times for particular reasons, and to that extent as notions can carry some resonance and meaning by those seeking to invoke them (e.g. Gallagher [2000] on 'white' racial identity and Quraishi [2005] on the invocation of Muslim identity).

Identity claims and ascriptions can be tied in with notions of affiliation and dis-affiliation then. However, again, this may be far from a simple affair, as often, 'belonging' and 'not belonging' may index different groups, at different times, and for different purposes. Alongside race, variables such as class, age, gender, and notions related to race such as faith and ethnicity may form the basis for affiliation, and for identities, as might wider cultural frames of reference. This means that identity might best not be viewed as monolithic or as necessarily meaning the same thing in different social or cultural contexts. This can create complex, challenging − and sometimes contradictory − notions of identity. We shall discuss this further below when we address the notions of 'intersectionality' (Chapter 7) and 'transnational identities' (Chapter 6, Case Study 2).

The point here is that, although identity is complex, and not solely based on race, race can often become an − the − identity issue, and consequently an interactional one, both for those wishing to ascribe it to others and those wishing to claim it for themselves. As Clayman and Gill point out:

> Human interaction lies at the very heart of social life. It is primarily through interaction that children are socialized, culture is transmitted, language is put to use, identities are affirmed, institutions are activated, and social structures of all kinds reproduced. (Clayman and Gill, 2004: 589)

Clayman and Gill's comments then point to not only the centrality of identities to interaction, but to the relationship between the institutionalised and the institutional we noted above.

The Experience, Meaning and Practical Accomplishment of Race, Racism and Racialisation in Everyday Life

As something of a prelude to our discussion of what we have termed the sociologies of everyday life below, we would like to emphasise three core features of everyday life.

First, in Chapter 1 we outlined a number of ways in which racism can be experienced. Across the 'daily round' (see Goffman, 1961) in both private space (domestic settings, etc.) and the public realm (streets, neighbourhoods, workplaces, malls, entertainment sites), race and racism can be variously experienced, from quite nuanced and implicit aspects of behaviour, through marginalisation and exclusion, to overt and even violent 'attack' (see Chapter 6, Case Studies 1 and 2). The same applies of course to the more institutional contexts pointed to earlier (such as carceral and total institutions [see Quraishi, 2005, 2010a]. We have already pointed to ideas about social construction and will touch on these issues in the following chapter, but a central domain that you will need to access in your research into race and racism as experience is the subjective one. As we shall see in the following chapter, accessing experience necessarily involves exploring this subjective domain. Persons are often able to provide 'versions' of everyday experience, or offer 'accounts' of actions or behaviours (their own and others'). By definition, this can often lead to varying or even contradictory accounts or versions of events, behaviours and actions, and just as such things as identities and affiliations can be complex and contradictory, so can these accounts and versions of the everyday (see Cuff, 1994).

Second, experience is not simply a flux of stimuli from the external world to which no sense is given. It is, rather, treated as *meaningful*. This focus on meaning is crucial when understanding race and racism in and as part of everyday life. Persons, places, actions, attitudes and events are imbued with particular meaning, by particular groups, sometimes for particular purposes. Again, via a range of research methods, these meanings can be revealed in the behaviours, actions and utterances of particular persons and groups. By definition, meanings are not universal, and competing meanings – competing definitions – may operate and emerge. Again, social research can go some way to accessing and appreciating these.

Finally, we have touched on the notion of social construction already in this text. However, tied in with notions of experience and meaning are more precise notions of everyday life as being a *practical accomplishment* (Garfinkel, 1967). That is, it is something that is done, made recognisable and worked out by persons in and through their everyday use of identities and interactional competences. Looking at social construction in this sense allows us to, perhaps most radically, see how the issues we have talked about over the preceding pages are played out in the immediacy of face-to-face – race-to-race – encounters.

Researching Race, Racism and Racialisation in Everyday Life

The Research Promise

What we have suggested as key considerations when researching race and racism in everyday life, then, and what this opens up for you as a researcher of race and racism, is a world consisting not of external immutable categories, classes and correlations (as some Enlightenment thinkers might have liked to have us believe), but of experiences, meaning, perspectives, discourses, affiliations and disaffiliations, institutional and institutionalised practices, identities and interactions and practical accomplishment. As we have suggested, these must be accessed and made sense of by you as a researcher. The 'promise' lies in the fact that thoughtful, sensitive and appropriate research can provide you with a well-trodden way of doing this.

Ontological and Epistemological Considerations

We undermined above the ontological (attitude to what constitutes 'reality') and epistemological (attitude to what constitutes 'knowledge') foundations of earlier thought and discourse about race and ethnicity. Moreover, we concur with Gunaratnam (2003: 13), who challenges the 'scientific' basis of truth claims of research on 'race' by drawing attention to the ways in which the meanings of 'race' have been socially and culturally constructed. The stance taken here then has its ontological and epistemo-logical foundations not in the 'hard science' of *positivism* (that underpinned the science of race – see Chapter 1), but in the what is generally referred to as the *interpretivist* approach to carrying out social research. A full discussion of interpretivism is beyond the scope of this chapter, but the general approach to understanding the social world can be traced back to the German sociologist Max Weber (see Weber, 1949). Unlike positivist social scientists of the time, Weber insisted sociologists tried to achieve *Verstehen* (German for 'understanding'), that is, the meaning taken from and underpin-ning social action held by members involved in those actions themselves. This general attitude to doing social research has informed a range of distinct but interrelated ways of analysing social reality, some of which we shall discuss shortly. In essence, in adopt-ing an interpretive stance, your aim will be to attempt to understand and appreciate those meanings, experiences and perspectives from the *point-of-view of the actor(s)*; as we noted above, the focus being not on the objective but the subjective.

The Quality of Race, Racism and Racialisation in Everyday Life

In order to research these aspects of the social world in general, and of race and racism in particular, *qualitative* (as opposed to *quantitative*) methods are conventionally used. We should note that, although we are advocating qualitative research here, we do rec-ognise that quantitative research and data can be useful to you as a researcher. For example, statistics on demographics or race/ethnicity/faith-related issues can provide useful overviews of, for example, incidences of racially motivated behaviour, and allow for important contextualisation (see Chapter 6, Case Study 1) for the qualitative researcher or even help in the recruitment process by identifying relevant populations or forming a basis for 'sampling' (again, see Chapter 6). Indeed, the processes that underlie these data can themselves be data for analysis insofar as they reveal how racialisation and ethnicisation have underpinned and guided official and institutional racial and ethnic categorisation and grouping, played a key role in the social, political, legal and institutional construction of race, and the potential problems, contradictions, inconsistencies and 'glosses' that this may give rise to (see Chapter 6). Of course, quan-titative data may be subject to secondary type analysis (see Chapter 5).

A frequent distinction made between qualitative and quantitative research is between *words* and *numbers*.[5] Indeed, although not restricted to 'words', as we have indicated, the 'spoken construction of realty' is central to qualitative research. Indeed, you will find that many of your data – or your 'evidence' - consist of words gained and gleaned from various social encounters and from various sources – those uttered *for* you, *to* you, in your *presence* and even *by* you. However, you may also encounter such qualitative data as images, photographs, film, or even cartoons and caricatures. All these things need to be examined for how they are experienced, the meaning they convey or are attributed with, and the uses they are put to.

An equally important distinction we would like to make is not to do with data as such (although reflection on this may constitute data – see below), but with exposure to, immersion in and empathy with the persons, groups and social processes with whom you may come into contact, observe and experience during the course of your research. It is this 'human' aspect of qualitative research that is perhaps a more important point of departure from quantitative approaches to researching race and racism. To varying degrees you will be exposed to those experiences, meanings, actions and interactions of persons, groups, organisations and institutions you wish to study. There is, then, an important personal dimension to consider. What this means is that conducting qualitative research can be a demanding, stressful or even dangerous experience. These issues are perhaps most relevant if you are conducting ethnographic–style research (see Lee-Treweek and Linkogle, 2000).

The Personal Side of Researching Race, Racism and Racialisation in Everyday Life

We have already emphasised the subjective domain of race and racism in everyday life, and pointed to your need to access this in your research. *Personal* experience should be borne in mind when starting down the road of qualitative research. As social researchers we should not of course, and cannot, talk about everyday life as some completely alien domain, that we know nothing about or – perhaps more importantly – have no feelings, attitudes or values towards. In recognition of this, one thing we would like to give some emphasis to is the *reflexive* side of researching race and racism. What we mean here is your ability to look back to yourself to see how you are impacting on the research process, and how, in turn, it is impacting on you. Such reflexivity should be central to any research into race and racism (Gunaratnam, 2003). Your feelings, values and prejudices about race matters should not be glossed over or ignored. Indeed, even if conducting 'value free' research is itself an 'ideal type' of activity (see Weber, 1949), reflexively and critically incorporating your personal dispositions, and how they may affect the research, should be something you as a researcher must be prepared to do (see Vera and Feagin, 2004).

This might first relate to the dispositional and prejudicial 'baggage' you bring to your research (which you undoubtedly will – see Becker's [1967] 'Whose side are we on?'). For example, you may carry with you to your research a range of racially or ethnically informed values or prejudices (Scheurich and Young, 1997) – in fact, as you have presumably some interest in race and racism and may well see these as 'problematic' as a reader of this book, this will likely be the case. You may also have very strong feelings about race and ethnicity issues. This could range from a determined intention to 'stamp out' racial and ethnic discrimination to a belief that 'political correctness' is undermining the rights of indigenous members of your own culture, locale or community. You may well have some axe to grind, torch to carry, or soapbox from which you wish to present your work. We are not suggesting that a wholly value free (see Weber, 1979) research is possible, however, as a researcher of race and racism we would argue that naively ignoring these possibilities, or worse, denying them, would not only be deluding yourself (and your potential readership), but could in fact be quite dangerous in that it may 'colour' your research at various stages. More directly, they may well negatively impact on social encounters and interpersonal relations you have with those you come across during your research.

A second aspect of reflexivity might pertain to your own biographical features. You will, by definition, have your own racial and ethnic identity(ies) (albeit, as we have suggested above, ones that intersect with other demographic variables), and these may well carry meaning for you and those you encounter. Your own race may have a noticeable bearing on your research (see e.g. Duneier, 2004; Egharevba, 2001; Quraishi, 2008b). Indeed, you may find that others – including your research informants – ascribe certain identities to you in and through 'in the field' racialisation and ethnicisation processes. It may be that these aspects of your biography – your embodied identity – facilitate or hinder your research. Your status as *insider* or *outsider* may influence what those you are researching are prepared to say or do in your presence. For example, your own perceived racial identity may result in your informants withholding any racist behaviour or attitudes (see Zinn, cited in Twine and Warren, 2000) or, alternatively, they may feel safe 'with you' to express such feelings (see Islam, 2000) (indeed, in past research 'racial matching' was employed to ensure researcher and respondent were 'of the same racial kind', so to speak [see Twine and Warren, 2000: Ch. 1]). For example, you may find that being 'white European', 'African American' or 'British Asian' makes rapport building or communication easier or more difficult, or even facilitates or hinders your access to the people and places you want to include in your research in the first place (see Chapter 6). Such recognition and negotiation of inside–outside status is a feature in several studies of race and racism (Gallagher, 2000; Young, 2004).

Third, you should also be reflexive about what we would term your research identity (what is commonly referred to as your *role* – see Chapter 5). Again, you need to be aware of what you 'mean' to your informants, that is, who (or what) you are perceived to embody or personify, not necessarily at a biographical or personal level, but at an institutional one, and any associated power issues. This is another way in which institutions and identities interact and co-construct each other, and how they can impact on the interactional. For example, in this sense, you may be perceived as first and foremost (your 'master status' [see Hughes, 1945]) a social worker, a teacher, a university academic, etc. This may have a bearing not only on some of the issues we have just outlined, but may point to important ethical issues (see the following chapter).

These issues of reflexivity will become more important the more exposed to and immersed in your research 'field' you become and the closer you get to the people you wish to engage with, study and write about (see our discussion of ethnographic work in the following chapter), but they are things you should be aware of in the context of (or even as outcomes of) your research.

The Problem of Race, Racism and Racialisation in Everyday Life

Conceptual and Theoretical Problems

Primarily, we have argued along with most contemporary social scientists that the concept of race is a socially and culturally constructed one, rather than being a biologically determined class of person(s) (see Chapters 1 and 2). As we have pointed out in our historical discussion, humankind has used the term to refer to a category of persons, and this has involved the typification of such persons and has ultimately impacted the social, political, legal and moral organisation of those persons. We have argued that race becomes problematic, that is, in and of itself a complex, often arbitrary, sometimes challenged notion, that is drawn upon in a range of contexts by different persons and, ultimately, means different things as people go about using the notion. In this sense, not only is race a socially constructed phenomenon, but, in effect, has no meaning of its own outside the *context of its use*. Moreover, arguments around intersectionality, discussed in Chapter 2 (see also Chapter 7) suggest that the concept of race may be further complicated, as it can only be better understood as it intersects with other concepts – ethnicity, class, gender, age, etc. In this sense race – and the notion of racism (see Garner, 2010; Miles and Brown, 2003) – are far from 'black and white' issues.

This in itself might seem to create a conceptual problem for you as a race and racism researcher, particularly if you want to do anything other than purely descriptive work. Ironically, the problem is perhaps more acute in quantitative research, which often seeks, for example, 'empirical indicators' of a predefined concept that need to be clearly outlined and defined at the start of a project. In qualitative research, conceptual problems are not prescribed and 'sought' in the same way, but allowed to 'emerge' out of the data, as the data are collected and analysed. In this sense, *a priori* application (or even understanding of) concepts is precluded (see the following chapter). This in one sense also allows you to avoid problems of essentialism as discussed in Chapter 1, and those of reification.

'Real World' Problems

Conceptual problematics are only part of the story though. As Thomas and Thomas (1928) once noted, if something is defined as real, it is real in its consequences. Even though we have challenged the validity of race as an objective one, the reality of the concept of race in terms of how persons choose to define the notion can have very real effects. To that extent, race and racism can become 'everyday problems' for those who inhabit and pass through the various sites and settings that constitute everyday contemporary society. Whether it is marginalisation and exclusion or physical assault, race and racism may be a 'real' problem for many in contemporary society. Indeed, simply 'having to' behave in ways that avoid any accusation of racism may be a problem for some (Augoustinos and Every, 2007). This is one way in which the abstract domain of theory and concepts and the practical domain of everyday experience, meaning and practice can often be misaligned. Race might not mean anything at a conceptual level, but may be fundamentally meaningful at a real world level.

Again, we should add that much rests on perceptual issues, that is, if and to what extent victims or perpetrators of such behaviour perceive it to be an instance or example of racialisation or racism. We have already touched on how persons or groups can 'self-racialise'. This process is also tied in with the idea of being a 'victim' of racism. Indeed, even if what others might perceive or define to be quite obvious racist acts to have taken place, targets of that behaviour may respond variously, from self-allocation to rejection of victim status (see Chapter 6, Case Study 1).

'Research' Problems

Finally, the starting point for any research is some sort of 'research problem'. Your research problem may be grounded in some identifiable real world problem. For example, in the context of the current discussion, such real world problems might be issues of race that are experienced as such, meaningful, occur in everyday life, invoke identities and arise in interaction. Alternatively, you may start out with some pre-dominantly conceptual problem. The two 'types' of problem will be inextricably linked. In this sense, research problems might be conceived of as the *meeting point* of conceptual problems and real world problems, and your job, to some extent, will be to more closely align them. Indeed, as a researcher of race and racism you will be focus-ing on both realms and, as a qualitative researcher, this may often involve simultaneous research activity (see our discussion of analysis in qualitative research in the following chapter).

Researching race and racism as real world problems will involve, then, a movement down the 'ladder of abstraction' to consider race and racism on the ground. In doing this you may have no interest in critiquing conceptualisations or revising and develop-ing theory. This may be the case if you are conducting your research for or in the context of some organisation (e.g. if you are a teacher researching in the school setting, a medical practitioner working in the context of some service provision, or a social worker evaluating some form of practice). However – due to the inductive nature of qualitative research – you may find yourself climbing back up this ladder to shed light on notions of race, highlighting key concepts, and even contributing to some wider theoretical understanding of it. As we have suggested, crucially, this will be 'grounded'

(Glaser and Strauss, 1967) in your data. Again, this is one way in which the abstract of conceptual and theoretical discussion, and the real of everyday life can be aligned.

This problem may be formalised in the shape of some 'research question'. In qualitative research questions perform a particular function. A distinction is often made between research questions and hypotheses, the latter referring to a statement that will be 'tested' in and through some sort of 'fixed' research design; the former to a general concern based on some identified problem. A fuller discussion of the differences between qualitative and quantitative design is beyond this text, but suffice it to say that, due to the essentially inductive and emergent nature of qualitative work, research questions – in fact any questions – tend to very quickly be *informed* and *transformed* by the emergent collection and analysis of data.

Finally, you may want to direct your focus not towards conceptual clarification or theoretical development and critique, but towards addressing those real world problems themselves. Again, this is most likely if you are a professional or practitioner (Katz and Moore, 2013) (although academic researchers also have an eye on how their work can be directly applied to improve real world situations of course, and some would argue that this is the whole point of academic work). If this is the case, your work might have some definite evaluative dimension (of, for example, new policy or initiatives in the workplace, community, etc.). What is referred to as 'action research' has gained favour over recent years, particularly in the fields of education and health and social services. The qualitative position and particular methods we outline in Chapter 5 are often well-suited to such types of research work and proactive engagement.

Research Planning Problems

All of the issues we have discussed above will bring you to the point of planning actual research. Research must be planned (from initial conceptualisation through submission of research applications and bids for funding), conducted (from small scale 'pilots' to full blown studies) and disseminated (through a range of means to a range of audiences). In Chapter 6 we shall illustrate and discuss these various aspects of the research process through our presentation of three case studies. In the following chapter we shall discuss some of the factors that you will need to take into account in the planning of your research into race and racism.

The Sociologies of Everyday Life

Finally, to conclude this chapter, we want to say something briefly about what might be termed the 'sociologies of everyday life' (see Dennis et al., 2013). These are theoretical and methodological approaches to understanding the things we have talked about above – experience, meaning, actions, institutions, identities and interactions, and the practical and pragmatic uses of race in everyday life, etc. – that act as general frames of reference for much social and sociological research. We mention these briefly due, in no small part, to our own disciplinary backgrounds and interests. However, we would like to think that these general perspectives to understanding everyday life may have some bearing on and relevance to your own particular research. If nothing else, they point to the importance of experience, meaning and practice we have emphasised above.

Phenomenology

Experience is the domain of phenomenological approaches to everyday life. Alfred Schutz is regarded as the central figure in the field of phenomenology. Very much influenced by the philosophy of Edmund Husserl, Schutz's central concern was with the nature and accomplishment of not just individual experience, but shared experience – of what is referred to as 'intersubjectivity' or a 'reciprocity of per-spectives' (Schutz, 1973). The successful achievement of intersubjectivity is greatly aided by what Schutz saw as '*typical sequences and relations*' of actions (Schutz, 1964: 80). As part of everyday reality, social actors come into one another's presence with a shared stock of knowledge about these actions, sequences and relations. Moreover, this knowledge can be and is routinely conveyed via a shared vernacular language – what Schutz saw as '*the typifying medium par excellence*' (Schutz, 1973). In this way, intersubjectivity is achieved in and through 'typified' and 'typifying' everyday ver-nacular language.

The consequences of understanding experience – and social organisation – as a typifying activity for race and racism research should be plain to see. Indeed, with language at its heart, how persons are prepared to 'talk about whilst typifying' persons, places and events should reveal much about their shared stocks of knowledge, their understanding of their lifeworlds, and, of particular importance to you, the place race takes in those stocks of knowledge and shared understandings.

Symbolic Interactionism

We have referred in our preceding discussion to the social construction of race, and pointed to notions such as definition, the meanings given to things and the centrality of language to the social world, and that definitions and meanings can have particular 'real' consequences. These issues are of concern to symbolic interactionists.

Symbolic interactionism was very much influenced by pragmatic philosophy, that is, the idea that the meaning of things resides essentially in their practical use(s) or actual consequence(s) (see Peirce, 1992). For pragmatists, any 'thing' with no use or consequences, in effect, did not have meaning. This idea of things having mean-ing was taken up by the sociologist Herbert Blumer. Blumer (1969) outlined three central premises: things are acted upon according to their meaning; meaning is derived from social interaction; and meanings are interpreted. A second influence on symbolic interactionism was George Herbert Mead, who focused on the notion of the self in society. For Mead, persons develop identities based on their own perceptions of themselves, or rather, on how they perceived others to perceive them (similar to what the philosopher George Cooley [1902] called the 'looking glass self'). Thus, we are presented with a picture of the world not simply as experienced, but as experienced as meaningful, and of selves and identities as being meaningful things that go to constitute that world.

Symbolic interactionists would be keen to point out that no thing has any intrinsic meaning, but that this meaning is worked out in interaction, and can be subject to claims, ascriptions, impositions, resistance and negotiations (see Strauss, 1978). To that extent, the social world is not simply, as we have argued, socially constructed, but interactionally constructed, communicated and negotiated.

Not infrequently, symbolic interactionists have concerned themselves with studies of marginal identities, stigmatised groups and 'outsiders'. The term 'outsiders' can be applied to certain groups often seen as different and more often than not in some way threatening – to traditional culture, economy, safety – or as 'enemy' (although in recent discussions based around such things as home-grown terrorism the notion of what might be termed the 'enemy within' has entered popular discourse around race and ethnicity). Moreover, this has often focused on the social processes involved. A classic example of this was Goffman's examination of the 'moral career' (a concept used in other studies), a central concern for Goffman being the interaction between the individual and the institution (of particular relevance to the context of Case Study 2, discussed in the following chapter). A number of studies have also adopted a symbolic interactionist approach to race in particular (Gillborn, 1995).

The issues of affiliation and disaffiliation mentioned above are also evident in symbolic interactionist work. In his classic study *Outsiders*, for example, Becker examined the 'dual-notion' of this term and showed how, as well as powerful groups ascribing the status of outsiders on marginalised groups, those marginalised groups can also actively seek to establish themselves as different from the mainstream, dominant group. Thus, as symbolic interaction, we can see how the social world is socially constructed and interactionally communicated and negotiated, with the meaning and interpretation of things lying at its heart.

Ethnomethodology and Conversation Analysis

Finally, the notions of routine, taken-for-granted, everyday interaction that have run through this chapter are perhaps no better investigated than in the field of ethnomethodology. The emphasis given among ethnomethodologists is on the practical accomplishments that persons display in the social world. However, more specifically, the role of language as used in the mundane, routine everyday is taken up by conversation analysts (see Hutchby and Wooffitt, 2008). Again, following Schutz, scholars working in this area are interested in both the everyday application of language and, in part, its typifying features. For example, as we shall see in the following chapter, naturally occurring everyday conversation often uses what are referred to as 'membership categories' (see Hester and Eglin, 1997), that is, mundane ways of categorising persons, but ones which can be redolent with meaning and implication.

These sociologies of everyday life furnish us with important sociological understandings of *experience*, *meaning* and *practice* and can be applied to the analysis of any contemporary context. We are not suggesting that you turn your attention to consider these general perspectives out of the context of your current research concerns. As we have noted above, their inclusion here reflects as much as anything our own disciplinary dispositions. However, their centrality to examining the social and interactional organisation of the everyday means they may provide useful academic steers on your research into race and racism.

Summary

In this chapter we have extended our focus on contemporary society with a closer examination of race and racism as part of everyday life. Alongside consolidating our comments in Chapters 1–3, what we have tried to do here is to suggest ways in which you as a researcher into race and racism can start to identify a range of contemporary sites, settings and contexts in which race and racism might reveal themselves and in which your research might be carried out. We have placed some emphasis on the ways in which race and racism are experienced, given meaning and practically achieved in any given social or cultural context, and in the way they inform interaction and form the basis of identities. In something of a preparation for the following chapter, we have discussed more explicitly the ontological and epistemological issues that have been implicitly touched on in Chapters 1–3, and outlined a series of theoretical approaches to understanding everyday life that allow for an examination of some of the issues mentioned above. One central argument we have advanced is the need to conduct qualitative research if one is to fully appreciate and understand race and racism, and avoid some of the pitfalls mentioned in previous chapters. Finally, we have drawn the reader's attention to what we referred to as the personal side of researching race and racism. This is particularly important to us, as we have found, and shall illustrate variously in the discussion of our case studies in Chapter 6, that researcher presence is something that is omnipresent in research into race and racism.

We have covered a lot of ground in this chapter, but the aim has been not to excavate deeply but rather to sketch out the landscape of race and racism in contemporary society. The 'deep mining' of particular points of this landscape is something that you will yourself set about in your own research project. Some of the tools you may need to go about this endeavour will be the focus of the next chapter.

Notes

1 Ironically, in seeking to tackle racism, governments and other bodies and agencies have required some working definition of race and ethnicity in order to preclude, prescribe or punish acts of racism – in effect, needing to racialise in order to deracialise.

2 Of course, as Essed (1991) also notes, we should recognise that not all racism is 'everyday' (e.g. more overt racist behaviour and events).

3 Indeed, racial categories can also be 'sung about' as part of everyday – often 'normalised' – language use, the prime example of this type of racial articulation being, in the UK, the football chant.

4 Indeed, post–World War II, any notion of race has tended to have been eradicated from the domain of science.

5 A rather dated, but still useful overview of this distinction is presented by Halfpenny (1979).

5

RACE, RACISM AND QUALITATIVE METHODS

Keywords: *qualitative methods, everyday language, ethnography, qualitative analysis, research ethics, dissemination of findings*

Introduction

Up to now we have presented overviews of the historical context of race and racism (Chapter 1), definitional and conceptual issues (Chapter 2) and legal frameworks (Chapter 3), before discussing the relevance to and problem of race and racism in and as part of contemporary society (Chapter 4). In the light of our discussion so far, we have pointed to the general ontological and epistemological standpoint which we feel is necessary to conduct research into race and racism. In this chapter we want to look more specifically at some of the qualitative research methods that you might use in conducting your research – as we termed it in the previous chapter, excavating the landscape of race and racism in contemporary everyday life.

This chapter is not an 'introduction to social research' *per se* then, which would be well beyond the scope of the chapter (or the book as a whole), but more of an exploration of some key issues that you are most likely to come across as part of your research.[1] The aim here is to furnish you with some methodological and procedural knowledge that will allow you to explore some of the issues dealt with in previous chapters, and are ones which we shall, in part, illustrate through our use of case studies in Chapter 6.

The questions raised in this chapter are:

- What are some of the 'key methods' used to collect qualitative data?
- How might 'ethnographically sensitive' work yield insights into race and racism in contemporary sites, settings and contexts?
- What are some of the 'key issues' to consider when conducting ethnographic work?
- How might spoken language reveal race and racism in contemporary society?

- How do qualitative researchers approach the analysis of qualitative data?
- What factors might have to be taken into consideration when deciding to disseminate the results of qualitative research into race and racism?

Documentary Records, Images and Artefacts

As we suggested in the previous chapter, the social world is a recorded, documented and mediated place. The issue of race can be the focus of such documentary activities and enterprises. Moreover, documents – often at an institutional level – come to be read routinely as accurate records and depictions of social reality – as 'fact'. As powerful definitional resources, they can be, and often are, not only meaningful, but *consequential*.

The term documents, at least as we are using it here, is something of a catch-all for a range of materials, from very *official* records to very *personal* items, from the strictly *private* to the openly *public*, from the easily *accessible* to the strictly *off limits*. The vernacular understanding of document points to written materials. Indeed, these will likely be the kind of documents you come across more than anything else in your research. However, the term can be extended to include any 'item' or 'artefact' that in some way forms part of the lifeworld of those persons or groups you are researching and specifically, indexes notions of processes of racialisation, and practices of racism.

Official Sources

What might be referred to as 'official' and institutional documentation can provide useful data in race and racism research. This may include contemporary documentation, or could include more historical documents; the latter can reveal some of the issues covered in Chapter 1, the former more contemporary forms of race and racism outlined in the previous chapter. Starting institutionally 'at the top', so to speak, governmental and even international legislation (see Chapter 3) can reveal how race is conceptualised and defined and point to the potential problems (problems for – e.g. underpinning anti-racist policy – or caused by – e.g. driving immigration policy – various racial and ethnic groups) that such legislation recognises and seeks to formally address. State documents such as official reports may also yield similar data (see Macpherson, 1999; Ministry of Justice, 2013a). We examined closely legislation pertaining to racist and discriminatory behaviour in Chapter 3. Legal documents (e.g. court proceedings or outcomes of inquiries) are another source of data. Indeed, legislative documentation reveals a very clear crystallisation of prevailing (governmental, legal) understandings of race and racism at any point in time (see e.g. the Racial and Religious Hatred Act 2006). 'Institutional' documentation such as official records or files kept about persons or groups of persons may also be a useful source of data (see Chapter 6). The ideas contained within and processes underlying these documents may filter down and be institutionally translated into organisational documentation, such as written company policy on matters such as equality and diversity in the treatment and recruitment of members of racial and ethnic minorities. Ideas contained within these may even be formulated for public consumption in the form of mission statements and the like. At a practical level, documentation may be given a pedagogical slant in the form of staff guidance, training courses, or a punitive one in the form of disciplinary procedures. Whenever and wherever race 'appears' in such documentation – in those documentary contexts – it will reveal how the notion has not only been conceptualised, but practically employed, and of course, the nature and extent of any discriminatory ways in which the concept has been used (for example, in the UK, every local authority produces guidelines on how to tackle racist incidents in schools and they are compelled to do so by virtue of the Race Relations [Amendment] Act 2000).

As we shall see below, 'accessibility' is an inherent issue in all research, and not all of this type of documentary material will be immediately accessible to you. Indeed, much like the focus for investigative journalists and the like, an added dimension to accessibility of documentary material is the possible distinction between the 'public' face of anti-racism practices and the 'private' reality (a front-stage/back-stage distinction that is endemic to contemporary western society [see Goffman, 1959]). Indeed, some 'internal' documents, such as minutes of meetings or e-mails can reveal interesting data for race and racism researchers (and if 'leaked' can be the cause of some embarrassment, as evidenced in the furore caused by the 2010 'Wikileaks' incident).

Of course, there may be quite overt racially oriented political dimensions to the documentary evidence you collect, that is, documents may be used to explicitly and quite openly represent and convey meaning, or 'send a message' about race (see Ministry of Justice, 2013b). This can include mainstream politics, such as political manifestos and other literature, transcripts of political speeches or even imagery used for political purposes, but can also include more subversive and discriminatory notions of race and ethnicity. The text used in the period of the Third Reich in Nazi Germany is a clear example of this (Herf, 2006). However, more contemporary examples include literature produced by right-wing groups such as the English Defence League (EDL) and the British National Party (BNP) in the UK as well as other extremist and radicalised groups (see e.g. Blee, 2000; Fielding, 1982). Falling into this broad category of written racialisation might also be lay politicisation of racially charged messages, manifest in such things as graffiti (see Chapter 6, Case Study 3).

Media and Images

We have already pointed to the role the news media play in racialisation (see Chapters 1 and 4). 'Institutional' and often 'politicised', rather formal and quite specialised documents are perhaps less interesting than what might be termed cultural documentation. These are important because they not only contain notions of race, and display contemporary racism but, more importantly, are designed for public consumption, and are, inevitably, consumed, often quite willingly, unthinkingly and uncritically. Obvious cultural documents that might contain notions of race and have some hand in processes of racialisation are newspapers, in particular the tabloid press. They are to some extent the 'pulse of perceived reality' for many at any moment in time and can quite often be seen to be openly and proactively engaged in racialisation (Hall, 2000; van Dijk, 1991). The popular press and news media fuel popular discourse and populist notions of race and, as was shown in Stanley Cohen's (2011) classic text *Folk Devils and Moral Panics*, seek out persons belonging to groups that pose a threat to the moral and social order. For example, since the atrocities of 9/11 and 7/7 in the UK, fears surrounding young, disaffected Muslim males and processes of radicalisation have been fed into the news media on a regular basis, presenting notions of the Muslim 'folk devil' (Patel and Tyrer, 2011; Quraishi, 2005, 2013; Webster, 1997b; see Chapter 6, Case Study 2). More recently in the UK, the notion of 'Asian grooming' of minors has 'hit the headlines', leading to public and political sensitisation and resultant discourses (Moore et al., 2008; Sian et al., 2012). Of course, there is also a connection between the media and the political realm, with popular discourse sometimes driving political decision making.

However, the more insidious and invisible racism is, the more dangerous it can be. Indeed, racialisation and the notions that underpin these processes can reach the point of entertaining and even amusing us (Weaver, 2011). A myriad of forms of popular culture may evidence this. This type of documentary material should be readily and easily accessible to you. You might draw on televised popular culture for example. In the UK, the 1970s were marked by notably politically incorrect forms of televised sitcoms such as *Rising Damp* and *Love thy Neighbour*, and before this programmes such as *The Black and White Minstrel Show*, which were often explicitly racist but extremely popular, as were a host of then popular comedians who regularly appeared on prime time television (Bourne, 2005). Those days are now behind us, but popular and simplified notions of race still exist in popular culture. Cinematic film also routinely engages in – indeed has a long history of – racialisation. For example the historic practice of 'blacking up' whereby white Hollywood actors would darken their skin to play black characters (Stam and Spence, 1983); to the more recent stereotypical depictions of the Muslim as terrorist (Mandel, 2001; see also Cripps, 1977; Silk and Silk, 1990). The music industry is also often highly racialised, and this spills over into fashion and subcultural styles (see e.g. Back, 2000).

Finally, a range of new communications and media mentioned in Chapter 3, such as social networking, social media and blogs, have changed the landscape, meaning and uses of media in contemporary society.

Personal Documents

One thing we emphasised in the previous chapter was the personal aspect of race and racism (including how they are immediately and locally experienced). Indeed, this is when race and racism are most acutely 'felt' as such. Such immediate and personal experience is often recorded and reflected in a range of personal documents. These can include such things as diaries, letters, photographs or other private documents (see Thomas and Znaniecki [1918] for a pioneering use of these types of documents in their study of immigrant populations). These can give an insight into experiences of race and racism from a very personal perspective and over a long period of time. Such materials can be used to good effect when conducting case studies or using what is referred to as a biographical or life history method (see Shaw [1966] for another classic example of this method). 'Personal' documents might also include official records and files kept not by particular individuals, but about them (see Chapter 6, Case Study 2).

One issue that should not be overlooked when considering how race is 'documented' at a personal level is the fact that race is an 'embodied' phenomenon, that is, arises out of bodily attributes (skin colour, eye shape, hair type, etc; see Goffman, 1963) often leading to what we shall discuss in Chapter 6 as 'at first sight' categorisation or 'immigrant imagery'. Moreover, the body can be actively and deliberately marked, modified or masked as having particular (or not having) racial qualities (Gilman, 2010). To that extent the body itself can serve as a document of race and racism, marked, for example, in tattoos,[2] scars, signs of assault (see Chapter 6, Case Study 2) or punishment or blemishes, alterations or modifications[3] of the skin or body (either imposed or made out of choice).

Approaching notions of race and ethnicity and processes of racialisation as lived and experienced, evidenced in and through documentary items, will bring you close to the human aspect of race and racism. However, as we alluded to in the preceding chapter, we advocate a greater degree of exposure to these experiences and the interpretations, meanings and actions that inform and are informed by them. This movement from documentary to experiential lies at the heart of qualitative research and requires a particular set of issues to be appreciated, practicalities to overcome, and methods to be employed.

Utterances, Language and Meaning

In the previous chapter we gave some emphasis to the role language plays in everyday life. Citing Schutz, we referred to this as the typifying medium *par excellence*. We also noted the use of language in the context of documentary materials. Much of what we have talked about so far can be reflected in the way persons or groups are prepared to talk about their experiences, the meanings they attribute to things and the way they interpret them, and their motivations and intentions, actions and behaviours. When we consider the spoken or 'uttered' word a huge array of possibilities for studying race and racism in a contemporary and everyday context opens up for us. Again, ultimately this involves engagement with – and exposure to – those whom you wish to study.

Qualitative Interviews

As we emphasised in Chapter 4, central to research into race and racism should be the exploration of the relationship between race, subjectivity and 'lived experience' (Gunaratnam, 2003). As a researcher, you will need to in some way access these experiences. A prime method for doing this is the qualitative interview (see Spradley, 1979). Actually, referring to the qualitative interview is something of a misnomer as, unlike questionnaires or surveys, no two interviews in qualitative research are ever the same, so we can't speak of *the* interview. However, their ubiquitous use as a key part of qualitative research attests to their power in accessing the experiences, attitudes, beliefs and potentially revealing prejudices of people in any social group.

Interviews are usually conducted on a face-to-face, one-to-one basis (although they can be conducted over the telephone, or, nowadays, even online). They tend to be semi-structured, or even unstructured, in nature (especially in ethnographic encounters – see below), with the former usually involving some loose interview schedule and the latter some sort of *aide memoire* (see the Appendix for an example from our own research). Qualitative interviews should allow as much as possible to emerge from the informants' own articulation of experience and allow the subject to relay experience via accounts of lived events as part of his/her everyday life. Essed (1991) is worth quoting at length here:

> *Experiences are a suitable source of information for the study of everyday racism because they include personal experiences as well as vicarious experiences of racism. In addition the notion of experience includes general knowledge of racism, which is an important source of information to qualify whether specific events can be generalized. These experiences of racism are made available for academic inquiry through accounts – that is, verbal reconstructions of experiences ... reconstructions of experiences in such accounts provide the best basis for the analysis of the simultaneous impact of racism in different sites and in different social relations. Accounts of racism locate the narrators as well as their experiences in the social contexts of their everyday lives, give specificity and detail to events, and invite the narrator to carefully qualify subtle experiences of racism.* (Essed, 1991: 3–4)

You should remember that you are in effect asking a lot of any person who agrees to be interviewed, as you may find yourself *exploring* – and your informant *exposing* – not only private experiences, feelings, attitudes, beliefs and behaviours, but also quite personal aspects of biography and life history (see Kvale, 1996). Because of this, you need to ensure that your informants (and you) are comfortable in such encounters as there may be a range of issues that make such encounters difficult or even impossible. The qualitative interview is not an 'interrogation' and you will need to build up a *rapport* with your informant as well as gain their trust (Glesnec and Peshkin, 1992; Mann and Stewart, 2000). Indeed, informants can often subjugate themselves if they feel in any way under pressure to 'perform'. Ironically, one disadvantage of gaining too much trust and establishing too much rapport is that informants can often 'spill out' and divulge extremely personal matters, sometimes of no (immediate) relevance to your research focus. Of course, the opposite may be the case, and your informants may 'clam up'. This can happen in any research project, but, in the context of the current discussion, as we noted in the previous chapter, issues of race and racism, and *in situ processes of racialisation and ethnicisation* may have an impact on either of these possibilities (Egharevba, 2001). However, we have argued at various points in this text that the social world is socially constructed and we have found that informants usually work with interviewers to co-construct a *recognisably successful interview* (although, of course, this will not always be the case as some informants will work to construct an unnecessarily awkward one!).

Although you should respect the words of your informants, it is always good to be aware that their comments will be subjectively charged (indeed, this is why you are accessing them). Furthermore, you are never guaranteed that your informants will allow you access to their experiences or true beliefs, attitudes or behaviours through the interview encounter, especially in respect of things you are unable to observe directly. Thus, although an important tool for the qualitative researcher, qualitative interviews also run the risk of providing a one-dimensional and sometimes uncorroborated set of data.

We shall talk a little more about research settings below, but one consideration you will need to take into account is the difference between what are commonly referred to as non-naturalistic and naturalistic settings. We are using the terms here to refer to those physical settings that are alien to those whom you are studying in the case of the former, and those settings that form part of everyday life for those persons or groups in the case of the latter. Non-naturalistic settings will be unfamiliar to the interviewee but more controllable, the latter (which we shall discuss shortly) will be familiar to the interviewee but less controllable (indeed, the researcher should avoid interference with such settings as much as possible [see Lincoln and Guba, 1985]).

Qualitative interviews can yield bountiful data on personal beliefs, attitudes, prejudice, experience and biography and provide insight into the social reality you are investigating. Indeed, they often provide access to what would otherwise be inaccessible (or unobservable), for example other places, times, periods or events that form part of your informants' personal experience or life history. Most importantly, they give your informants the possibility to articulate these issues *in their own words*, and on their own terms.

Focus Groups

An extension of the individual interview is the group interview (oddly, the paired interview seems to be seldom used in qualitative research). However, group data gathering would commonly take the form of focus groups (see Hughes and Dumont, 2002).

Naturally Occurring Language

The notion of persons conveying the everyday in *their own words* is perhaps no more clearly demonstrated than when one considers naturally occurring talk. That is, talk as *part of* the mundane, routine activity of day-to-day life. Such talk can reveal the way persons describe, typify and account for their experiences of race and racism (see Chapter 4). The field of conversation analysis (see Sacks, 1992) draws its empirical basis from the recording and analysis of naturally occurring talk-in-interaction (see our discussion at the end of the previous chapter). Naturally occurring conversation can reveal the social construction of race and racism at a very mundane, taken-for-granted level, in and through the primary mode of communication – and social construction – that is, ordinary language. A nice example of how naturally occurring talk can reveal race and racism is in the way what conversation analysts call 'membership categories' (see Hester and Eglin, 1997) are used. These are ways in which persons 'select' particular ways to describe particular persons or groups. There are myriad ways of describing any person or persons. However, some terms that are used are clearly associated with the construction of race and various forms of racism (see below).

Observations, Fieldwork and Ethnographic Encounters

The emphasis on lived experience and everyday interaction that we feel underpins the social construction of race, processes of racialisation and practices of racism often calls for a more direct engagement with, exposure to and contact with the lifeworld (see Schutz, 1973) of the persons you wish to study. Again, drawing on the notion of the broad distinction between naturalistic and non-naturalistic settings, the former refer to those places (physical, social, cultural) and times that the persons you are interested in researching inhabit as part and parcel of their normal everyday activity; the latter refer to any other setting (usually, one that has been set up or contrived for the purposes of the research); in the former you enter the lifeworld of the persons you are studying; in the latter they tend to enter whatever lifeworld you have constructed for the purposes of the research.

The closer you move towards being an actual participant in the settings and contexts you are interested in, and the greater the extent of exposure to those settings and contexts, the more you move towards conducting what is referred to as ethnographic work. The term ethnography or ethnographic study refers to research which is conducted in naturalistic settings and involves the researcher exposing him/herself to the *day-to-day* experiences and contingencies of those he/she is studying (the data collection aspect of this is generally referred to as 'fieldwork'). The etymology of the word literally means 'writing culture', the underlying premise that we cannot understand the social world by studying artificial simulations of it in such things as experiments (Hammersley and Atkinson, 1983: 9).

Contemporary ethnographic work has a long history, beginning with the Chicago School of Sociology (see Bulmer, 1984). Researchers working in Chicago at that time viewed the city as a natural laboratory (Park and Burgess, 1925), and were very much interested in community organisation within the burgeoning (and new) urban environment and the relationship between urban geography and social problems (see Chapter 6 for a discussion of some of these issues with specific reference to contemporary British society). They were also interested very much in the experiences of ethnic and racial groups who had migrated to the city (see e.g. Drake and Cayton, 1945; Frazier, 1932; Park, 2004 [1950]; Thompson, 1939).

The popularity of ethnographic methods increased over the twentieth century, based on the recognition that, as we saw in the previous chapter:

> ... *any group of persons – prisoners, primitives, pilots or patients – develop a life of their own that becomes meaningful, reasonable, and normal once you get close to it, and a good way to learn about any of these worlds is to submit oneself in the company of the members to the daily round of petty contingencies to which they are subject.* (Goffman, 1961: 7)[4]

Following a period of relatively little work focusing directly on racism (Twine, 2000), in the past two decades both research into and teaching of issues pertaining to race and racism have been on the increase (Bulmer and Solomos, 2004). Indeed, there are some classic and contemporary studies of race and racism that provide fine illustrations of ethnography in action (Brown, 2001; Carlile, 2012; Cole, 2005; DuBois, 1996 [1899]; Luhrmann, 1996).

Many ethnographic studies involve extended time spent in the 'field'. However, even limited use of the ethnographic method (using ethnographic methods but with limited exposure and for a limited duration of time compared to full blown ethnographic studies) can provide valuable data and enhance your research experience.

Social Worlds, Social Settings and Research Sites

There are many different types of sites, settings and social worlds (see Chapter 4) in which researchers have explored race and racism, from normally closed off worlds (e.g. inside the police or criminal justice system [Cheliotis and Liebling, 2006; Genders and Player, 1989] – see Case Study 1 in the following chapter) to public streets (see Duneier, 1999; Liebow, 1967). Your choice of setting will be guided by the particular 'problem' (see Chapter 4) with which you are approaching your research. You may, for example, be interested in general areas of social activity – general social worlds – such as education, criminal justice, religion, leisure, science, politics, law, the workplace or everyday life. Such activities tend to be organised in particular places, at particular times, so designed for the social construction of these realms of activity. Thus, class-rooms or lecture halls, police stations and prison cells, churches, mosques, synagogues and temples, laboratories, a range of workplaces, and various spaces in the public realm, such as town and city centres, shopping centres or those designed for specific leisure and sporting activities such as pubs, clubs and sporting arenas may be the focus of your activities (see e.g. Cashmore, 2001; Farrington et al., 2012; Jay, 2009; Meeks, 2010). For example, in one of our case studies discussed in the following chapter, the notions of place and time (in this case public houses at weekends) constituted very salient sites for racialisation processes, and ultimately overt acts of racism. The importance of such places will tend to become evident as the lifeworld of those you are studying unfolds during the process of data collection and analysis and new directions for your focus emerge.

Access

Whenever students interested in conducting qualitative, ethnographically sensitive work ask us, as tutors, 'what shall I research for my dissertation?' our first answer is often 'whatever you have access to'. This may sound flippant, but it is a valid recommendation. For you as a qualitative researcher of race and racism, access to naturalistic settings may become an issue in itself. There may be legal reasons why certain settings are not open to you or off limits, it may simply be a matter of convenience or practicality, or, as we suggested in the previous chapter, the ques-tion of access may be influenced by your own biographical features which may well include your race. It may be that your race helps you gain access (or you assume it will) or works against you (again, see our own example of this in Chapter 6). For example, if you are a member of a visible ethnic minority and you wish to evaluate attitudes of a majority white institution, your race may prevent respondents from 'speaking openly' about their views. Of course, the same applies if you are white and wish to elicit the views and life experiences of visible minor-ities. Remember also that you must maintain access. Nothing is guaranteed and you may be required – or decide to – withdraw from the field at any time. Whatever the specific circumstances of your research, access may well be some-thing that requires negotiation, compromise, and sometimes, luck.

Getting to the Right People

The beginning of your research will necessarily involve the identification of some 'population' you want to focus on. This may seem straightforward, but one issue that immediately crops up is how 'membership' of such a population is defined – or rather, socially and culturally constructed, and by whom. Indeed, as should by now be quite apparent, the use of any 'racial' category itself is grounded in racialisation, whoever does this (authorities, members themselves, you as a researcher 'for the purposes of the research'). You will then need to recruit persons belonging to your chosen population. There are several techniques for sampling persons at the start of qualitative research. You might, for example, use posters or leaflets to recruit participants (see Chapter 6), and this may involve a range of particular sites and settings, particular to the racial group you are interested in (see our discussion of sampling in mosques in Chapter 6). Again, this may rely on racialisation *of* or *by* members of those populations. For example, by responding to calls to participate in your study, members of racial groups will be involved in processes of self-racialisation (Murji and Solomos, 2005). Even more problematic may be relying on others to select, recommend or choose persons for you (and this type of 'snowball' sampling does often occur in qualitative research, particularly in what are generally classed as 'hard to reach' populations).

Although a necessary part of your research, sampling and selection of persons may gloss over important distinctions between individuals or groups, and potentially places and times. Alternatively, attempting to recognise increasingly nuanced differences between groups or persons may result in an ever increasing (and unmanageable) number of categories or classes of persons which you need to include in your sample.

Finally, in qualitative research, although you may begin with a person or group of people you want to talk to or observe, you may find yourself 'sampling-as-you-go', so to speak. That is, deciding who to speak to or observe – and when and where to carry out these research activities – as the research progresses. Therefore, at the outset of qualitative research your main aim will probably be to get the (snow)ball rolling rather than delineating your full cohort in advance. In this sense, sampling is intimately tied in with (ongoing) data analysis, and to that extent forms one side of a coin which marks the *iterative* character of much qualitative research.

Plurality of Perspectives

As we have suggested in the previous chapter, it is important to remember that in conducting your qualitative research into race and racism (indeed, any qualitative research) you need to access a range of experiences and perspectives on whatever issue – whatever problem – it is you are interested in. For example, in the context of the current focus, this will include not only identifying, recruiting and gathering data from those who have been, for example, marginalised and even discriminated against or victimised, but also those who have or may be leading racialising processes (whether directly or indirectly). Accessing a range of perspectives allows us to understand, for example, not just the outcomes of, but the motivations for racist beliefs, attitudes and behaviour. Indeed, just as racism itself can take a myriad of forms and manifestations, so too can motive for such behaviour (see Chapter 6). From an ontological and epistemological perspective, what this also does is open up the idea of 'multiple truths' operating around race and racism. Perspectives should be a plural notion.

Roles and Rapport

Assuming that you are not already a member of the social world you are investigating, you will need a reason for 'being there'. The issue of role very much ties in with covert and overt issues in ethnographic work, that is, whether or not the people you are researching are (fully) aware that, above all else, you are conducting research. However, when conducting fieldwork this is often not a 'black and white' matter. For example (unless you wear a brightly coloured shirt with 'I am a researcher' in bold letters on the front), you may be overt to some members, but covert to others, or overt some of the time but covert at others (see our discussion of ethical issues below). Of course, racial or ethnic features of your person that 'stand out' may give you away as an interloper. Extreme cases might be a white European conducting research in a Black segregationist group, or a Black African/Black Caribbean person in a White supremacist group. Under normal circumstances the maelstrom of every-day life in effect precludes an 'all the people give informed consent all of the time' approach, so be aware of this and actively seek to minimise its impact, rather than seeking to exploit it.

As we noted above, building rapport with those with whom you have direct face-to-face contact is essential in race and racism research (Young, 2004). In ethnographic work this interpersonal feature of research can become all the more important. This may start with negotiating access to the field, with some sort of gatekeeper or key holder (see esp. Duneier, 1999). Once in the field, you may find that you not infrequently need to be 'vouched for' by existing members, and 'kept in'. During your work you will then interact with many persons and will need to get them and yourself 'onside', so to speak. Again, this may be hindered or facilitated by your own or others' racial or ethnic features or prejudices. Even if others find these features insurmountable barriers, you must try your best to build and maintain good relations in the field.

Finally, when your research is concluded you must also consider your exit strategy. Simply leaving research sites may cause a number of problems. For example, members of such sites may feel abused, abandoned or duped in some way. When work is finally published they may feel misrepresented after the fact. At a more general level, groups or communities may experience research fatigue (essentially worn out through being over-researched). You are under some obligation then not to 'spoil' the research field in which you are working. Indeed, some ethnographers continue their relationships with their informant long after the ethnographic work has finished (e.g. in his study of African American street vendors, Duneier [1999] invited his key informant to present college lectures for him).

Encountering, Immersing, Observing

The key benefit of ethnographic work is *participant observation*. Whereas speaking with or listening to people may reveal aspects of experience and forms of behaviour and processes of racialisation that cannot be observed by you, so observation can reveal features that are not (or cannot be) spoken about. It is in and through observation that, perhaps more than anything else, the taken-for-granted features of the social world can be revealed and examined by you as a researcher. In the context of race and racism this can carry added significance since, as we have argued in Chapter 4, much of this may be part of the routine, day-to-day fabric of whatever social setting you are investigating, and to that extent, *invisible-through-routinisation* to members of that setting (although the effects may be very tangible and observable).

Gold (1958) famously outlined the various stances a researcher could adopt when observing, from complete observer at one extreme, to complete participant (in the lifeworld and activities being observed) at the other. Unless you are adopting the stance of complete (and detached) observer (think of the scientist behind a one-way mirror or observing via a CCTV camera) the term is a bit of a misnomer, as you will tend, at one point or another, to draw on all your senses as you not only see, but hear, feel and even smell or taste things as part of your experience in the field (see Pink, 2009). We feel we must stress that observation in qualitative sociological research is not − and should not be regarded as − observation *of*, but rather observation *in* social settings and contexts. Moreover, your observation should be not of particular persons in a pseudo-psychological fashion. It is a case of moments of social reality and construction and their men, not particular men and their moments (Goffman, 1967). This is vitally important to remember − you are not people watching but process and practice watching.

Finally, alongside written observations, the use of the photographic − or even video − image may also be useful to you in your research into race and racism (see Christian et al., 2010; Pink, 2007). As we have noted above, cultural images and film can be used as data. In an ethnographic context the use of the camera can yield powerful and revealing images. Prime examples of this in the study of race can be found in the work of Mitchell Duneier. Collaborating with Pulitzer Prize winning photographer Ovie Carter, Duneier's images in Sidewalk powerfully illustrate the plight of African American street dwellers in the sidewalks of contemporary New York (Duneier, 1999; see also Duneier, 2004, 2006; Liebow, 1967).

Achieving Empathy and (not) 'Going Native'

If any group of persons develops a meaningful life once you get close to the petty contingencies of members' daily rounds, the whole point of ethnography then is to try to see the world you are investigating as it is experienced, understood, interpreted, given meaning, acted upon and socially constructed by its members. Via this process you will learn and appreciate the meaning given to actions, events and objects (including persons) in that world. Moreover, you are trying to achieve some sort of intersubjective interpretation and empathetic understanding − some *Verstehen*. Seeing the world as your informants see it, and empathising with their views may jar with your own biases, but, as we argued in Chapter 4, it is important to try to suspend your own values and see the world as your informants see it. As we have already noted, suspending your own values and prejudices may be a personal challenge. However, this is essential if you are to *understand-through-empathising*.

Having said this, as with much ethnography and qualitative work, you must avoid what is termed 'going native', that is weaving yourself into the fabric of the reality of your informants to such a degree that you are unable to see things from the critical and interpretive distance of the researcher – that they become invisible through routinisation not only to the persons or groups you are studying, but to *you*.

A final point to note is that in cross-cultural settings (see Liamputtong, 2010) one can very easily 'put one's foot in it' whilst attempting to have a hand in the activities of cultural groups. In such settings you as researcher may need to show 'cultural sensitivity' as regards such things as the *'social, familial, cultural, religious, historical and political backgrounds'* (Jackson and Mead Niblo, 2003, cited in Liamputtong, 2010: 87) of those with whom you come into contact. Again, not only will this aid interpersonal interaction, but will be essential to your interpreting action and appreciating experiences in a way that they are understood to those you are studying.

Putting Yourself in the Picture

Academics often air concerns about the effect of the researcher on the setting or context – to what extent he/she as an embodied participant in those settings and contexts 'contaminates' (see our comments on naturalistic settings earlier). Observation in qualitative research often involves a sort of reverse contamination, and we think should do, in that you will have your own experiences and perceptions impacted on as part of the research process. One relatively underused aspect of ethnographic work – one that directly allows you to draw on your own experiences – is what is referred to as 'auto-ethnography' (see Kenny, 2000).

Ethical Ethnography

Finally, central to ethnographic work in general are ethical considerations. Ethical issues will guide your management of your research, from preparation through execution, to completion, and afterwards. This goes beyond a lay interpretation of ethics to address some quite specific and practical aspects of the research process, and there will often be a set of formal ethical codes of practice laid out by professional bodies in or affiliated to your disciplinary area.[5] Ethical issues then are something you should think about from the outset.

As you will have gathered from the preceding section, during the course of your research you will be *told, hear, read* and *observe* many things. You will need to ensure that whatever people reveal to you, whatever you observe or whatever materials (documents or records) you acquire are kept confidential. At a practical level, and as your research progresses (and after it has concluded), all audio and video recordings, transcripts, fieldnotes, documents and other data should be kept securely stored. Hard copy material (including data storage media such as DVDs/CDs/pendrives/external HDs) should be kept in locked cabinets. Digital files should ideally be in some way password protected. This will usually involve anonymising (although see Duneier, 1999) *names*, *places* and even *times*. Not only is this a legal requirement and basic human right, but it will also ensure the well-being of your informants. This may be particularly relevant in race research (for example, female Muslims talking about intimate matters or far-right extremists expressing political viewpoints may have their well-being seriously threatened should their identities become known).

A primary concern is the issue of informed consent. Both aspects of this requirement must be obtained, i.e. *information* must be provided and *consent* obtained (often requiring the drafting of a consent form - see the Appendix (Resource 8) for an example of such a form used in our own research). It may sometimes be the case that participants in your research in some way misinterpret this part of your work. For example, some years ago, one of us was involved in interviewing young ethnic minority offenders. At first, these persons were under the impression that they 'had to' be interviewed, and some even thought it was part of their punishment. They had to be informed several times that this was not the case, and they could withdraw at any time if they wished.

A related issue here that you need to keep in mind is any power issues that might be at play. For example, in our own experience of researching into sensitive topics, even though we have taken rigorous steps to ensure informants were well informed and explained the consent-withdrawal basis of the research, we have experienced informants who have felt 'obliged' to participate in research, based on a range of power issues they perceived to be at play in the contexts and settings in which the research was carried out (see Chapter 6).

As we have noted, your research may involve exposure to and contact with people in the immediacy of face-to-face encounters. The notion of well-being extends here. You must ensure that your informants do not feel uncomfortable or in any way under pressure to take part in the research or, for example, answer questions they are uncomfortable with (much will depend on your sensitivity as informants may feel uncomfortable about expressing their uncomfortableness!). So tread carefully, and always be aware that you *are* treading.

Of course, you have an ethical obligation to yourself. This may sound back-to-front research-wise, but it is important to remember, as we have suggested, that you yourself may be racialised (just as you may be sexualised, classified, or age-ified by those persons with whom you come into contact [Quraishi, 2008b]). Be aware of this, as it can be a feature of qualitative research – particularly when researching sensitive topics or 'hard to reach' groups or settings – that it can cause stress, worry and even danger to the researcher (see Lee-Treweek and Linkogle, 2000).

On the more practical side of things (but still ethically charged), payment and rewards for participating can be thorny issues. A classic example of the problems associated with this can be seen in Vanderstaay's (2005) study of African Amercian gangs. Vanderstaay paid $100 to one of his informants, who subsequently went to spend this money on drugs and was involved in a fatal shooting. You should think carefully about whether you want to do this and if so what form such payments and rewards should take. Again, you should also be aware of potentially culturally sensitive issues pertaining to this.

Finally, although the intention (sometimes requirement) of most research is that it be disseminated or published in some way (see below), there may be ethical issues that cause you to delay or even suspend publication. There may be various reasons for this, not least the risk of potential harm or threat to those you studied or even yourself (cf. Patrick, 1973) (see below).

A general maxim then would be 'remain ethically sensitive at all times'. Ethical issues may seem 'obvious' and unproblematic, but in the live action of research they can easily be overlooked (or inadvertently suspended!).

Analysis and Dissemination

Data alone, be they documentary, image or artefacts, interviews or focus groups, naturally occurring conversation or observational, will not necessarily speak 'for themselves'. They require some form of analysis, interpretation, presentation and dissemination. Again, it is beyond the remit of this chapter – or this book – to provide a comprehensive overview of types of qualitative analysis (see Lofland et al., 2006; Miles and Huberman, 1984; Saldana, 2000; Silverman, 2001 for excellent examples of how to conduct analysis on qualitative data). Rather, we want now briefly to signpost some ways in which the above data types may be analysed.

Handling and Interacting with Data

Qualitative research of any sort (not just extended ethnography) can (and more often than not, will) generate huge volumes of data, be it boxes of documentary items, pages of interview transcripts, or volumes of fieldnotes, and these need to be made sense of – to be analysed. Analysis of qualitative data can be quite demanding on the researcher and is to some extent 'unteachable'. What we mean by this is that much depends on the researcher's 'insight'. This is not an attempt to mystify the procedure, but it does point to the very human aspect of qualitative research in general that we have pointed to in this and the preceding chapter. Moreover, as we have noted above, analysis is part and parcel of the ongoing research experience (rather than something you simply 'do at the end'). Qualitative data collection and analysis are *iterative* in nature, which means you analyse, sample and reanalyse 'as you go'.

The degree of formality you might use in analysing qualitative data can range from looking for *themes* in your interview transcripts, fieldnotes or documents/artefacts to attempting to identify distinct codes and concepts and build these into some sort of 'grounded' theory (see below). There are nowadays dedicated software packages (known as Computer Assisted Qualitative Data Analysis Software, or CAQDAS) that will help you to conduct such analyses on large data sets.[6] Interestingly, in actual published work based on qualitative data there is often a marked absence of explicit description of how qualitative data analysis was carried out.

Qualitative Content, Emergent Themes and the Construction of Meaning

We started our discussion earlier in this chapter by looking at documentary sources. There are several ways that these sources might be analysed (see the texts cited above for excellent examples). One good way to analyse documents – particularly printed news media – is via what is referred to as content analysis (see e.g. Krippendorff, 2004). For example, a number of researchers on Islamophobia have utilised content analysis of print and other forms of media (see e.g. Saeed, 2007).

Images, cartoons, photographs and videos can also be analysed for their 'content'. One useful way to analyse this type of data for their 'meaning' is through semiotic analysis. Semiotics refers to the science of signs. Although derived from linguistics, semiotics can be useful in the analysis of imagery and photographs (see e.g. Bignell, 2002; Godazgar, 2007).

Data generated from interviews and focus groups are often subject to some sort of thematic analysis, as mentioned above. At a basic – but sometimes sufficient – level you effectively scan the data – in the form of interview transcripts – for reoccurring themes. These can be ones that your informants explicitly cite, or ones that you feel reside in your data (see Essed [1991] who develops a useful framework for analysing verbal accounts of racism in race research). Whatever themes you focus on, they must reflect as much as possible the reality of the lived experience that you claim they represent. One way of doing this is to use terms – or *in vivo codes* (Glaser and Strauss, 1967) – that are used by the people themselves. For those researchers drawing on naturally occurring conversation (or even interview encounters), very particular types of analysis can be used. The field of conversational analysis as pioneered by American sociologist Harvey Sacks (see Sacks, 1992) provides some quite sophisticated ways to analyse talk. One way of doing this (and one that is of particular relevance to those involved in race and racism research) is the use of membership categorisation analysis (see Hester and Eglin, 1997). For example, at the time of writing this book, the 'N–' word was receiving much media attention in the UK following its use by a popular TV celebrity. This is a prime example of a 'word' that can, and often is, used to categorise pejoratively members of black communities (see Watson, 1997).

Observational data from fieldnotes can be also subject to similar thematic analysis. In the case of this type of ethnographic data, again, there may be no need to analyse your data with the aim of contributing to or generating theory. Rather, such thematic analysis may be sufficient for you to present a 'thick' description (Geertz, 1973) of the sites and settings in which you have researched.

Generating Theory

More formally, the question of concept and theory development can come into the analysis of qualitative data. However, this is different to quantitative based studies' relationship to theory development (or the status of generalised theory of some objective social reality *per se*). As we noted above, from a social constructionist perspective it is too blunt to suggest there are 'facts' that exist outside of people's ability to socially construct them – to talk, act and negotiate them into being. As Hammersley tells us, in much qualitative research:

> *The search for universal laws is rejected in favour of **detailed descriptions** of the concrete experience of life within a particular culture and of the social rules or patterns that constitute it.* (Hammersley and Atkinson, 1983: 8; emphasis added)

Having said that, your work may well generate particularly important, or 'key' concepts. Again these can be not only important to any wider statements you want to make, but can – and should – reflect the experiences, perceptions and meanings of race and racism of those whom you are researching. For example, we use the key concept of 'no-go zone' in the following chapter, which is derived from and directly reflects the experiences of a particular group of persons in a particular cultural and spatial context.

Even though the relationship of qualitative research to theory is different to quantitative work, it is not (and should not - see Chapter 4) be detached from it. Your work may still involve the application of theoretical concerns. For example, in the following chapter we show how a particular theory or perspective of race – critical race theory (Crenshaw et al., 1995) – has been applied to the study of a particular ethnic group. One advantage of using wider theoretical discussion in this way is that your work can be interpreted within a wider academic discourse of race and racism, rather than simply providing a description of or an insight into a particular group or set of practices. At a looser level than might be used in quantitative conceptual use, what are referred to as 'definitive' concepts and 'sensitising' concepts (Blumer, 1954) might also be identified, that is, concepts that function as, in effect, 'eye-openers' rather than 'building blocks' of any formal theory.

More formally, 'grounded theory' can be used to analyse data from qualitative studies (both data from fieldnotes and from qualitative interviews). This involves careful coding of your data leading to the development of concepts and categories and ultimately some theoretical propositions that are derived from (grounded in) a close and detailed analysis of your data based in comparison and contrasts of phenomena that you observed or are reported (see Glaser and Strauss, 1967; Strauss and Corbin, 1998).

More specialist forms of analysis do exist, but require some degree of specialist training and often empathy with the particular ontological, epistemological and procedural foundations that underpin them. Good examples of more radical types of analysis are practised by ethnomethodologists (which heavily influenced the way conversation analysts discussed above do their work). Both these forms of analysis look at the mundane sense making practice in social interaction.

Presentation and Dissemination

When writing up, we would like to emphasise two things. The first is that you should always give (social, cultural, political and historical) context when writing up and presenting your work. This is vital and, as you will see in our case studies in Chapter 6, essential to fully understanding how the notion of race operates and how it realises itself in any given cultural, institutional or everyday context. A thorough contextualisation is essential in any comparative work across cultures. Second, we noted above the importance of language, and more specifically, of verbal accounts. In writing up your research we would urge you to draw on verbatim extracts from interviews (after having followed necessary ethical guidelines). The extent to which we will use verbatim interview extracts in the following chapter attests to the importance we put on them.

Unless you are carrying out your research 'for the fun of it', you will want to – or, if funded or doing your research in a work setting or practice/policy context, be expected to – present, disseminate or publish your work. This final stage of your research should not be underestimated as you will have some important decisions to make. As Essed (2004) notes, with race and racism research there will always be consequences of publishing your work both inside and outside the academy.

The first of these decisions will of course be whether to disseminate your findings at all, or, perhaps more realistically, which 'bits' to disseminate. Such decisions will most likely rest not on the quality of your findings (you do not think they are 'good enough' to disseminate), but on the potential consequences of dissemination. For example, if you feel that there may be potentially negative consequences for any of the people you are studying or that they may be put in harm's way at all, you may decide to withhold your findings (see e.g. Pittaway et al., 2010). This of course may also apply to any such potential consequences for yourself (see Patrick [1973] for a classic example of this dilemma). A second factor will be to consider your intended audience. This will rest largely on what you think your intended audience will find intelligible, relevant, useful or interesting. As Hammersley (1992) notes, '*the kinds of research questions and findings that might be of interest to practitioners and researchers are likely to be somewhat different*' (cited in Bryman, 2004: 277). Thus, in the case of practitioners, your writing will need to have some relevance to practice within that particular institutional and organisational context, and for policy makers your work may need to be couched in legislative or legal frameworks. Your work might even take the shape of or inform published texts and guides whose key aim is tackling racism, perhaps directed at certain institutions, organisations or practitioner contexts (see e.g. Clements and Spinks, 2009; Dadzie, 2005; Dominelli, 1997; Thompson, 1997). A common mode of dissemination is in the form of a report, containing a list of recommendations for practice and policy, with very little theory. This is not always easy to do, especially if you are trying to 'translate' findings from academic work that might be heavily conceptual and theoretical into recommendations which are highly practical and applied. Your own exposure to organisational and institutional practice and contingencies will no doubt aid this translation. It is however a process that can have its difficulties. For example, in a piece of research one of us was involved in once, we had to present sociological findings to a group of chemists and physicists looking to improve cosmetic products. The translation of sociological theory into hair care practice was not an easy task!

Writing for other academic researchers may come a little easier to you, as you will have just emerged from the research experience and so can write extensively about all aspects of your work, from highly conceptual aspects to biographical and reflexive ones. Your 'recommendations' here will most likely be limited to 'recommendations for future research' or suggestions as to how concepts or theoretical standpoints may be reconsidered on the basis of your findings (see Chapter 6). Of course, there may be a range of academic conferences, journals (including specialist ones looking at racial issues[7]) or even book chapters in and through which your work could be disseminated to a wider academic audience.

Writing for the public will probably not be a demand placed on you in your research. You may however be asked to write documents for public consumption (anything from flyers and posters to information packs and brochures). You may even have your work disseminated through the media (TV, newspapers, documentaries). Again, these will need to be pitched in a certain way and are likely not only to contain little if any theory, but also to contain little in the way of explicit policy recommendations or guidelines for institutional practice. Instead, a 'user-friendly' model of communication aimed at raising awareness of race issues and suggesting steps people can take to avoid or respond to instances of racism may be called for. You may need to take steps however to avoid oversimplification, sensationalisation or even misrepresentation of your work (see Silverman, 2010).

Whichever 'market' you are aiming your work at, we believe the presentation of it must serve a dual function. It needs to be both informative and interesting (see Lofland et al., 2006); representative and readable (see Atkinson, 1992). There is a certain tension implied here, and Atkinson (1992: 5) has suggested that *the more readable the account, the more it corresponds to the arbitrary conventions of literary form: the more "faithful" the representation, the less comprehensible it must become*. However, you need to remember that qualitative research is about people, about human experience and identities, and the social construction of race, racism and racialisation. Because of this, your work must aim to 'connect' with your audience in some way.

One final consideration is the potential reception of your work. We have already noted the problem of achieving value free research. There may also be an awareness of this on the part of the audience, which may lead to accusations of bias or hidden agendas (see Becker, 1967).

Summary

Although continuing our emphasis on contemporary and everyday contexts, our focus in this chapter has turned quite deliberately to qualitative research methods. As we noted at the outset, the chapter does not constitute a 'catch-all' of qualitative research methods, which would be beyond the scope of a single chapter (or even a book of this size), but rather has had as its main aim the presentation of what we regard as important issues for you to consider in your research.

We began the chapter by examining documentary sources, several of which have been pointed to in earlier chapters. Following this we spent some time examining the centrality of language in the context of research work, from formal interviews to naturally occurring conversation. The bulk of the chapter examined ethnographic work and the various contingencies that can arise when exposing oneself to and immersing oneself in the lifeworld of those persons and groups in naturally occurring sites, settings and contexts. Following this we presented a brief overview of ways in which qualitative data might be recorded and analysed. Finally, we concluded by discussing issues pertaining to dissemination and publication.

What we would ask you as a potential researcher into race and racism to do is to think about the nature, practice and methods of qualitative research both in general, and as they might pertain to your own research and practice in particular. In order to go some way to illustrate some of these methods, and some of the contingencies of qualitative research mentioned in this and previous chapters, in the following chapter we shall outline three particular case studies, which have to a large extent influenced the writing of this book.

Notes

1 One of the best general introductions to social research is Bryman's (2012) text *Social Research Methods*. For introductions to qualitative research more specifically, we suggest looking at Silverman (2006, 2010) for equally comprehensive and accessible introductory texts.
2 The concentration camp tattoo being a classic example of this type of racial 'branding'.
3 A classic example of this being the speculation around the late Michael Jackson's change in skin colour over his adult life.
4 We are of course not naively claiming that you can ever truly know and understand what it is like to a member of the culture you are investigating, but you can expose

yourself to the '*daily round of petty contingencies to which they are subject*', as Goffman termed it, in the hope of making some sense of them, and observing how they are made sense of by those you are studying.

5 For example, in the UK, those issued by the British Sociological Association, or British Psychological Society.

6 See http://www.surrey.ac.uk/sociology/research/researchcentres/caqdas/.

7 Good examples of academic journals focusing on race and ethnicity are *Ethnic and Racial Studies* (Routledge), *Journal of Ethnic and Migration Studies* (Routledge), *Ethinicties* (Sage).

6

RACISM RESEARCH:
THREE CASE STUDIES

Keywords: *racist attacks, intersectionality, transnational, 'no-go' zones, racialisation of urban areas, Muslim prisoners, Pakistan*

Whilst reading these case studies we ask you to reflect upon the following questions prompted by this chapter:

- How have some of the methods outlined in the previous chapters been deployed in the present case studies?
- How do the research philosophy and perspective adopted inform the research questions for these case studies?
- What type of practical and ethical challenges arose from undertaking the research and how might you think about overcoming and addressing them?

In the previous chapter we provided a broad overview of qualitative research methods which you may find appropriate and useful in your own research. We now want to demonstrate how some of these methods have been applied in three particular cases of research into race and ethnicity. More specifically, this chapter provides an insight into issues of racism and identity amongst BME and Muslim populations. The idea behind this chapter is to provide the reader focused examples of how research on racism is conducted as well as the intellectual and political impact of social science scholarship in this field. As we outlined in Chapters 4 and 5, race and racism research may be carried out in a range of contexts and settings. For example, scholars have undertaken work exploring the impact of racism in a wide range of spheres including education (Mason, 2000; Modood and Berthoud, 1997; Pathak, 2000); the media (Gilroy, 2002; Webster, 1997b); prisons (Beckford et al., 2005; McDermott, 1990); and policing (Bowling, 1999; Holdaway, 1996). The range of work reflects the pervasiveness of racist discrimination and its ability to impact upon many aspects of the daily lives of minorities.

The three case studies presented here are taken from our own research on BME and Muslim populations. The first case study provides a current 'in-progress' research project ahead of fieldwork being undertaken and therefore presents the reader with a useful insight into how a project is conceptualised, constituted and what is addressed in a typical institutional application for ethical approval.[1] The case study and subheadings have been presented in the format in which a university would expect a typical application to an ethics committee to adopt.

The second case study is based upon primary research with Muslim ex-offenders, with a focus on transnational identities and the implications of this for criminal justice practitioners. The example constitutes a pilot study, which is a useful mode of research capable of testing parameters for enquiry ahead of a more comprehensive or lengthier examination.

The study invites exploration of the intersectionality (see Chapter 2) of religious and racial or ethnic identities. We would like to draw your attention to two important caveats when reading this case study. First, as previously mentioned, researchers should be aware of the pitfalls of drawing upon essentialist notions whenever a particular ethnic minority population is studied. In other words, by framing discussions about a religious population (Muslim) against notions of deviance (crime, criminals or prisoners) the researcher runs a risk of reifying the very connections he or she is wishing to challenge and debunk. The ethical and moral dilemma for academics in this field is whether to engage and provide a counter-vocabulary or narrative to the racialised associations or simply to protest by disengagement. It is our opinion that the former strategy of critical engagement is preferable to the silent protest of the latter.

Second, the field of research in criminology which examines the influence of religion upon offending and deviance can run the risk of providing over-judgemental conclusions about the levels of religious observance and comprehension of religious jurisprudence amongst offenders. This issue is particularly pertinent to the examination of what has become known as the 'Hellfire thesis' in criminology, founded by Hirschi and Stark (1969). The 'Hellfire thesis' examines the extent to which the belief in divine judgement impacts upon the propensity for an individual to commit crime or deviance. The main faith of focus has been Christianity and the bulk of the research has been in the USA. The limits of this approach centre principally upon how 'religiosity' or 'piety' is measured. Turning to the issue of Muslim populations in the UK, researchers have deliberately excluded the notions of religion as a deterrent to deviance, instead concentrating upon how faith informs identities and intersects with dimensions of gender, class and ethnicity (Quraishi, 2013). Nevertheless, the case study presented here was specifically framed in part against an objective to capture how a sample of Muslim former offenders viewed, comprehended and articulated their relationship with Islam. More importantly, well-established Islamic jurisprudence makes a demarcation between secular and religious crimes or transgressions. The case study also aimed to therefore capture the complex ways in which Muslim offenders negotiated, constructed and qualified their lived experiences against these religious norms and laws. Therefore, although comments upon relationships outside of marriage may appear outmoded or harshly condemnatory, a finding or theme which frames these experiences is nevertheless useful for social scientists examining the impact of faith and spirituality and its contemporary meaning for social actors (Spalek and Imtoual, 2008). Therefore, the case study should be read with the aforementioned in mind since the intention was not to present a view of 'flawed' or 'bad' Muslims which somehow explained the circumstances the respondents found themselves in.

The third study is based on the ways in which minorities residing in urban locations socially and racially construct their physical environment in terms of 'no-go zones' expanding upon literature in geography, criminology and victimology.

What we would like you to do is think about not only the objectives and substantive findings to emerge out of these three studies (which is undoubtedly the aim of any research) but also the methods employed and research processes. Following the presentation of these three studies we will briefly reflect on their significance in the light of our discussion over the preceding chapters.

CASE STUDY 1

Rationalising Racist Attacks: A Case Study of Greater Manchester[2]

Project Focus

The study is concerned with the rationalisation process and the conclusions that victims draw from after having experienced a racist attack. It examines how black and minority ethnic[3] victims of racist attacks carried out by members of the 'white'[4] majority in Greater Manchester process the incident. In particular, there is a focus on the factors (i.e. triggers) they consider to be relevant in the immediate lead-up to the incident and the degree to which they retrospectively view the incident as having been solely about racial discrimination. An important dimension to the study is the incorporation of an intersectional lens through which a fuller account of victim experiences can be captured. Intersectionality acknowledges that 'race' does not operate in a vacuum but intersects with other aspects of a person's identity such as gender, class, age or faith which makes certain individuals more vulnerable to discrimination.

With a focus on the victim of racist attacks and their interpretation of the incident, this study aims to:

1. Detail their perception of triggers;

2. Outline factors motivating reporting decisions;

3. Examine their self-allocation or rejection of 'victim' status;

4. Consider victim assessment of reporting experiences and support agencies.

On its completion, the study will offer local criminal justice agencies and victim support organisations a set of policy/practice recommendations on encouraging greater reporting of racist attacks and how to better tailor their services to supporting victims.

(Continued)

CASE STUDY 1

(Continued)

Project Objectives

Following the aims outlined above, the objectives of the study are:

1. To revise understanding of offender motivations for racist attacks;

2. To outline victim perceptions of motivations for racist attacks;

3. To capture victim perceptions of 'intersectionality' and its impact upon the victim's experience of racist attacks;

4. To establish recent data on victim reporting levels;

5. To understand victims' motivations for reporting;

6. To detail the meaning of the 'victim' status, and to consider its influence on reporting decisions;

7. To gather victims' views on reporting experiences;

8. To offer an insight into victims' assessment of support agencies.

Research Strategy

Researching racist incidents in general is difficult, to say the least. Existing studies have tended to use police records and victim surveys, if only as a means of quantifying the problem (Bowling and Phillips, 2002): for example, those emerging from analysis of the British Crime Surveys, such as Aye Maung and Mirrlees-Black (1994), Clancy et al. (2001), FitzGerald and Hale (1996) and Percy (1998). However, this is problematic when we consider the extent of under-reporting. Other studies have sought to understand the experiences, impacts and coping mechanisms through use of more qualitative methods, such as interviews and focus groups, and liaisons with specialist community support groups: for example, Chahal and Julienne (1999), Chahal (2003), Gordon (1990), ICAR (2004), Sibbitt (1997), Virdee (1995) and Witte (1996); and more recently, there has been an examination of the perpetrators of racist incidents themselves, for instance, Bjorgo (1993), Connolly and Keenan (2001), Gordon (1994), Khan (2002), Ray and Smith (2004) and Sibbitt (1997).

In addition to secondary data analysis, i.e. review of existing literature and government policy, the study will primarily use qualitative data from semi-structured interviews, each lasting approximately 30 minutes, with a total of 50 respondents: those of BME background who have been victims of racist attacks in the Greater Manchester area, in the last three years. Although interest in gender, age and class variables are relevant, the study is not strictly a comparative study, therefore there is no set quota. However, respondents from diverse backgrounds will be sought, to offer additional insight. A total of 50 respondents is considered to be an achievable size, practically manageable, and will generate approximately 25 hours of narrative, from which detailed data and criminological analysis on the subject can be made, and the study aims met.

The sample will be recruited via drawing on already established links with local ethnic and faith-based community groups. An interview schedule (see Appendix, Resource 7) will be used, which contains a series of questions, the answers to which should provide meaningful data about how victims experience racist attacks.

Respondents will be interviewed in a comfortable space, i.e. a local cafe, library or on university premises – depending on which space is most safe, accessible and relaxing for them. At the start of each interview, respondents will be asked to sign a consent form (see Appendix, Resource 7), detailing the purpose of the study, data protection issues and their rights to withdraw at any time.

For reasons of accuracy and reliability in the data collection process, tape-recording is seen as necessary. The recordings will only be used by the researchers and held long enough for transcriptions and detailed notes to be made. After this, all recordings will be destroyed. In light of the study's aims, a number of pre-listed themes, expected to emerge from the data, will be considered in the data analysis, with room being left for any new emerging themes to be considered. This themed analysis approach will be used within a framework of anti-racist critical analysis, and draw upon labelling and symbolic interactionism. In between the analysis and write-up stages, follow-up interviews may, if needed for clarity of information, be undertaken with respondents. Here, respondents would be given a transcript of their interview narrative, along with some initial analytical notes. This allows the participant sight of their initial narrative, not only to correct any errors, but also so that they can re-engage with their narrative, and confirm or even dispute interpretation and analysis of it. This is seen as supporting the empowerment objective of the research.

What is the Rationale Which Led to the Project?

Defining and Explaining Racist Attacks

In particularly looking at race, a *racial group* is defined as '*a group of persons defined by reference to colour, race, nationality, or ethnic or national origin*' (Race Relations Act 1976, §3). In this respect the occurrence of racially motivated crimes can be viewed as such where the perpetrator's criminal conduct is motivated by hatred, bias or prejudice, based upon the actual or perceived race, colour, nationality, or ethnic or national origin of another individual or group. Here, the term *racist incident* is also often used, which is defined as '*any incident that is perceived to be racist by the victim or any other person*' (Macpherson, 1999). The range of such racially motivated crimes and racist incidents may vary widely, so as to include, for example, murder, graffiti, verbal abuse and common assault. Occurrences which are especially violent in nature are often referred to as acts of *violent racism* (Bowling, 1999). Indeed, McVeigh argues that the very nature of such crimes, which makes them '*most distinctive ... is that it is clearly **about violence**'* (McVeigh, 2006: 11; original emphasis). This is because there is the constant experience and fear of violence, either through its actual use or through its threatened use. Indeed,

(Continued)

(Continued)

in looking at the experience and policing of racist incidents in Britain, Gordon argues that '*the scale and intensity of the violence is now such that many black people have begun to use the term "racial terrorism"; believing that this is a more accurate description of the onslaught of violence now being faced by black communities*' (Gordon, 1990: 16). Clearly, such racially motivated crimes and racist incidents, whether committed in a singular or repeated pattern, are nevertheless hostile, offensive, terrifying, derogatory and humiliating for the victim. In this sense they therefore can be seen as a *racist*[5] *attack*, the consequences of which can be emotional, psychological or physical. For example, in their study of the type of racial harassment experienced by a sample of 74 people across the UK, Chahal and Julienne found that racial harassment and victimisation affect partner relationships, children's safety and relationships, visiting people, use of space, health and well-being, feelings of security and, indeed, all other aspects of routine living (Chahal and Julienne, 1999: 25–32). Research has also found an under-reporting of racist attacks due to reasons of a lack of faith in police, police racism, fear of repercussions, mistreatment of victims and attacks being too numerous to report (Bell et al., 2004; Christmann and Wong, 2010; Gordon, 1990; Jarman and Monaghan, 2003b; Skellington, 1996; Smith and Gray, 1985; Virdee, 1995).

A number of particular factors are considered significant in the occurrence of racist attacks. First, there exists within the UK (and in other places like it, such as Australia, the USA and France, to name a few), a fear of the supposed 'non-native' body.[6] This refers to all those who are considered to be outsiders, born outside the country, who seek or make attempts to enter it – either for refuge, employment and/or residence. Although the movement of such bodies is varied and, taken in perspective, minimal,[7] it is the inward movement of BME bodies in particular that generates concern, fear and hostility. Here panic exists about the motives and presence of economic migrants[8] and asylum seekers and refugees[9] – especially those considered to be '*undeserving refugees*' (Sales, 2002). Within the current climate of fear and hostility (in relation to a period we mark out as a 'War on Terror' context), these groups are all, in the public imagination, categorised as 'illegal immigrants'. As Sivanandan (2006: 2) notes: '*the two trajectories – the war on asylum and the war on terror – have converged to produce a racism which cannot tell a settler from an immigrant, an immigrant from an asylum seeker, an asylum seeker from a Muslim, a Muslim from a terrorist. We are, all of us Blacks and Asians, at first sight terrorists or illegals. We wear our passports on our faces or lacking them, we are faceless.*' All BMEs then are represented through an '*immigrant imaginary*' (Sayyid, 2004), subjected to blame, anger and enhanced risk of victimisation. This literature clearly echoes the conceptual developments made by critical race theorists and particularly Black feminist socio-legal scholarship which first espoused the concept of intersectionality (Crenshaw, 1991). Therefore, traditional categories of black, white or Asian are rendered insufficient for full accounts of how minority populations experience discrimination. It is incumbent upon academics, therefore, to incorporate intersectional identities in race research, so the focus shifts away from broad, crude homogeneous racial categories (black, white, etc.)

to more meaningful intersections with other important aspects of personal identity such as immigration status, faith and gender.

The 'immigrant imaginary' is also supported by misrepresentations in the media, especially news outlets, which present Britain as a fair and tolerant society, but one which is being 'swamped', 'infested' and 'abused' by members of the BME population – for instance see Pilkington's (2003) analysis of the British press in the 1980s, and more recently the work of Moore et al. (2008). Such negative representations of BME people in the press is full of blame, hate and suspicion (see Malik [2002] for a detailed discussion on this). In recent times this has taken a more sinister turn as those identified as '*brown bodies*' (Patel, 2013) are reimagined within the post-9/11 terror panic, which alongside the recent debates about multiculturalism and 'community cohesion' – see for instance David Cameron's speech at the Munich Security Conference in February 2011 (*New Statesman*, 5 February 2011) – are constructed as 'the enemy within', who not only self-segregate, but support anti-western and anti-British, by which we here read anti-white, society – thus we see the popularity of notions of white victimhood. For example, in an article headed: 'The enemy within', the story read: '*home-grown terrorists. ... The danger seems ever present ... there is an enemy within Britain who wants to destroy our way of life. Most of this relatively small group of fanatics are British-born Muslims who have been educated here and brought up within our tolerant democracy. ... The great challenge for Britain is how to stop this and minimise the future risks. Nobody should underestimate the scale of the problem or the time needed. We already have a generation of disaffected Muslims who see any excuse, whether it is war in Iraq, Afghanistan or Lebanon, as a reason for killing their fellow citizens*' (*Sunday Times*, 13 August 2006, cited in Patel and Tyrer, 2011: 10). Patel and Tyrer (2011) note that this too has other implications; for instance, it supports the claims of the right-wing press that BMEs are dangerous pollutants which need to be targeted, controlled and removed. Here they ask us to consider the claims of the BNP about the supposed Asian rape gangs who were preying on white girls (*Sunday Times*, 18 January 2006, cited in Patel and Tyrer, 2011: 10), and how through a powerfully selective and fabricated narrative, a discourse of 'racist common-sense' was promoted. Indeed, such biased and careless reporting, which leads to the generation of moral panics, can actually be blamed for increases in racist attacks. For example, journalist Paul Foot, commenting on the situation in late 1980s Britain, noted: '*race hate and race violence does not rise and fall according to the numbers of immigrants coming in Britain. It rises and falls to the extent to which people's prejudices are inflamed and made respectable by politicians and newspapers*' (cited in Bowling, 1996: 198). Similarly, Gordon (1990: 36) notes: '*racial attacks and racist incidents do not occur in a vacuum but take place in a social and political context*'. This is a social and political context that is based on power relations (Chahal, 1999).

Racist Attacks in Greater Manchester

Britain has witnessed pervasive racist attacks perpetrated against the BME population since the establishment of significant migrant communities from the former

(Continued)

(Continued)

Commonwealth, much of which has seen victims forced to cope with it alone or without police help. Of particular concern though is the literature which suggests that victims adopt a '*normalisation*' of the attacks (Connolly, 2002), seeing it as '*a fact of life*' (Jarman and Monaghan, 2003a: 3). Similarly, Donnan and O'Brien's (1998) study of Pakistanis living in Northern Ireland found that such experiences were '*a "normal" and expected part of being a member of a minority ethnic group, an integral and inevitable element of the migrant experience, and thus not something which can be effectively addressed or dealt with*' (Donnan and O'Brien, 1998: 204). This leads to problems in under-reporting, which mean that the true extent of racist attacks is very difficult to measure (Skellington, 1996). However, although scarce and incomplete, the available data do give us some rough estimation of the degree of racism and racist incidents. Whilst the current trend in the official recording of racist incidents is downwards, there were 47,678 racist incidents recorded by the police in England and Wales during 2011/12 (Home Office, 2013).

In terms of the study's sample site, Greater Manchester, racist attacks are depressingly plentiful, illustrated not least by recent press reports:

> '*Racist' powder attacks closed hospital A&E and police station.* (Bainbridge and Thompson, 2010)

> *Racist yob jailed for attack on bus driver.* (*Bolton News*, 8 October 2010)

> *CCTV stills released following racist attack.* (*Rochdale Observer*, 7 June 2011)

> *Somali driver attacked in cab.* (*This Is Lancashire*, 10 January 2010)

> *Racist abuse drunks confronted students.* (*Bolton News*, 16 July 2011)

> *Police quiz pupils after boy injured in 'race attack' outside Bramhall High school.* (Qureshi, 2011)

> *Refugee who fled Pakistan violence is beaten up by young thugs.* (Gray, 2011)

As a metropolitan county created in April 1974, and located in the North West region of England, Greater Manchester comprises 10 metropolitan boroughs (Bolton, Bury, Oldham, Rochdale, Stockport, Tameside, Trafford, Wigan and the two cities of Manchester and Salford).

Rationalisation of Racist Attacks by Victims

There are a number of possible factors or motivations that are seen to act as a trigger to a racist attack. The research on offenders documents some of these – see for instance Ray and Smith (2004), and later, Ray et al. (2004). In particular, Law's (2010: 139) 'Typology of race hate motives' is useful in our consideration of how victims may process the incident. In focusing on reasons for offender motives, Law outlines seven main categories, which we argue connect to the perception of the attack by the victims, which then goes on to inform their rationalisation, and ultimately their reporting of it. Law's categories are shown in the following table.

Ideological	Those in pursuit of their values, which often includes the perpetrator insisting that they are the 'real' victim	'Because it fits with our world view'
Bigots	These are intolerant adherents of populist, mundane or casual prejudice, drawn from immediate social context and encounters	'Because we hate them'
Emotions	An unearned easy feeling of superiority, from which pleasure may emerge. Other emotions of anger, hate, disgust may also act as a driver for release of anxiety.	'Because it's fun'
Criminal-materialist	Action that is motivated by direct gain, such as stealing property.	'Because we want/ get something'
Territorial-political	Strong attachment or loyalty to spaces and their social/political identities, lead to feelings of a need to defend territory.	'Because it's "our" place'
Social group norms	Conformity to the expected behaviour of a formal or informal group.	'Because we all think it's OK'
Bureaucratic, disciplined or military	Legitimate organisations which require routine compliance with racist action, i.e. genocide, ethnic cleansing, etc.	'Because we're told to'

Although much research has been undertaken on victims, highlighting that in addition to feelings of fear, there is also a strong sense of anger (Goodey, 2005), Christmann and Wong (2010) highlight how victims of hate crime nevertheless undertake a cost–benefit calculation, either consciously or unconsciously, and that this then goes on to impact on their decision of whether or not they report the offence to the police. Informing this calculation is also the degree to which one is more readily perceived to be 'an ideal victim', which includes the view that they are innocent and have played no part in their victimisation (Spalek, 2006: 22). It is suggested that one's race, ethnicity and religion (as well as other social variables) also influence the 'ideal victim' status, and often these have served to evoke feelings of blame by self and/or others for their victimisation.

Taking from this, we argue that a cost–benefit calculation clearly takes place in constructions of victimhood, but that it does so at a much earlier stage of the victimisation

(Continued)

(Continued)

process – this being when the individual is assessing the incident (usually during or immediately after it), and what he or she interprets to be the reason for its occurrence – in other words, their rationalisation of the racist attack, which may include trying to explain it in a number of ways, including:

- Mistaken identity;
- Drunkenness;
- Neighbourhood demographics;
- Local, national and international events;
- Media news stories;
- Changes to immigration policy;
- Economic uncertainty or crisis.

This study therefore will offer a more detailed understanding on the reporting of racist attacks, in particular how those who experience such attacks identify themselves and whether this motivates reporting. The research will add to existing knowledge by providing an empirically sound and criminological insight into key crime, justice and victimisation matters in the area of racist attacks and victims' needs. It will do this by directly accessing, via a series of interviews, the voices (as to enable insight into actual views and experiences) of those who have experienced racist attacks. It is hoped that this study will produce an insightful and theoretically informative narrative from the perspectives of key subjects involved. This will then be used to expand criminological understanding on the subject, as well as informing discussions on policy development and best practice in terms of criminal justice intervention, as well as enhance the position of victims.

The Sample

The sample will be recruited via drawing on already established links with local ethnic and faith-based community groups. Given that race, crime and victimisation issues are the researchers' areas of expertise, we have a set of contacts who have expressed interest in the research, as well as highlighting their recognition of the need for such research to be carried out. We are confident that research access to a sample of 50 respondents can be achieved. We will work with leads (gatekeepers) within these already established contact organisations and community groups to make contact with individuals who have in the last three years experienced at least one racist attack. Individuals will be given an information sheet (see Appendix, Resource 7) detailing the purpose of the study, along with an invitation to be involved in the generation of data/knowledge.

The study will gather data via interviews with a total of 50 respondents. This sample size is considered to be achievable, practically manageable, and will generate enough detailed data for criminological analysis on the subject to be made.

It is recognised that research into this area does require very serious pause for thought of the ethical matters associated with (1) researching such a politicised and sensitive subject and (2) researching marginalised groups. Ultimately the protection and safety of the research participants must be upheld, both in adherence to the Human Rights Act (1998) and in accordance to the principles of good social research. Given that the research topic is one that is located within a particularly sensitive and political context, it is understandable that respondents may be suspicious of the researcher and/or their motives, which may go on to hinder access or research cooperation. Understandably, the respondents will ask questions about how their interests (including safety, anonymity and accuracy of voice) will be served by the research, undertaking even their own form of vetting work (Noaks and Wincup, 2004) of the researcher, their institution and/or the funding body. Combating these difficulties is not easy. To begin with, gaining access is time-consuming and difficult, and its achievement is not always guaranteed. The researcher must be truthful about the research purpose and the work involved from the respondent (Noaks and Wincup, 2004). Informal gatekeepers may exist, and their influence on securing access must here be given careful consideration, given that they hold the power to enable or block access. Noaks and Wincup (2004) advise that the role and influence of the gatekeeper(s) be considered at all stages of the research, including after access has been granted. In this sense, access is viewed as an ongoing relationship rather than a one-off event that occurs at the start of the research (Denscombe, 1998, cited in Noaks and Wincup, 2004: 60). Research access may also be enhanced if the gatekeeper or respondent has an immediate practical incentive, for example copies of the final report or a summary of findings, a workshop to discuss the findings, or access to professional advice or academic services. This could be offered in addition to the dissemination of findings in academic and policy making bodies – which would offer the research participant an avenue for their voice to be heard in these important and influential arenas.

The Centre for Social Research at the University of Salford (of which the researchers are members) uses guidelines from the British Sociological Association (BSA) (1998) and the British Society of Criminology (2003) for its ethical review and governance. Adherence to these guidelines is strong, and the need to 'creatively produce ethics' (Plummer, 2001: 227) as the research unfolds is viewed as unnecessary and potentially damaging. The guidelines provide fundamental ethical guidelines for how the researcher should conduct work throughout all stages of the study (Noaks and Wincup, 2004). The guidelines will also be used to create appropriate boundaries of involvement and detachment, which is useful when dealing with any discussions of personal issues.

Also, there is an ethical responsibility to protect the confidentiality of participants through such means of safeguarding anonymity. This is especially true for those who have already experienced discriminatory victimisation, such as the sample here, where

(Continued)

(Continued)

participation in criminological research may place them in a vulnerable position. From the outset a guarantee of confidentiality will be given to all respondents.

Accessing and providing an avenue for under-researched, marginalised and hard to reach groups, add to the empowerment of these voices – a vital objective of this research given that historically social science has treated this group in neglectful, abusive and misrepresented ways (Patel and Tyrer, 2011). This legacy brings some methodological risk, meaning that problems of access and cooperation may also arise (Noaks and Wincup, 2004), where respondents may be concerned about how they may be represented, especially in matters of 'race' and crime, which has the very real potential to add social scientific weight to them being formally demonised and criminalised (Patel and Tyrer, 2011). There is also the problem of research fatigue (Clark, 2008), which often occurs when certain groups are over-researched – a claim that has been made about BME groups (Afshar et al., 2002; Butt and O'Neil, 2004) – which is linked to frustration emerging from high levels of research participation, and little evidence of delivering change directly to the researched group (Patel and Tyrer, 2011). To address these concerns, it is useful to take direction from Patel and Tyrer (2011) and Phillips and Bowling (2003) who offer the following recommendations:

1. Acknowledge that the research relationship is structured by power relations;

2. Pursue multiple truths;

3. Value inclusionary research participation in knowledge production;

4. Develop rapport and trust;

5. Develop an ethos of non-exploitative research (Phillips and Bowling, 2003: 273–276);

6. The social science researcher should acknowledge the ethnic biases of their discipline;

7. And recognise that social science can be as a source of potential harm (Patel and Tyrer, 2011: 139).

Informed Consent

Informed consent, which is voluntary and based upon the participant having been informed of the research purposes, dissemination plans, financial support and participant rights, will be sought and recorded on a consent form (see Appendix, Resource 7) before any interviews are undertaken.

Data Protection

Also, in ensuring that confidentiality and anonymity conform to the Data Protection Act (1998) pseudonyms will be used; certain details will be coded, omitted, or carefully described so as to avoid disclosing the identification of the respondent; and all details about the respondents, including personal details, contact details and the original copies of the tape-recorded interview sessions and notes taken from the interview sessions will be password protected and locked away in a secure location and destroyed when no longer needed.

Professional Ethics Code

Outcome of Ethics Application

Following deliberation and evaluation by the University College Level Ethics Committee we received the single comment below:

> **Panel's comment:** *'Some of the questions may cause disquiet or upset the participants as they are being asked questions about an attack. The interviewers need to address how they will manage this, and what will be put in place to support the interviewees.'*

The research team met, reflected upon the issues raised, modified the strategy and replied to the Committee with the following response:

> *The emotional and mental well-being of the respondents is of paramount concern to the researchers. The researchers will seek to ensure, to the best of their ability, that participants are kept safe from any short or long-term disquiet or upset that may be caused by questions about their experiences of racial victimisation. The researchers will attempt to protect the respondents' well-being by explaining the focus of the research to them and informing them in a clear and comprehensible way that they will be asked questions about the attack in a one-to-one interview setting. They will be advised that they can draw on the support of the gatekeeper victim support organisation at any time during research participation, as well as any of the listed specialist support groups and organisations that will be additionally provided to them by the researchers at the start of each interview. Respondents will also have the option of being able to withdraw from the interviews/ research at any time. In the event that respondents express upset during the interview, but wish to continue participation, they will be offered alternative methods of expression previously utilised by the researchers whilst working with other vulnerable groups. For example, respondents can submit diaries containing written accounts, sketches, poems and other forms of expressive narrative which convey their experiences. This will allow the continued use of the personal narrative research method, but in a way that places a particularly sensitive respondent in greater control over when and how to express their narrative.*

The Ethics Committee accepted this addition which was incorporated into the ethics application and ethical approval for the project was then granted.

(Continued)

(Continued)

Procedure

Following ethical approval, the researchers have embarked upon a complex process of developing access to likely participants. This process relies upon utilising existing research contacts or 'gatekeepers' known to the research team as well as forging new pathways to recruit participants. One strategy has been to contribute to a forum on hate crime in the locality, to publicise the research across the group and to invite institutional contributions from public and third sector organisations such as housing associations, multi-faith groups and charities. In addition to physical representation on such forums, the core strategy is to write to likely participants gleaned from professional networks providing them with a general overview of the project (see Appendix, Resource 7).

Many of the professional and institutional contacts have been collected by the research team as a result of previous contact and experience and teaching links, which may not be available to all researchers embarking upon such projects. If such connections and links are not at your disposal then you will need to approach likely gatekeepers for your research, e.g. formal organisations, research and strategy personnel, directors of voluntary organisations. Similarly, you should consult and approach individuals in your organisation likely to have access to a greater pool of appropriate professional contacts. The early negotiation stage to recruit appropriate samples in qualitative research is a challenging task as reflected in our previous discussion in Chapter 5 on issues of access.

Following a successful meeting with the director of a well-established local NGO, the research team were introduced to practitioners routinely liaising with victims of racial hate crimes. The practitioners were briefed by the researchers about the aims and objectives of the project and then to invite 'respondents' to contact the researchers in order to conduct interviews.

Summary

This case study has demonstrated how a project can be conceived and has outlined the steps routinely taken by researchers to transform a conceptual premise or research question into an empirical project. The example illustrates the complex task of getting gatekeepers on board, satisfying institutional and professional ethics committees and developing the 'apparatus' and 'documents, such as participation invitations[10] and interview schedules, to enable an empirical study to function.

CASE STUDY 2

Transnationality in the Lives of Muslim Ex-offenders[11]

Introduction

This case study is drawn from a larger qualitative study examining the experiences of Muslim ex-offenders from northern England. Although this study did problematise the link between race and faith (Quraishi, 2005), for the purposes of the current discussion the focus will be on how, when, where and by whom 'race' was raised as a subject focus in the research. As with Case Study 1, this case study employs some of the methods and nicely illustrates some of the themes and issues outlined in previous chapters.

A central aim of the project was to document and critique the ex-offenders' experiences of discrimination, victimisation and exclusion to identify gaps in support from the voluntary sector and criminal justice professionals. The project both confirms and qualifies the little which is known about the experiences of victimisation and criminality amongst British Muslim populations.

The study also provided an exploration of the importance of transnational identities and contexts to the complex lives of South Asian Muslim ex-offenders in the UK. It also contributes to the literature which explains how British Muslim populations have become subject of a populist discourse which irresponsibly intertwines debates about immigration, crime, segregation and terrorism in the UK (Kundnani, 2007).

Background

The study by Beckford, Joly and Khosrokhavar in 2005 is the first substantial evaluation of the qualitative experiences of Muslim prisoners in the UK and France. It explores issues of Muslim self-identity but also the way in which the closed institution of prison treats religious minorities. It provides a unique insight into the challenges of multi-faith and multi-ethnic policies against an evaluation of the institutionalisation of Islam (Beckford et al., 2005). One under-researched area the study highlights is the levels and processes of conversion in prison to Islam significantly amongst British Black Caribbean males (Quraishi, 2005). Whilst precise figures of conversion are presently unavailable, an analysis of classification of ethnicity against religion in prison demonstrates that whilst South Asian Muslims represent the public face of Islam in broader British society, this is less true for the male prison population (Quraishi, 2005, 2008b, 2013).

This raises interesting questions regarding how prisoners who convert to Islam in prison are treated once they are released. How do they categorise themselves? What obstacles face converts to Islam upon release from prison as compared to Muslim prisoners 'born into the faith'? Whilst they may have felt part of a community in prison how far do these experiences transfer to their interaction with established Muslim communities in Britain?

The Home Office has funded research into the experiences of black and Asian offenders on probation but this has evaluated interaction with the Probation Service and the respondents are categorised on grounds of ethnicity rather than faith (Calverly et al., 2004). The present study complements the very few studies which have been undertaken in the UK within this field.

Muslim Populations and Crime in the UK

Very few criminological studies exist which specifically evaluate Muslim populations in Britain. In part, this is an outcome of the way in which official criminal statistics have been produced and documented in the UK. The dominant use of classification based on ethnicity rather than faith identities is the product of statutory obligations upon

(Continued)

(Continued)

key criminal justice agencies pursuant to the Criminal Justice Act 1991. Scholars have emphasised the problems of recording ethnically diverse populations under homogeneous classifications within the criminal justice system (FitzGerald, 1997; Spalek, 2004). Whilst there has been a concerted effort on the part of the Home Office to move towards a uniform 16-point classification system across the criminal justice system, the full outcome of this remains to be seen.

Therefore, with the exception of prison statistics, researchers wishing to evaluate Muslim populations and crime are prompted to make educated evaluations of statistics based on the ethnicity, rather than the faith, of the offenders. Since the UK Muslim population is overwhelmingly represented by people declaring South Asian ethnicity (namely Pakistani and Bangladeshi), it is reasonable to assume that crime studies on Pakistani or Bangladeshi populations can translate to studies on principally Muslim populations (Quraishi, 2005).

There are common themes across the few criminological studies on South Asian Muslim populations in the UK. The discussions are based upon relatively low levels of offending amongst South Asian populations in the UK historically. In part the conformity of the past was attributable to the way in which crime statistics recorded people under the generic 'Asian' category. Once scholars were able to disaggregate the statistics for Asian offenders based on 'Indian, Pakistani or Bangladeshi' a clearer picture emerges. For example, we see over-representation in incarceration rates per 100,000 population for Pakistani males (Home Office, 2006). It is not surprising, therefore, that some of the earliest studies in this field were undertaken with specific reference to Pakistani populations.[12]

A common theme across some of these studies was the assertion that whilst Muslim populations had experienced relative conformity and under-representation in official criminal statistics in the past, this would be less true for the future. The cause of a potential increase in the processing of criminality amongst Muslim populations includes a consideration of demographic factors which place Asian Muslim youth statistically within the peak age of offending; shifts in how Muslim populations are constructed as deviant; and, more recently, proactive targeting by the police as part of anti-terror strategies (Quraishi, 2005).

Academic contributions also emphasise that offending by Muslim populations must be contextualised against incidents of victimisation, marginalisation and social exclusion within the urban populations where most Muslims reside (Spalek, 2002; Wardak, 2000).

In addition, it is important to be aware that criminologists have often directed people to view crime in terms of cyclic historical behaviour. Therefore, it is worth noting that some crime was present amongst first-wave South Asian Muslim migrants to the UK from the 1960s onwards. Incidents of such crime and infractions of religious norms is often masked by a process of historical amnesia which needs to be addressed in order to bring any contemporary offending by Muslim youths into context (Quraishi, 2005).

Muslims in Prison and Radicalisation

The incarcerated Muslim population in the UK has attracted significant media attention. Whilst the media have focused upon the potential for Muslim prisoners to become radicalised within prison, various studies have been more cautious in suggesting a causal relationship between prison experiences and radicalisation. The following discussion outlines the key challenges prompted by a rising Muslim prison population and the contributions made to understanding the ramifications of this within the UK.

The Statistical Background

The Muslim prison population has experienced significant expansion since records began. Between the years 1995–2005 the Muslim prison population grew by more than 150% (Home Office, 2006) and presently accounts for approximately 14% of the prison population in England and Wales (Ministry of Justice, 2009, 2011; Morris, 2014). In September 2000, on average, the female and male Muslim prison population represented 3% and 7% respectively of the total prison population (Guessous et al., 2001). The prison population should be contrasted against the percentage of Muslims in the general British population. The Census of 2001 revealed that 2.7% (1.6 million out of a total population of 58,789,000) of the UK population declared Islam as their faith (Office for National Statistics, 2003b). This therefore illustrates significant over-representation of Muslims in prison as compared to their density in the general population.

The British Muslim population is ethnically diverse; however the majority of Muslims claim South Asian ethnicity with Pakistani (658,000) and Bangladeshi (260,000) populations accounting for approximately 918,000 of the 1.6 million Muslims in the UK. Furthermore, 8.5% of the Indian population in the UK are also Muslim (Office for National Statistics, 2003a). Therefore, one may expect the ethnic composition of British Muslim populations to be reflected in the incarcerated population. However, in 2001, the Home Office released statistical analysis of the prison population based on religious affiliation and ethnicity, which revealed that, in 2000, Black Muslims in prison constituted 34% of the total Muslim inmate population whilst Asian Muslims constituted 42% (Guessous et al., 2001). The percentage of Muslims who declared Black ethnicity in the Census 2001 is very small, with Black Caribbean Muslims recorded as 0.29% and Black African Muslims as 0.09% of the total Muslim population of the UK (Office for National Statistics, 2003b). Although no statistics on conversion to Islam in prison have been published, the evaluation above suggests that many black prisoners are converts to Islam and qualitative research illustrates that some black prisoners convert whilst in prison. The statistical picture is partly responsible for government and media engagement with this issue.

Media and Government Perspectives

The British media have produced many articles raising concerns about potential radicalisation amongst Muslim prisoners and problems prompted by a rising Muslim prison population (Doward, 2008; Ford, 2008; Pidd, 2008; Travis, 2008a, 2008b). The articles are, in part, reactions to the release of official reports and observations from prison-related organisations and watchdogs including the Prison Officers Association, Independent Board of Monitors and HM Inspectorate of Prisons.

The concerns raised centre upon the perceived vulnerability of prisoners to radical influences from extremist inmates (including those detained pursuant to terrorist offences) and in some rare cases from prison imams. It is worth emphasising that the

(Continued)

(Continued)

reports tend to focus on maximum security prisons or those where the Muslim prison population is particularly large, and speak less of the prison estate as a whole. HMP Belmarsh has figured prominently in the media on account of some of its high pro-file inmates whilst HMP Wandsworth has attracted attention over allegations of rival Muslim factions and disagreements between Muslim prisoners and an imam.

The government perceives the problem of radicalisation as a genuine and escalating issue with the Ministry of Justice predicting a 10-fold rise in the number of terrorist suspects held in prisons in England and Wales over the next 10 years (Travis, 2007). Policy has been recently extended by the Home Office to provide a nationwide 'deradicalisation' programme and the deployment of £12.5 million for countering terrorism including counter-radicalisa-tion in prisons (HM Government, 2008; Travis, 2008b). Furthermore, the Metropolitan Police Authority has acknowledged the operation of discreet 'deradicalisation' teams headed by Islamic scholars to de-programme extremist prisoners theologically in some UK prisons (Metropolitan Police Authority, 2007). The establishment of such teams has been criticised by some scholars as representing the conflation of threats from al-Qaida with the political and religious views of peaceful adherents to Salafism in the UK (Spalek and Lambert, 2007).

Studies of Muslims in Prison

The first detailed evaluation of Muslim prisoners was undertaken by Beckford et al. (2005). Whilst this study did not specifically set out to evaluate radicalisation or extremism, the fieldwork period straddled 11 September 2001 and hence necessarily engaged with some of the ramifications of this event upon prison management. The study was comparative with France and, *inter alia*, provided a qualitative evaluation of the experiences of Muslim prisoners in three UK prisons in relation to issues of discrimination, racism and access to religious support. The study also evaluated how prison staff, including chaplains, inter-preted the rise in Muslim prisoners and whether this presented the prison estate with particular challenges. The main conclusions of this study highlighted significant experi-ences of discrimination as perceived by Muslim prisoners and imams as well as an assertion that Islam was effectively being institutionalised in prison via the creation of the Office of the Muslim Adviser to the Prison Service and the appointment of full-time Muslim chap-lains (Beckford et al., 2005). The research did not find any significant levels of radicalisation or extremism amongst Muslim prisoners in the UK nor in the preaching or approach taken by full- or part-time imams over the course of the study (Beckford et al., 2005).

Another study which was undertaken examined the experiences of Muslim converts in two English prisons (Spalek and El-Hassan, 2007). This work explicitly challenges the populist assertion that converts to Islam in prison are vulnerable to extremist ideology. The study claims that converts utilise Islamic teachings not only to cope more easily with the conditions of incarceration but also for the provision of a moral framework in preparation for their life post-incarceration (Spalek and El-Hassan, 2007).

The latest and most comprehensive study has been undertaken by Gabriele Marranci, who spent four years interviewing over 170 Muslim prisoners and ex-prisoners from Scotland, England and Wales (Marranci, 2007). As with the two previous studies, Marranci claims the potential for prison imams to radicalise prisoners has been exaggerated and he found no evidence to suggest prison imams were facilitating radicalisation. Marranci emphasises the positive role prison imams play in countering extremism in prison; his study also highlights the complexity facing the prison authorities in formulating coherent and practical guidelines to identify behaviour amongst Muslim prisoners which signals 'radicalisation'. Whilst rejecting radicalisation amongst prison imams, Marranci does conclude that some disassembled militant organisations try to 'talent scout' young former Muslim prisoners (Marranci, 2009: 3). Furthermore, he expressed extreme concern that some of his respondents had 'formed an Islamic gang' having converted their group to Islam (Marranci, 2009: 2). Importantly Marranci's study claims that prison authorities, by overemphasising extremism, have neglected the more pressing problem of challenges facing the reintegration of Muslim ex-offenders into society.

The material briefly discussed here should be contextualised against broader and well-trodden debates within criminology about the impact of prison populations upon other parts of the criminal justice system as well as upon the constructions of suspect populations. The historical relationship in the UK between Muslim (South Asian) populations and crime has been one of relative conformity and under-representation in official criminal statistics. Many factors have been offered to explain the rise in the recorded Muslim prisoner population since the 1990s, including demographic contexts and extra-legal factors in policing and sentencing (Quraishi, 2005, 2006; Spalek, 2004). An exploration of the way in which particular populations are processed by the criminal justice system has the potential to reveal discriminatory practices which contribute to the over-representation of such populations in official criminal statistics. Youthful working-class urban populations have always been the subject of over-policing. The Muslim British population has a youthful demographic profile and the majority reside in urban areas. Therefore, if recent counter-terrorism strategies are also factored into the equation, a drift towards over-representation of Muslim male youth in criminal statistics is a likely consequence.

Finally, how can the anomaly between media and government perspectives about Muslim radicalisation in prison and the contributions from studies be explained? It could be the case that the researchers have not been privy to government intelligence about the extent of the problem, or that the fieldwork was not primarily in maximum security prisons housing terrorist prisoners. The qualitative nature of the studies enabled them to reflect upon often mundane, pastoral issues coupled with experiences of discrimination which are the central concerns for many Muslim prisoners. Muslim chaplains are not viewed as the agents of radicalisation but more accurately as intermediaries in checking extremism.

The picture is undoubtedly complex but a moral panic over radicalisation only reduces such complexity and acts as a distraction from engagement with the pressing issues of faith-based initiatives in rehabilitation and resettlement for a predominantly non-radical Muslim prison population.

Methodology

This example is based on a pilot study which has provided the first step towards a more comprehensive study of Muslim ex-offenders across different geographical parts of the UK

(Continued)

(Continued)

and possibly for international comparative research. The principal qualitative data gathering process was via semi-structured interviews with Muslim ex-offenders.

The project demonstrated the complexities and challenges of access to a population considered to be sensitive and vulnerable. Furthermore, the project very aptly illustrates ambiguities in the way in which individuals processed by the criminal justice system are categorised. As previously mentioned, prison remains the only institution in the criminal justice system which classifies individuals according to their religion. Hence, there are valuable statistics which illustrate religious affiliation amongst the incarcerated population. No other arm of the criminal justice system records faith identity, so when it came to identifying Muslim ex-offenders the task was far from straightforward.

The consent and cooperation of the relevant Probation Service was fundamental to the fieldwork stage. Following correspondence and a meeting at the regional headquarters of the Probation Service, the researcher was permitted access to confidential offender data and to an independent Offender Support (OS) service responsible for advising the Probation Service on cultural and religious needs of clients on a case by case basis.

The fieldwork gathering stage commenced on 24 April 2009 and concluded 28 October 2009. The OS service was consulted on two dates (24 April 2009 and 3 September 2009) and informed the researcher that they did not classify clients according to faith. However, it was assumed that clients with Arabic names and declaring Indian, Pakistani or Bangladeshi ethnicity would most probably be Muslim. Furthermore, the clients were personally known to the support staff who confirmed whether a particular client was Muslim or not. The OS service had approximately 40 Muslim clients in their caseload over this period, 35 of these were approached yielding 10 interviews.

The files included details about the offences committed, sentence and which probation office and individual probation officer was responsible for the supervision of the client. The next step was to contact the probation officer responsible for each client and ask them to forward an invitation to participate in the project. There were 10 districts and 16 probation offices in this geographical region. A message had been cascaded via Probation Service headquarters through the internal staff e-mail system informing all probation officers about the project and the request to participate. Once the probation officer acknowledged that the client was in their workload they would forward the request to the ex-prisoner and then reply directly to the researcher to inform whether or not the client wished to participate or not. If the answer was in the affirmative the researcher would then have to set up an interview date for the mutual convenience of all.

Furthermore, it was decided that the interviews take place at the Probation Services offices. The reason for this decision was multi-fold. First, the buildings contained appropriate interview rooms. Second, the client was already obliged to visit their probation officer as part of their sentence and so agreeing to meet them on the same date would mean they would not incur additional travel costs. Third, it would mean the respondents would be in a familiar environment. Fourth, for the safety of the researcher and clients it was deemed prudent to meet respondents out of earshot but within close proximity to other members of staff.

A disadvantage to meeting in Probation Service rooms was that, despite assurances to the contrary given by the researcher, there may have been a tendency for respondents to assume that the Probation Service had commissioned the research or was in some way influencing the project. Indeed, the fact the interviews had to be arranged via individual probation officers may have also influenced decisions to participate in the research or indeed to choose not to. In some cases, the records at the OS service were slightly behind latest developments regarding clients and a number of potential respondents had either been transferred to a different probation region or their sentence had come to an end by the time the probation officer had been contacted.

All of the 10 respondents agreed to audio-recording and for full participation in the project. In keeping with the remit of a pilot study, the project concentrated largely upon the qualitative responses from ex-offenders rather than from practitioners. The study does, however, include an in-depth interview with the service manager of the OS service, since this was the sole conduit for the cultural and religious support needs of Muslim ex-offenders in the probation region selected for the study.

Findings and Emerging Themes

Family Fragmentation and Complexity

The government has recently acknowledged the negative impact that the imprisonment of a mother or father has upon children (Ministry of Justice, 2007). Whilst it was not the specific focus of the present study, it was apparent that the respondents often lived complex lives: for example, Emran was married but separated with two children; Abdul's parents were separated and he lived with his mother; Bilal was separated following an attempted polygamous relationship; Choudry was single but had a six-year-old daughter; Helal was in a relationship but not married to his partner and had one child; Iqbal had two children with a partner to whom he was not married; Javed was not married and had a son aged five. It is worth reminding the reader here that this theme needs to be read against the caveat in the introduction. Specifically, that part of the remit of the project was to examine how Muslim ex-offenders interpreted Islamic jurisprudence and religious laws against secular norms. So whilst the respondents' lives were not particularly remarkable for their relationships, as compared to other ex-offender populations, they were significant when examined against an assessment of how they interpreted Islamic religious norms and prohibitions, which include restrictions on particular sexual relationships.

Research has indicated that 65% of boys with a convicted father go on to offend, although it is not known whether the disruption caused by imprisonment leads to this or whether other factors are at play (Glover, 2009). However, less is known about the specific family support needs within BME populations (Social Exclusion Unit, 2002). There was also evidence, in the present study, of the imprisonment or offending impacting upon younger siblings. One respondent, the eldest son, claimed his imprisonment meant his younger brothers were less responsive to parental discipline. The following excerpts from interviews with the ex-offenders provide examples of the complexity of their domestic lives. For example Bilal talks about the pressure he faced when he undertook a relationship with another person whilst married:

(Continued)

(Continued)

> *The girl I was living with at the time that's what she wanted me to do is, divorce. If I got given a divorce that would be the end of my life for my kids as well. Being selfish, I probably wanted the best of both worlds and I wanted to be able to see my kids and live the life I was living, after having constant rows.*

Gul explained how his imprisonment had impacted upon his relationship with his mother who was separated from his father:

> *I was out [of prison] for about three or four weeks and she [my mum] threw me out on the streets. I'm thinking, I'm losing my head and I thought, I'll just go to my dad and my stepmum. I'm happy with them both.*

Choudry had experienced significant domestic disruption including formal involvement from Social Services:

> *The mother of the child, I've had domestic issues and stuff. At the time, Social Services were involved and everything. At that time, I never really – it was tried to participate and communicate properly in order to get access, because I was a bit naive and I wasn't really thinking properly.*

Finally, Javed's account details how his imprisonment meant he was not able to exert his usual disciplinary influence on younger siblings:

> I: *How do you think this affected your brothers, you know when you went inside?*

> R: *They got a bit more free-ness [sic], especially the one that's younger than me, he's in college, he's seventeen going on eighteen, because when I was out I used to be strict on him, when he can go out, what he can do, who he can go out with and when I went, because I went for a total of a year, and I came back and all my friends were saying you need to sort your brother out, he's gone out of hand, he's doing this, he's doing that. They go, he's trying to be you, he's trying to be like you but he's never going to be like me, he was trying to get that like popularity, what I used to have, all my friends they like all look up to me, and he wants like all his friends to look up to him.*

Perceptions of Discrimination

The responses may be distinguished between experiences from within prison to those when released. Although some prisoners did cite specific incidents of racism or anti-Muslim behaviour in prison there was little sense of explicit discrimination or racism from officials impacting upon the individuals interviewed. This is in contrast to published research on discrimination towards Muslim prisoners in British prisons (Beckford et al., 2005). The few incidents of racism in prison seemed to centre upon either racist language or perceptions of inaction on the part of the prison officers and management to requests such as moving to another prison or being released on licence. However, respondents also discussed the pervasiveness of discrimination in wider British society rather than at the hands of practitioners whom they encountered or were supervised by. It is worth noting, however, that in the perception of the OS service manager discrimination was evident towards their clients from probation staff, warranting formal intervention on two occasions.

Gul articulates a common theme in contemporary accounts of racism, that it is more likely to be subtle, indirect and hidden rather than explicit or spectacular:

> Obviously, when I was locked up. It's just one of those things there. You know that the officers in there they are racist, but they will play games with you. They won't say to your face, but they will make time hard for you. Obviously...

For Helal, being a victim of racism was closely tied to whether you were visibly a minority or did not speak English. Discrimination here was more about failing to be represented or being neglected rather than about direct verbal or physical racist abuse:

> Yes. You see with me now, I never witnessed it [racism] myself. I can speak English and I can respond. But there is [sic] people in there who can't speak English and not just Pakistanis. There is Chinese in there and there is Indians in there, there is all sorts in there, yeah? They tend to treat you in prison nowadays that if that community with you are all right, I get what I want. If they can't communicate with you, they don't get nothing.

The following extract from an interview with Iqbal gives voice to the everyday mundane discrimination routinely tolerated by visible ethnic minorities:

> When I was in Cat D I had a problem there with racism and stuff and I was obviously fighting in the Cat D and stuff. That's about it. Other than that ... you have the odd few people, you walk around and they are saying, you Paki this and stuff. You get that. A lot of people discriminate and that. Nothing serious.

Similarly, Bilal's account speaks of being a victim of racism as very much a common aspect of his experiences growing up in a particular location in northern England. Bilal clearly identifies the area he grew up in as traditionally 'white' and alludes to the formation of resistance and reaction to such racism as he and his friends grew older:

> I've suffered racism. I grew up in ****** and I remember it was very sort of English dominated when we first moved into that area. I got called all sorts, Paki and stuff like that. Times changed and obviously when we grew older and older and fought back.

It also appeared that, once removed from the institutional setting of prison, the perceptions of discrimination from officials were also less evident. Indeed, particularly noteworthy are accounts of where respondents felt that the Probation Service and individual probation officers in particular were sensitive to their cultural needs. The community sentence for one

(Continued)

(Continued)

respondent included working in the kitchens of a care home. He was very grateful that his probation officer ensured that he was not obliged to handle non-halal products as part of this sentence and this was without him having to make the request. It is unclear in this instance whether the probation officer was acting in response to guidance from the OS unit or on her/his own volition. It is worth noting that those in the sample, by virtue of the methodology, were already identified as having cultural and faith-based needs and support hence one may expect them to be less critical than those not referred to the OS unit.

Transnational Lives

An important theme to emerge from the interviews was the transnational dimensions in the lives of Muslim ex-offenders. Scholars of contemporary race and religion have acknowledged the importance of transnational contexts to the concepts of identity, citizenship and belonging (Levitt, 2003; Seddon et al., 2003; Vertovec, 1999; Voyer, 2013). Undoubtedly, Muslims in the UK comprise multiple transnational communities defined as *'groups based in two or more countries that engage in recurrent, enduring and significant cross-border activities, which may be economic, political, social or cultural in character'* (Castles, 2003: 20).

The responses from ex-prisoners demonstrated the importance and influence of extended family networks in Pakistan which impacted upon the day-to-day lives of British Muslims (see Ballard, 2002; Taylor et al., 2007). Respondents maintained physical links with Pakistan, travelling there for business, to visit family or to attend funerals, sometimes for periods of up to one year. The impact of such connections and obligations was felt across many aspects of their lives, including interruptions to school education, breaches of bail terms and even as a rehabilitative exercise to distance the individual from the crime and sentence. There is little discussion of the significance of such transnational dimensions in criminological literature on community sentencing.

Transnational contexts illustrate the flaws in considering ethnic minority populations as a uniform homogeneous group always subject to exclusion, marginality and inequality. Without undermining the need to address inequality and discrimination experienced by BME populations in Britain, transnational contexts provide an important arsenal for the anti-essentialist debate. Transnational contexts explain in part how the intersectionality of ethnicity, class, caste and gender operate in practice. Viewed through a transnational lens we can begin to comprehend how, for example, sections of the British Pakistani community can occupy both marginalised and privileged positions. Scholars have highlighted that although many South Asian migrants to the UK came from rural and often impoverished regions of the Indian sub-continent, some of the very same migrants have come to enjoy significant affluence as money earned in Britain flowed back to their countries of origin. Migrants reinvested in rural villages and areas such as Mirpur in north Pakistan, in turn developing the physical infrastructure of these regions whilst acquiring trophy properties as part of the competitive jostling between families for honour, prestige and esteem (Taylor et al., 2007).

It is clear that the complexity of identities, national, racial, religious or cultural, often leave the individual challenged in terms of their sense of belonging. The extract below from an interview with Iqbal clearly illustrates the challenges faced by minorities seeking acceptance in British society whilst similarly facing exclusion in their country of ethnic origin.

I'm happy. I'm British. My parents are Pakistani, that's where we come from, Pakistan my mum and parents and stuff, but I'm British. I'm British. They don't want to hear that. Go back to your own country, go back to your own country. Where do I stand? You come here, oh, go back to your own country, we don't want you. You go back to your own country for a holiday and they say, no, you are British and this and that.

The findings articulated here must be read against some important caveats. First the project is a qualitative pilot and so there are limits to how far we can treat the findings as relevant to the broader Muslim ex-prisoner population. Second, the lack of faith classification for ex-offenders means researchers must resort to less accurate classifications of ethnicity rather than faith. This necessarily means that Muslims who have converted, particularly those with white or black ethnicity and who have not necessarily adopted an Arabic name, are untraceable in the present system post-incarceration. Third, in the Probation Service area chosen for the project all cultural and religious needs of black and minority ex-offenders were dealt with by a single referral agency which had a legacy of dealing principally with Pakistani clients. This fact accounts for the sample consisting overwhelmingly of Pakistani British nationals born into Islam and does not reflect the ethnic diversity amongst the Muslim prison population as a whole. Despite the caveats above, the project does provide a useful platform from which to launch a more in-depth investigation and perhaps one which compares across different Probation Service regions and jurisdictions.

In terms of future directions, the study most definitely illustrates a neglected research field. Although the respondents did not express a need for faith-based support services, ironically they were already receiving such support by virtue of the OS unit. One interpretation of this position is that the processing of support appears seamless between the voluntary unit providing the assistance and the Probation Service paying for the input. During the course of the project the contract for the OS unit for BME ex-offenders was not renewed owing to the conclusion of an internal quantitative audit of the service by the Probation Service and a lack of referrals from probation officers from black clients, rather than Pakistani clients.

This is unfortunate, since the OS represents another example of the pressing need for criminal justice practitioners to utilise cultural and religious knowledge to assist in offender management. In the absence of such services, the onus is likely to shift in-house relying upon Muslim or BME staff to provide insight on religious and cultural practices.

Summary

The present project was unable to test some of the issues it originally set out to investigate, namely the experiences of those ex-offenders who have recently converted to Islam and whether this group are in greater need for cultural and religious services than those already part of established Muslim communities and extended family networks. Furthermore, although the sample consulted did reflect unsettled domestic lives, only one lived in secure housing owing to the nature of his offending. Upon investigation it emerged that the Probation Service in the area studied had contracted accommodation services to a private company. This meant that they were unable to assist in formally setting up interviews with people in secure hostels.

(Continued)

(Continued)

The project has provided a very useful platform from which to commence a more in-depth study of the same issues but as between different Probation Service areas and court jurisdictions. A firm methodological reference point has also been established to inform any future similar research. Criminology is often deemed reactive rather than proactive; the project demonstrates a reaction to the statistical rise in Muslim males in prison. However, adopting a proactive strategy, a similar or larger project should explore the interpretations of Muslim female ex-offenders, many of whom are foreign nationals.

Although Asian youth are under-represented in crime statistics as a whole, as a result of both demographic factors and the construction of Muslim communities as suspect populations, the proportion of British Muslims entering the criminal justice system is likely to rise (May et al., 2010; Spalek, 2010). Furthermore, following developments from the Preventing Extremism Together (PET or PREVENT) strategy, British Muslim populations remain the subject of government scrutiny and interest (Home Office, 2005).

CASE STUDY 3

The Construction of Racial 'No-Go' Zones[13]

The final case study details the articulations of a sample of South Asian Muslims from Lancashire, UK and Karachi, Pakistan in relation to their construction of the urban space in which they reside. In particular, theories of how urban spaces are 'racially constructed' and the impact of this on our understanding of racial and politically motivated violence are examined. The theoretical inspiration for this case study originated from the writings of Chicago School scholars such as Robert Park touched on in the previous chapter, but more specifically from the works of Webster, Hesse et al. and Keith, who each explore the dynamic relationships between urban space, racial identity and victimisation (Hesse et al., 1992; Keith, 2004; Park, 2004 [1950]; Webster, 1994, 1997b). The study evaluated the construction of certain 'no-go' zones in the UK and Pakistan as perceived by Muslims. The comparative dimension enabled an exploration of the divergence and convergence of processes accountable for a racially constructed interpretation of urban environments (Alexander, 2000; Desai, 1998). Such processes were contextualised against the broader experiences of social exclusion, victimisation and racism experienced by Muslim youth in everyday life (Quraishi, 2005; Spalek, 2002, 2005).

The complex relationships between urban space, ethnic groups and crime has prompted substantial academic enquiry since the founding contributions from the Chicago School of Environmental Criminology. The Darwinian influenced ecological model of a city espoused by Robert Park has been criticised by scholars of race for its positivistic determinism (Bowling and Phillips, 2002). Within this perspective, the process of migration was framed within problematic concepts of invasion, dominance and succession. However, the concepts of 'social disorganisation' and 'cultural transmission' in Shaw and McKay's thesis enabled the emergence of liberal (sub)cultural theories exploring neighbourhood contexts, criminal areas and processes of economic and ethnic segregation (Bottoms and Wiles, 2002; Shaw and McKay, 1942).

Whilst the debates about criminal concordance and urban spaces have been highly charged, a more constructive discourse has emerged in relation to concepts of racial victimisation and social geography (Back, 1996; Hesse et al., 1992; Sibley, 1995; Smith, 1989; Webster, 1994). Within this discourse the significance of viewing racist offending alongside racist victimisation is explored. Concepts of 'territorialism', 'neighbourhoods', 'ethnoscapes' and 'no-go' zones contribute to the diversity of how urban spaces become identified and personified along ethnic and cultural lines (Campbell, 1993; Massey, 1998). The focus in the present case study is the concept of a 'no-go' zone as perceived by Muslim youth within two diverse social geographies in Lancashire, UK and Karachi, Pakistan.[14]

Methodology

The selection of the community study format was influenced by the established methodological tradition of community studies in criminological and sociological research as outlined in Chapter 4. However, a second persuasive factor in selecting the specific communities in Lancashire and Karachi was the embrace of a particular theoretical perspective that, we would argue, is central to understanding race and racism in contemporary society. Critical race theory (CRT) argues that the socio-legal academy has downplayed and silenced issues pertaining to indigenous, displaced and ethnic minority people. The perspective is by no means governed by a canonical set of doctrines or methodologies but certain CRT scholars have adopted novel and unique methods of breaking the perceived silence of suffering minorities (Crenshaw et al., 1995). Methods tend to be ethnographical, qualitative and biographical. These works reject the prevailing orthodoxy that scholarship on ethnicity or race should or could be neutral or objective (Lawrence, 2004; Zuni-Cruz, 2001). In line with this philosophy, the specific community locations selected for study were due to the biography and familial links of the researcher.

A series of qualitative interviews in Karachi were carried out in April 1998, January 1999 and February–April 2000. In total 21 tape-recorded semi-structured interviews were undertaken in Karachi. The interviews were split between two locations: five interviews were conducted with female students at the Area Study Centre for Europe at the University of Karachi whilst 16 interviews were conducted with residents of the community in Sharifabad, Federal B Area, Karachi. At the university, the director of the Area Study Centre for Europe introduced the aims and objectives of the broader study as outlined by the researcher and volunteers were invited for interview from students enrolled on postgraduate courses. These interviews were conducted in English. The Sharifabad interviews were all conducted in Urdu and translated by the researcher. Two respondents stipulated Punjabi ethnicity, 19 stated Mohajir ethnicity and one respondent declared mixed Punjabi/Mohajir ethnicity. The sample was well educated with nine graduates, five

(Continued)

(Continued)

postgraduates and three employed in skilled clerical professions; six declared that they were unemployed.

In Lancashire, interviews were conducted in 1999, with 16 contributors to tape–recorded interviews. Volunteers were requested via posters and leaflets in local community centres and three mosques. The face-to-face interviews were supplemented by the distribution of 120 anonymous postal return questionnaires, of which 35 completed questionnaires were returned. The majority of the respondents declared Pakistani ethnic origin but the sample included four people with Bangladeshi ethnic origin. Many of the Pakistani respondents narrowed their place of origin to 'Attock' or 'Campbellpur' or simply 'Punjab'.

Defining 'No-Go' Zones

A key concept to emerge from the interviews was that of the 'no-go' zone as a subjectively construed phenomenon dependent upon the complex relationship between lived experiences of frequenting and residing in urban locations coupled with imagined or projected perceptions about other unfamiliar urban spaces. The emphasis is upon a 'no-go' zone being synonymous with crime (see Back, 1996). In the case of Muslims in the UK and Karachi, it may be understood as constituting a physical space avoided for the perceived significant likelihood of becoming a victim of crime whilst frequenting the area (Quraishi, 2005).

In the UK, academics have concentrated upon deviance pertaining to racist victimisation when exploring 'spacism' and offending, although contributions also focus on social space and violence against women, as well as general categories of street crime (Stanko, 1990; Webster, 1994). Whilst not discounting the theoretical limitations to comparative criminology,[15] the experiences of respondents in Karachi as compared and contrasted with those in Britain illustrate the processes through which urban spaces become racially or ethnically personified.

The Pakistani Context: Karachi

Karachi is a sprawling conurbation constituting Pakistan's most populated city. As with all large cities, the historical and contemporary patterns of migration define the residence patterns of the current population. The most significant political event regarding the demographic history of Karachi was the Partition of Indian in 1947. Partition led to the arrival of thousands of refugees from the central and northern provinces of India. The influx was so dramatic that Karachi's population rose from 420,000 in 1948 to over 1 million by 1951 (Fernandes and Fernandes, 1994). Over 60% of Karachi's population at this time were immigrants, bringing with them a social and cultural heritage distinct from both the indigenous Karachiites and the rural peoples of Sindh. The significance of this migrant population to the contemporary political life in Karachi cannot be overstated. Upon Partition, the Mohajirs,[16] as the migrants subsequently became known, began to dominate politics, commerce and the social life of Karachi, and indeed of Pakistan as a whole (Mahmud, 1997).

A study by the Pakistan Institute of Development Economics in 1994 estimated that 1.40 million migrants settled in Karachi during 1947–58; of these 1.14 million came from India and 0.26 million from Punjab and the North West Frontier province in the new Pakistan (Fernandes and Fernandes, 1994). Despite the political decision by General Ayub Khan to move the nation's capital from Karachi to Islamabad in 1960, the city of Karachi continues to sprawl. The city's status as a true 'Eldorado' for migrants remains firmly so, and it has become host to waves of migrants from India, Bangladesh, Afghanistan and various parts of rural Pakistan (Kool et al., 1988).

This rapid expansion has not resulted in corresponding planned development and therefore the infrastructure of the city is suffering from heavy over-subscription. In Karachi, between 2.5 and 3 million people live in *kaatchi abaadis*[17] or squatter set-tlements, and the national squatter population is around 45 million (Human Rights Commission of Pakistan, 1997).

The Ethnic Construction of the Mohajir Population

Prior to the Partition of India in 1947 the Urdu-speaking Muslim minority, subsequently known as 'Mohajirs', had formed communities in urban areas of north central India where they constituted 20% of the population (Mahmud, 1997). Mohajirs had been closely associated with the Mughal Empire which meant they had relatively high levels of literacy and had acquired an elite status within Indian society. It was from within this ethnic group that the All Indian Muslim League was founded in 1906 (Moorhouse, 1983). Indeed, it can be said that the principal political articulation of the concept of a separate Muslim state came essentially from this group of people who adopted Chaudri Rahmat Ali's term via the Pakistan Resolution in 1940. In 1947 the Mohajirs constituted some 20% of the 8 million that migrated to Pakistan following Partition, but only constituted 5% of the total population of the new Islamic Republic of Pakistan (Mahmud, 1997).

The majority of the Mohajirs settled in Karachi declared it a capital and began to dominate the politics, commerce and culture of the newly formed country (Hussain, 1996). According to Tayyab Mahmud, the case of the Mohajirs represents a unique attempt by a state to create a nation (Mahmud, 1997). The initial dominance of the Mohajirs was short-lived as their attempts to deny federalism grew increasingly weaker and ineffective. Opposition to their dominance was demonstrated, for example, by the stripping of Karachi's capital status in 1960. The Mohajir dominance lasted for approximately 20 years post-Partition and then began to implode for a number of reasons. Partition had created mass upheaval, displacement and economic deprivation for the majority. Those who had managed to succeed financially were increasingly viewed to be enlarging the gulf between the affluent and impoverished. The ethnic groups marginal-ised by social division began to mobilise via resistance movements. At the same time the financial gap between rich and poor began to alienate the intelligentsia, professionals

(Continued)

(Continued)

and urban student groups to whom the denial of civil liberties became increasingly intolerable (Mahmud, 1997).

It is worth noting that the label of Mohajir was initially construed in derogatory terms, for it connotes refugee rather than the status of nation builder. The initial reaction by Karachi's Urdu-speaking political representatives was to deny the currency of the term Mohajir for it undermined the permanence and ability of this population to claim legitimate Pakistani citizenship. With the overriding of civilian governments and successive military dictatorships the once elite Mohajir population has experienced marginalisation, particularly with regard to government policies deemed discriminatory (Shaheed, 1996). The frustrations of the Mohajirs were politicised via the formation of the Mohajir Qaumi Mahaz (MQM, Migrant National Front) in 1984. The party subsequently splintered into two factions culminating in the formation of the Haqiqi (real or true) MQM and the renaming of the original MQM to Muttahida (people's) National Front in the 1990s.

The political dynamics of groups in Karachi frame a turbulent recent history of ethnic and politically motivated violence (Hussain, 1996; Shaheed, 1996). The conflicts can be viewed within three categories: first, the annual clashes between two major sects of Islam, Sunnis and Shi'ites; second, the periodic clashes against Ahmadi[18] groups; and third, the more frequent clashes between different ethnic and rival political groups (Shaheed, 1996).

Some of the most destructive riots and disturbances took place in December 1986 between Mohajirs and Pathans[19] (Hussain, 1996). The catalyst for the riots was the government's Sohrab Goth Operation on 12 December 1986. Sohrab Goth was an area on the outskirts of Karachi known as being the location for the storage, distribution and sale of heroin. The community serving this area comprised mainly Pathans and some Afghan refugees; both groups occupied squats which provided tunnels for the illegal storage of drugs and weapons. The drugs mafia instigated propaganda to mobilise the Pathan community alleging that Mohajirs were to blame for the forced evictions at Sohrab Goth as part of a wider plot to evict Pathans from Karachi (Hussain, 1996). On 13 December, several hundred armed Pathan men commenced acts of murder, assault, arson and riot against Mohajir homes. This initial act claimed over 40 lives; the days following witnessed retaliation from the Mohajirs and unchecked rioting spread to many parts of Karachi for four days (Hussain, 1996; Shaheed, 1996).

The urban conflicts in Karachi are reflective of an ingrained crisis between the state and civil society. There is little public trust, dependence or respect for governmental institutions due to significant evidence of corruption, poor civic amenities and economic inequity. Furthermore, as Akmal Hussain highlights, the availability of firearms following the end of the Afghan war and the collapse of state authority in large parts of Sind has prompted civilians to seek community support mechanisms to redress injustice and provide protection from physical assaults (Hussain, 1996: 193).

'No-Go' Zones in Karachi

Given the political and urban history outlined above, the articulations of Mohajir residents of Karachi provide evidence of how certain areas become labelled as 'no-go' zones fuelled by ethnic sectarianism and politically motivated violence. The following extracts are from interviews with Mohajir residents of an area proximate to well-reported sites of sectarian violence.

Respondents in Karachi expressed that there existed certain 'no-go' zones in their neighbourhood and city as a whole. Such areas were to be avoided due to risks of becoming a victim of crime (Sibley, 1995).

Abdul[20] expressed that for him there did exist certain 'no-go' zones, namely Al-Akram Square (near Sharifabad) and Gharibabad, a *kaatchi abaadi* neighbouring Sharifabad. The principal reason for avoiding these areas was the belief that he might get caught and falsely arrested during a police raid on political activists who reside in these locations. Abdul also expressed an overwhelming perception of such locations as 'dangerous' even though he had not actually visited these locations:

There's a kaatchi abaadi and it's a very dangerous place because you are not sure of your security so if you just go there you don't know where you might get caught. Majority there are persons who are doing car lifting, especially in this area, they are the prime suspects of all that, people from Gharibabad ... it's because they are really involved in such activities. Because you must have heard or noticed or read in the newspapers, that some raids have been going on there by the police ... well they call themselves Mohajirs, but I really don't know whether they are purely Mohajir or Afghani and all.

Babu and Ali held similar views about frequenting such localities. Ali spoke of certain places 'never being safe' whilst Babu's fears were perpetuated by the reality of violent exchanges in these localities between law-enforcers and others.

Danyaal explained that, for him, vast warrens of narrow congested alleys and routes characterised the *kaatchi abaadis*. In his opinion, people could easily get lost in them and they enabled criminals to execute their activities within a hidden environment. Most respondents, when speaking about *kaatchi abaadis*, spoke with reference to feelings of perceived 'threat', 'danger', 'strangeness' and of 'safety' within these settlements. A common theme was how *kaatchi abaadis* impacted upon physical resources for 'legitimate' residents, for example:

I: *Are you happy with the kaatchi abaadis?*

R: *No. Kaatchi abaadis or unauthorised shops shouldn't be there. I'm not happy with them because the whole system goes bad, we lose track of the population,*

(Continued)

(Continued)

> *the planning fails. Water, transport and electricity and sanitation problems are exaggerated.*

Importantly, the few respondents who physically frequented areas commonly cited as 'no-go' zones spoke of no feelings of animosity or fear when visiting such locations. For example, Daanish spoke of his perceptions of localities others considered unsafe, which he has had to frequent:

> *There aren't such places for me because I reside in such neighbourhoods, where I have observed so much that the fear has been ground out of me. I go wherever now, and now there's nothing going on anyhow.*

Similarly, Hassan spoke of frequenting such localities in order to visit relatives:

> *No, not really, I go everywhere, no problem, I mean I have relatives there so I frequent these places, I don't fear them.*

Extensive fieldwork conducted in Karachi has facilitated the gathering of a detailed understanding of the complex meanings of 'no-go' areas for the residents. There was a general consensus about which areas clearly constituted a 'no-go' zone. These were most often characterised in terms of geographical identity, for example Liaqatabad or Gharibabad. It must be noted that the majority of the respondents were Mohajir and many of the 'no-go' zones, such as Landhi, were considered 'ethnically different' zones. Therefore, to a large extent, the zones demarked ethnically defined residence patterns. Risks to Mohajirs were considered higher in non-Mohajir dominated areas. The source of such perceptions often stemmed from first-hand experience of racially motivated violence against the Mohajirs in these areas. However, the majority of the respondents indicated little direct experience of frequenting the perceived 'no-go' zone.

A general perception of such 'no-go' zones centred upon the belief and observation that these were the sites of ongoing conflicts between groups such as rival political parties, police and activists, landowners and squatters and that simply being in these locations would automatically place the individual within the line of crossfire. This is a practical philosophy of simply avoiding areas reputed to have regular civil unrest. For example:

> I: *Are there any no go zones for you?*
>
> R: *Yes, Landhi, Korangi. Orangi Town, Lines Area Liaqatabad although it's not as bad there now.*
>
> I: *Why don't you go there?*
>
> R: *There's a lot of fighting going on, anything could happen, anytime, fighting, bullet flying anytime.*

Following the military coup of October 1999, the civil unrest in Karachi lessened considerably whilst rival political parties entered a 'honeymoon' phase with the incoming dictatorship. The police were also understood to be 'under military control' and hence corrupt practices, raids and illegal stop and searches were considered by the residents to be less frequent than in previous months.

The fact that certain 'no-go' zones had now become more accessible to the respondents is reflective of the reduction in the civil unrest and conflict in the city as a whole. However, many respondents still perceived these locations as problematic even in the absence of genuine unrest, and hence their status as 'no-go' zones has remained psychologically engrained (Sibley, 1995). For example, Esaah described the long-lasting nature of labelling a certain geographical area as criminogenic:

> Yes, Lines Area [Jacobline], but even though it's not a big threat now, it's remained in our heads that we should avoid that area.

The fact that certain areas can shift in and out of the 'no-go' classification illustrates the transitory and temporary nature of such perceptions for some areas. The *kaatchi abaadis*, however, rarely seemed to be considered areas where Mohajirs felt they could visit without serious risk of becoming victims of crime.

The British Context

Regarding 'no-go' zones in British research, Colin Webster (1994, 1997a), for example, has demonstrated the importance of deconstructing the urban environment in terms of racially defined zones. There are a number of British studies which have explored the experiences of black and Asian residents of urban areas as pertaining to 'no-go' areas. Claire Alexander's study of an Asian gang details the experience of prejudice and exclusion as experienced by Asian youth in London from youth facilities (Alexander, 2000). Webster's (1994) study provides a detailed exploration of inter-racial and intra-racial harassment and victimisation between and amongst Asian and white youth in Keighley, West Yorkshire. Webster asserts that Asian young people construct perceptions of 'dangerous places' which actually contribute to 'lower levels of racial harassment and attacks than would otherwise be the case as young people apply risk avoidance strategies in deciding where they can or cannot go' (Webster, 1994: 45). According to Webster, the 'local knowledge' in smaller towns informs a resident of 'the geography of danger' which is perhaps less applicable or predictable in larger metropolitan cities. The Karachi example illustrates that in the absence of 'local knowledge', the media play the role of informer. Hence, perceptions of certain areas are informed by politicised agents and those who control the media.

Working-class youths are viewed as defending a threatened identity whilst Asian youths react via resistance and retaliation. Certain urban spaces become associated with each ethnic group, whilst others remain contested (Webster, 1994).

(Continued)

(Continued)

The primary research mentioned in this case study was undertaken in the east Lancashire former mill town of Haslingden approximately 20 miles north of Manchester. There has been a South Asian Muslim population in Haslingden since the 1950s comprising mainly Pakistanis originating from northern Pakistan and Bangladeshis from Sylhet. When the research was undertaken Haslingden had a population of 14,443 of which 371 (2.57%) were Pakistani, 200 (1.38%) were Bangladeshi and 20 (0.14%) were Indian (Home Office, 1991). Haslingden is proximate to the larger northern mill towns of Rochdale, Burnley, Blackburn and Oldham which all have sizeable South Asian Muslim populations.

As in Karachi, British Muslim youth in Haslingden spoke of areas they considered 'no-go' zones. The prime reason for avoiding such areas was to reduce the risk of racially motivated conflict. In Haslingden the extra dimension of time was considered to be important in assessing risk. Night time was associated with drinking and respondents mainly classified locations near to public houses in the town centre as areas to avoid. For example:

I: *Are there any areas you wouldn't go in Haslingden?*

R: *Not really, probably Lower Deardengate at night near pubs, when all the white guys are outside the pubs.*

In Haslingden, some respondents expressed concerns about the likelihood of becoming the victim of racial abuse whilst walking to one of the local mosques. The following respondent explains a violent episode:

Do you see these teeth? Why are they missing? Because four men beat me up whilst I was on my way to prayers in 1991. I left my house … they beat me up, I fought to the best of my village fighting ability, I am neither a Karachiite nor a boxer but you have to defend yourself. I was going along when one of these guys said 'Muslim bastard!', he repeated this three times, on the fourth time I couldn't stand it any longer and said 'why are you swearing like that?' When they spoke like this I retaliated the same, one of them was a boxer, the police later told me he was a semi-professional boxer... I got £700 in compensation, an apology in court but where shall I get my teeth back from? I was only going for prayers.

Similarly another respondent described racial abuse he experienced whilst attending evening prayers at the local mosque:

Actually they trouble the elders more than the youth, they don't approach the younger people as much, but it did happen once to me. I was walking past the Commercial Inn one evening and I had traditional shalwar kameez[21] on, I don't usually wear them. There were many people stood outside the pub, as I passed by one guy spat his beer over me. I hadn't done or said anything to aggravate them.

I crossed the road and saw a bottle on the ground. I was thinking about picking it up but there were six or seven of them or probably more. I suppressed my anger but I was thinking of taking that bottle and smashing it on his head and then run, he spat on me for no reason. I stood opposite the pub thinking about this but I thought someone might recognize me so I didn't do it. But if we meet them in the back street and there are four or five of them they tend not to do anything. They pick on the vulnerable ones.

The above comments illustrate a contested area around the town centre and specifically proximate to public houses. The pubs demark clearly 'white space' not frequented by Muslim elders but an area which must be traversed in order to get to the local mosques. If we consider that congregations meet for five daily prayers, the potential for abusive exchanges is considerable.

This issues introduced here contribute to the broader experiences of exclusion and discrimination as perceived by British Muslims. Academic enquiry of British Muslims has produced an overwhelming discourse of victimisation and social exclusion (IHRC, 2001; Modood and Berthoud, 1997; Quraishi, 2005; Runnymede, 1997; Spalek, 2004; Wardak, 2000). The articulations of British Muslims illustrate how certain urban spaces may be subject to ethnically constructed territorial claims where there is often a genuine apprehension of the fear of racist abuse or violence (Alexander, 2000; Keith, 2004; Webster, 1994).

Summary

Perhaps the first point of reflection in this case study is the importance of the researcher's own biography in choosing, accessing and understanding the experiences of the informants. More generally, here we see a clear correlation between an emphasis upon lived experiences in the research questions and aims linked to a method (qualitative one-to-one interviews) which can satisfactorily produce appropriate data and answers.

In terms of the substantive findings, the chosen methods yielded important findings about the incidents and nature of 'no-go' zones in two differing cultural contexts.

Whereas in Karachi the areas avoided were also considered areas of the destitute and poor, in Haslingden the 'no-go' areas were considered mainly to be near public houses. The main perceived threat to Muslim youth was from white males drinking at such locations. Indeed, many of the respondents cited having to walk past the pubs during the evening as a significant point of anxiety. These findings are mirrored by research in West Yorkshire by Webster who asserts '*Young people's imagined fears and their actual victim experiences were found to have coalesced in a strikingly racialised geography of fear*' (Webster, 2007: 38).

Broad institutional practices within social policy and media construction have an influential part to play in the formation and perpetuation of urban localities personified as criminal and deviant. Whether the initial perception is sparked

(Continued)

(Continued)

by genuine criminal activity is therefore less relevant than the projection and 'holding-out' of a particular locality as a 'no-go' zone.

In Karachi, where ethnic and class segregation is particularly marked, it is easy to see how the perception of a 'no-go' zone is conceived and perpetuated as an integral aspect of power relations between the 'haves' and 'have nots'; for the latter the construction of their social and physical environment is largely out of their hands. There are locations in Karachi, such as *kaatchi abaadis*, which are essentially residential in nature, impoverished and poorly resourced. Nearly 2 million people reside in such localities in the city (Human Rights Commission of Pakistan, 1997). It can be understood that the need to frequent them by non-residents is indeed minimal. That is to say, for most residents of Sharifabad there is no need or reason to travel into a *kaatchi abaadi*. Not only do these locations represent a class barrier but also an ethnic barrier, as often these places are home to the newest migrants seeking refuge in Pakistan's largest conurbation.

Therefore, although the origin of a particular locality's reputation as a 'dangerous' place may well be founded on a 'once-in-the-past' reality of urban conflict and victimisation within it, there is a further process of perpetuation of this image by agencies such as the media. This is capable of determining whether a particular urban location becomes a 'no-go' zone for non-residents or outsiders.

The establishment of a 'no-go' zone is one way in which individuals navigate their social space as part of avoiding harm whilst simultaneously '*sorting people into groups which can get along with one another*' (Webster, 2007: 40). The creation of such ethnic boundaries in urban locations is reflective of a general agreement about the terms on which associations are considered safe or dangerous (Suttles, 1968).

Whilst the individual may be strongly influenced by institutional projections of a locality's reputation, he or she is still free to make a subjective assessment of the 'risk factor' of becoming a victim whilst frequenting a zone thus labelled. Such an assessment is weighed against a *need to frequent* as opposed to a desire or wish to frequent a particular locality. The 'no-go' zone for one person, therefore, is wholly capable of being the refuge of another and what determines this pertains to the complex connections between ethnicity, power and class.

One central idea to emerge from this research – the notion of 'identity' – arose in the second of the two case studies we outline here.

Reflection on the Case Studies as a Whole

What all of these case studies demonstrate is the complex nature and interplay of cultural and social constructions of racial and ethnic identities against formal or state categorisations of ethnic minority populations. With regard to the social construction of 'no-go' zones, here we learnt that social spaces are the subject of politicisation, criminalisation and racialisation. The physical urban space becomes personified with the ethnic and racial attributes of the dominant population residing within a particular locale. In a developing and uncertain political environment facing a collapse of civic trust, such as in Pakistan, the fragmentation along sectarian, class and politicised lines is reinforced by agents such as the media.

The case study on transnational contexts begins to explore how some ethnic minority populations may occupy competing social positions, both deprived in the UK, but empowered in their countries of ethnic origin. The case study highlights the flaws in social policies which view ethnic minority populations in homogenised terms arguing for more complex and deeper evaluations of the ways in which transnational contexts begin to explain the lived social reality for many migrant and displaced populations around the world.

Summary

In this chapter we have focused on three case studies to illustrate the practice of researching race and racism discussed in previous chapters. The discussion here to a large extent reflects, consolidates and illustrates many of the key issues developed over preceding chapters: the historical roots and legacy of race and racialisation; the legislative context; conceptual debates; the legacy in contemporary society; issues surrounding identity and belonging; and the qualitative approach to research practice.

Each of the studies presented outlines particular substantive issues pertaining to notions of race.

The first case study demonstrates how a project can be intellectually conceived, planned and developed into an empirical project. The research is clearly prompted by official engagement with racially motivated crime and its classification but more importantly with the way in which individuals 'experience' and make sense or rationalise racial victimisation.

The second case study represents a pilot study, which can be very useful when little is known about a particular research field. Such studies are important for enabling a researcher to plan for a more substantial project and address and overcome some of the methodological and practical problems encountered during the pilot. Indeed, sometimes the pilot brings into question the very viability of pushing further into the field and it is just as useful for the refinement, suspension or discontinuance of a research avenue as it is for justifying further enquiry.

In our third case study, our focus was on the social construction of public urban places and spaces, with an emphasis on how places and spaces can come to be defined and experienced along racial lines; in the second we looked at a quite different context – that of the 'total institution' of the prison and formal supervision via the Probation Service – and examined more closely the notions of how race – along with other variables such as faith, class, age and gender – inform identities.

Although the case studies represent three quite different institutional – and institutionalised – contexts, each study reflects the focus in the preceding chapters by being historically and culturally grounded. All three examples combine an historical background with a contemporary research focus, in turn highlighting the cultural and social contexts and prevailing political and popular discourses in which each study was carried out.

In addition, each study illustrates how a range of different methods, outlined in Chapter 5, have been applied; how a conceptual and theoretical understanding has been pointed to; and how some of the issues we discussed in the previous chapters (access, sampling, biography, ethical issues) have been managed by the researcher.

The nature of the data presented in this chapter has reflected the focus on accessing meaning and experience from a first-person perspective, and to that end, has been quite personal and candid in nature. However, what we have also demonstrated in this chapter is the uses to which quantitative data are put by various institutions and agencies, as well as the uses to which they may be put by you as a researcher of race and racism. As we noted in the previous chapter, while our focus here has been on qualitative methodology, we recognise the usefulness of quantitative data, particularly for providing contextualisation, as illustrated in this chapter.

Although the focus is partly on the experience of British Asians, again, in using case studies taken from a particular social, cultural, political and historical context, we have also tried to expand our discussion to more global issues pertinent to race and racism, and the practice of research into these phenomena.

Finally, we have pointed to particular theoretical and empirical debates around critical race theory and the notion of intersectionality. While our focus in this text is on race, these comments have nevertheless pointed out the relevance of the intersection of this central concept to additional ones such as class, age, gender and faith.

Notes

1 The authors would like to express their gratitude to Dr Tina G. Patel, University of Salford, co-applicant with Dr M. Quraishi on the 'Rationalising Racist Attacks' project, for consenting to allow the use of this project as one of the case studies for this text.

2 Reproduced with the permission of the University of Salford, College of Health and Social Care Ethics Committee.

3 Black and minority ethnic (BME) is used as a preferential term of reference, sometimes alongside more detailed terms of reference. This highlights labels that have been renegotiated and moved away from an essentialised notion of a singular or universal black identity.

4 Drawing on the work of Patel and Tyrer (2011), we consider the term 'white' as having been presented in race talk as neutral, and thus enjoying a position of power and privilege. It is also recognised that the term is bound up with the similar implications that are associated with essentialised notions of the term 'black' (see below) and therefore use the term reluctantly to refer to all those who are of non-black minority and ethnic status.

5 McVeigh (2006: 11) points out that to use 'racist' when talking about such crimes more accurately allows the incident to be contextualised in terms of its root cause, that of the existence of racism in society, a preferred use which they highlight was also supported by Macpherson (1999) in his recommendation for a universal racist incident definition. McVeigh (2006) highlighted the Macpherson Report's recommended use of 'racist incident', and how this is preferable over say 'racial' as the latter implies *'that racial violence happens because there are different racial groups in that society'*, whereas the first refers to the occurrence of racial violence due to actual racism in society (McVeigh, 2006: 11).

6 Use of this term does not indicate our support for it. Rather it is used to indicate populist lay thought. In addition, we use it here with inverted commas to highlight its sociological problematic and contested status.

7 For example, figures presented by Rogers from the Office for National Statistics show that in 2008 immigration was at 590,000 – a record figure. Significantly though, there were in the same year also a record number of people leaving the country – 427,200 in total (Rogers, 2010).

8 An 'economic migrant' is a person who voluntarily leaves his or her country of origin for economic reasons. This voluntary movement may be a temporary one, or a more long-term movement. 'Economic migrants' are often referred to as 'migrant workers', which suggests a movement that is more short-term in nature. It is argued that we have much to economically gain from the readily available cheap labour supply offered by migrant workers; for example, a Home Office study found that in 1999–2000, migrant workers in Britain made a net contribution of approximately £2.5 billion to income tax (Gott and Johnston, 2002).

9 Under the United Nations and international law, a 'refugee' *is a person who is outside his/her country of nationality or habitual residence; has a well-founded fear of persecution because of his/her race, religion, nationality, membership in a particular social group or political opinion; and is unable or unwilling to avail himself/herself of the protection of that country, or to return there, for fear of persecution'* (United Nations, 1951). If a person is found to be a refugee, the UK (one of the signatories of the Convention) is obliged under international law to offer support and to ensure that the person is not sent back unwillingly to the country of origin. Those who seek 'refugee' status are sometimes known as 'asylum seekers'. However, there is a slight difference. In a legal context in the UK, a person is a refugee only when the Home Office has accepted their asylum claim. While a person is waiting for a decision on their claim, she/he is called an 'asylum seeker'.

10 See Resource 7 of the Appendix for examples of these documents.

11 Adapted from Quraishi (2010a, 2010b).

12 See for example Mawby and Batta (1980), Wardak (2000) and Webster (1994).

13 Adapted from Quraishi (2008a). Springer and *The Asian Journal of Criminology*, 3, no 2, Dec: 159-71. With kind permission from Springer Science and Business Media.

14 The primary sources for this case study originate from research undertaken in Lancashire and Karachi between 1997 and 2000; see Quraishi (2005).

15 See Sztompka (1990) and Nelken (1997).

16 Mohajir – Arabic, literally meaning migrant or refugee, originating from the Flight of the Prophet Mohammed (p.b.u.h.), from Makkah to Medina in 622 AD; subsequently asserted as a distinct racial group by the Mohajir Quomi Mahaz (Migrant National Front) in 1984.

17 *Kaatchi abaadi* – Urdu, literally meaning raw population(s), shanty town(s), squatter settlement(s) acquired through adverse possession.

18 Ahmadi – adherents to a sect founded by Mirza Gulam Ahmad (1835–1908) of Qadian, Punjab. Orthodox Muslims have claimed them to be a 'heretic' group due to its founder's claim to be a prophet (Nigosian, 1987).

19 Pathans – Pushto-speaking ethnic group from Khyber Pakhtunkhwa (formerly known as the North West Frontier province of Pakistan).

20 Pseudonyms have been used throughout this study.

21 Traditional Pakistani attire.

CONCLUSION:
RACISM AND FUTURE DIRECTIONS

Keywords: *intersectionality, critical race theory, brokerage*

To conclude this text we would like to draw together some of the key issues covered in previous chapters and consolidate some of its main messages. We would also like to suggest some ways in which your own research can engage with the future directions racism research may take. We do not have any special researcher's crystal ball to peer into the future but we can make some educated forecasts here about the topics and issues which scholars of race could be engaging with over the next decade.

Researching Race and Racism: Key Themes and Messages

We began our discussion by introducing you to the *history and legacy of race* as a concept, the discredited science of race and the ways in which the *process of racialisation* perpetuates racial discrimination. We have emphasised throughout this text that the origins and vocabulary of racism are firmly rooted in *historical practices*, which have over-reached into contemporary society.

We then outlined the *complexity of race* as a concept, in terms of definitions and attributes. One key message we sought to convey was that race was best not perceived of as a monolithic notion, but rather as an *intersectional phenomenon*.

Despite such complexity, policy makers and legislators routinely seek to distil such conceptual divergence into *practical working definitions*, demonstrating both a widespread acknowledgement and recognition of the phenomenon of racism and *legal prohibition* of it.

We then moved on to demonstrate how notions of race and practices of racism can be seen to operate as *part and parcel of everyday life* in contemporary society. We drew attention to the notion of race and racism as *experienced, meaningful and practically accomplished* phenomena, and pointed to race *institutionally, interactionally and individually relevant.* We also pointed to the ontological and epistemological standpoints required for research.

Before examining our case studies, we provide a *methodological primer* for qualitative research into race and racism. We paid particular emphasis to *exposure to and immersion in* the lifeworlds of those who variously experience race and racism and the importance of obtaining a *plurality of perspectives* in your research.

At the heart of our discussion was the close examination of the themes and issues presented in the earlier part of the text via *three case studies of research* we have conducted into race and racism. These case studies allowed us to illustrate the *planning and piloting* of research, through *execution and output.*

Race is not only a complex, but also a malleable and evolving notion. The pervasiveness of racism is evident in contemporary media. Presently the US army is engaged in controversy over alleged racist regulations about the hairstyles of serving personnel (Cooper, 2014). The recent European elections have demonstrated a shift to the centre right of politics. In Britain, the ascendency of the UK Independence Party highlights a political rhetoric which conflates issues of migration with xeno-racism (O'Callaghan, 2014). With regard to criminal justice, the London Metropolitan Police are facing an enquiry following allegations of improper surveillance of the family of murdered teenager Stephen Lawrence.

Intersectionality

We would like to return now to the concept of intersectionality as briefly introduced in Chapter 2. You will recall, intersectionality directs scholars to acknowledge that race does not operate in a vacuum but interacts with other aspects of a person's identity such as with gender, class, age or faith. All persons are intersectional, whether or not they recognise themselves as such (Puar, 2011). Therefore, the challenge for researching racism is to engage with the ways in which these complex interactions arise, are maintained and change as well as to deconstruct the ways in which race is presented in homogeneous terms. The concept was created within Black feminist literature and some argue it has remained largely contained to the intersection of gender and race (Crenshaw, 1991; Harris, 1990; Nash, 2008).

We can identify three ways in which researchers may approach the study of intersectionality: anti-categorical complexity, inter-categorical complexity and intra-categorical complexity (McHall, 2005). Here we will examine each of the approaches in turn.

Anti-categorical Complexity

This approach asserts that social categories are simply arbitrary constructions of history and language. The discussions we have been outlining, particularly in Chapter 1, add significant weight to this view. The labels or categories defining one group as belonging to a particular race or ethnic group play little part in how individuals actually experience living in society. However, inequalities and oppression are connected to relationships which are defined by race, class, sexuality and gender. Therefore, the only way to truly remove oppression is to get rid of these categories which are currently being used to process, define and exclude complex populations. The categorisation leads to demarcation which in turn leads to exclusion and then inequality. Since society is in essence comprised of individuals with complex and varied identities, any attempt to boil down such complexity into limited categories leads ultimately to oppression. The emphasis in this approach is to analyse power and knowledge against mechanisms of exclusion and inclusion operating under several genders, sexes, sexualities and multi-racialisms (Knusden, 2006).

Inter-categorical Complexity

This approach acknowledges that inequality exists in society but the focus for researchers should be the relationships among the social groups and how these are changing over time. Here the existing categories for classifying populations are retained. The emphasis is upon studying structural relationships in many social groups and not within single groups or single categories. This approach builds upon quantitative rather than the qualitative methodologies favoured by anti-categorical complexity and intra-categorical complexity.

Intra-categorical Complexity

This approach represents a half-way between the previous two approaches. The shortcomings of existing categories of defining populations are acknowledged whilst questioning how boundaries are drawn. The importance of categories is not completely rejected, however, and instead the focus in this approach is upon people who cross the boundaries of constructed categories. There is an acknowledgement that some social categories represent robust relationships whilst others do not.

The first approach (anti-categorical complexity), which advocates a total abandonment of the categories presently deployed to classify populations, whilst projecting a noble if not idealised aim, is perhaps the least helpful in terms of practical advice when embarking upon a research project. The reality is that categories do exist and are deployed in the delivery of services, monitoring of performance and adherence to equal rights policies and legislation.

The second approach (inter-categorical complexity) reflects a good proportion of research about racism which is often prompted by an inequality often identified following statistical disproportionality based on categories of race or ethnicity. The focus on how relations are changing between social groups provides for a degree of flexibility, although the very definition of those social groups is an issue for some commentators.

Adopting the third approach (intra-categorical complexity) is also not without some methodological challenges. Whilst the focus on how individuals straddle and cross boundaries of group identities may provide excluded groups a voice, at which point do subcategories provide a useful analytical function? Indeed, what is to prevent the infinite creation and subdivision of intersecting subcategories of interests?

These criticisms and many more of the concept and usefulness of intersectionality to race research have been addressed by Richard Delgado in his insightful and percep-tive article 'Rodrigo's reconsideration: Intersectionality and the future of critical race theory' (Delgado, 2011). We shall now outline the main challenges to intersectionality as a workable research concept as articulated by Delgado.

First, returning to the issue of subcategories, once it is acknowledged that a cate-gory, for example 'Asian', contains subcategories (e.g. Indian, or Pakistani or Bangladeshi) it begs the question, what follows? In other words there are potentially infinitely divisible subcategories with no logical end point (Yuval-Davis, 2006). The problem is particularly acute for political and legal systems which necessarily advance upon the presupposition of groups with interests to protect and articulate. According to Delgado, there is in fact a danger that reliance upon smaller and smaller units of analysis can overlook larger scale processes that are working to the disadvantage of large classes. Furthermore, identifying new subcategories of groups may in fact work to undermine the interests of people you may wish to champion. In this regard, Delgado cites the practices of Canadian judges who sought to sentence Native American Indian women in a more punitive manner when committing certain crimes since they were setting examples for the broader indigenous community.

Next, there is the challenge presented to researchers about the way in which indi-viduals view their intersectionality; in other words, people do not tend to identify themselves within intersectional categories in the same way they do not claim they simply belong to one category.

Given categories of race are socially constructed, so are subcategories or intersec-tions of groups in everyday life. However, the subject position of any individual may blind them to the intersection of a group. Where one member of an ethnic group sees homogeneity, another may see diversity, so this prompts the question, how can the researcher address all subject positions satisfactorily? In other words, how can we know which groups are being left out of the research equation?

Other challenges facing intersectionality rest upon its ability to engage with a sig-nificant audience. That is to say, the remoteness and esoteric nature of the categories or identities create a distance between the speaker and the audience. When analysing legal cases of discrimination, Delgado highlights that they are more likely to succeed when resting upon single issue discrimination (e.g. racism) than upon multiple issues (sexism and racism). Delgado goes further by claiming that in some instances a reliance upon intersecting identities of discrimination may cause people to feel the claimant is 'milking them for sympathy', investing in 'powerlessness' within a sort of 'victim complex' (Delgado, 2011: 1273).

Another important challenge is the appropriateness of a focus upon endlessly refining smaller and smaller units of voice, given changing urban demographics. In some parts of North America and the UK, traditional ethnic minorities are no longer physically in the minority. The changes in population present a neo-colonial evaluation of contemporary society whilst acknowledging white privilege. There is an argument that researchers should concentrate less upon the endless division and subdivision of categories of identity and more upon the macro processes which are blocking the upward mobility of minorities whilst deploying token role models to perpetuate a myth of meritocracy. The latter concern is often termed 'brokerage' and mimics strategies deployed by colonial powers across the globe to govern the colonised.

Given the above, is there much to recommend research which seeks to explore intersectionality today and in the future? In its defence, whilst acknowledging the above caveats, there remains a need to provide a voice for the marginalised. According to Delgado it also *'reminds you to check from time to time, to see if your tools and concepts are leaving somebody out'* (Delgado, 2011: 1282). Furthermore, the concept has enabled some scholars to examine the social reality of *'identity demands'* upon *'intersectionals'* (Ramachandran, 2006: 300). What is meant by 'intersectionals' here are people who belong to more than one 'low status category' and are thereby subject to multiple identity performance demands which places them in a restrictive double bind or 'catch 22' (Ramachandran, 2006: 300, 303). Furthermore, it is clear that some intersections, arguably those which utilise the confluence between well-established or politicised identity categories (faith and ethnicity, gender and nationality or statelessness) have yielded fruitful scholarship (see Burman, 2012; Quraishi, 2013). It would be an injustice to be too dismissive of the merits of the original conception of intersectionality, as evidenced by meaningful contributions from some feminist scholars examining gender, race, class and postmodern imperialism. The questions asked are how different modes of governmentality and particularly increased militarisation are giving rise to differentially *'exploited, racialised, ethnicised, sexualised and religionised humans living in different parts of the world'* and what the ethical and political response should entail (Brah and Phoenix, 2004: 84).

The discussion above illustrates the complexity of advising research directions for the future.

It is clear that the concept of intersectionality has travelled much further than its original home in Black feminist scholarship and scholars from a wide range of disciplines have attempted to apply it to their respective academies. For example, the usefulness of an intersectional approach to studying race, gender, class and other categories of difference in political science is succinctly summarised by Ange-Marie Hancock in Table 7.1 below.

Nevertheless, the concept of intersectionality has many conceptual restrictions, as highlighted above, which make it particularly challenging to champion without reservation or caveats.

Table 7.1   Conceptual differences among approaches to the study of race, gender, class and other categories of differences in political science. *Source:* Hancock (2007: 64).[1]

	Unitary Approach	Multiple Approach	Intersectional Approach
Q1. How many categories are addressed?	One	More than one	More than one
Q2. What is the relationship posited between categories?	Category examined is primary	Categories matter equally in a predetermined relationship to each another	Categories matter equally; the relationship between categories is an open empirical question
Q3. How are categories conceptualised?	Static at the individual or institutional level	Static at the individual or institutional level	Dynamic interaction between individuals and institutional factors
Q4. What is the presumed make-up of each category?	Uniform	Uniform	Diverse; members often differ in politically significant ways
Q5. What levels of analysis are considered feasible in a single analysis?	Individual or institutional	Individual and institutional	Individual integrated with institutional
Q6. What is the methodological conventional wisdom?	Empirical or theoretical; single method preferred; multiple method is possible	Empirical or theoretical ; single method sufficient; multiple method desirable	Empirical and theoretical; multiple method necessary and sufficient.

Summary

Following our focus on the results of three empirical studies, this chapter presents a discussion of the arguments around critical race theory and the notion of intersectionality. After discussing the merits and limitation of approaching racial categories at both a conceptual level, and in terms of mobilisation and application in actual research, we conclude the main body of the text by reminding the reader of the rationale for conceptualising a study on racism via the lens we have adopted and indicated throughout this text.

First, we emphasise that race began in the period of the European Enlightenment as a pseudo-scientific concept, utilised to dehumanise and manipulate colonised populations and shifting into a socially constructed phenomenon in the nineteenth and twentieth centuries. We argue, whilst explicit racial determinism is now not widely believed nor sustainable, the legacy of the classification and taxonomies of a discredited

---

[1]Reprinted with kind permission of Cambridge University Press.

science of race nevertheless finds vent in a wide range of contemporary views, attitudes and opinions about ethnic minority populations.

Second, racism is dependent upon the process of racialisation; namely, the formal and informal social mechanisms through which people become defined as a group with reference to their biological and/or cultural characteristics. We concur with other researchers in this field, that racism therefore depends upon an historical power relationship (racialisation), a set of ideas about the distinctiveness of particular 'races' (ideology) and the corresponding forms of discrimination (practices) which emanate from racialisation and ideology (Garner, 2010). Hence the challenge for any research in this field is to decide upon which aspects, if not all three, of the above they wish to concentrate upon.

Third, the latest methodological development related to the study of racism is the articulation of the intersectional identity as outlined above. Within an intersectional perspective, the intertwined and complex relationships between different aspects of a person's social identity (class, gender, sexuality, age and faith) become vital dimensions to more fully comprehending the lived experiences of racial discrimination.

Finally, much has been written on the structural and macro forces which operate to classify and determine the status and racialised oppression of certain populations over others. In writing this text, we do not wholly contest the prudent arguments and scholarship which examines these macro dimensions and causes of systemic racism in contemporary society. However, we have advocated a micro approach for a number of reasons which we hope have been made explicitly clear throughout the text. Perhaps one of the main reasons for suggesting the pathways we have recommended is related to the issue of identifying viable everyday social contexts and settings routinely accessible to most individuals (the workplace, the neighbourhood, the class room) or more formal institutions which could potentially be reached (the police station, prison or hospital).

We conclude by reiterating our pledge and advice imparted to you in the introduction. We hope the text has provided you with knowledge and conceptualisation about the phenomenon of racism as well as a clearer understanding of how to devise a viable qualitative project to investigate it. May your endeavours be productive and illuminating!

APPENDIX
A RACISM RESEARCHER'S TOOLBOX

Resource 1: Ethnic Group Categories 1991–2001

Compatible Category	1991 Categories	2001 Categories
White	White	White – all three subcategories (four in Scotland)
Black Caribbean	Black – Caribbean	Black or Black British – Black Caribbean
Black African	Black – African	Black or Black British – Black African
Indian	Indian	Asian or Asian British – Indian
Pakistani	Pakistani	Asian or Asian British – Pakistani
Bangladeshi	Bangladeshi	Asian or Asian British – Bangladeshi
Chinese	Chinese	Chinese or Other Ethnic Group – Chinese
Other (not comparable over time)	Black – Other Other – Asian Other – Other	Mixed – all four subcategories (one in Scotland) Black or Black British – Other Black Asian or Asian British – Other Asian Chinese or Other Ethnic Group – Other Ethnic Group

Resource 2: Ethnic Categories Used in the UK 2011 Census

What is your ethnic group?

16 ⇨ Choose one section from A to E, then tick one box to best describe your ethnic group or background

A White
- ☐ English / Welsh / Scottish / Northern Irish / British
- ☐ Irish
- ☐ Gypsy or Irish Traveller
- ☐ Any other white background, write in

[write-in boxes]

B Mixed / multiple ethnic group
- ☐ White and Black Caribbean
- ☐ White and Black African
- ☐ White and Asian
- ☐ Any other Mixed/multiple ethnic background, write in

[write-in boxes]

C Asian / Asian British
- ☐ Indian
- ☐ Pakistani
- ☐ Bangladeshi
- ☐ Chinese
- ☐ Any other Asian background, write in

[write-in boxes]

D Black /African / Caribbean / Black British
- ☐ African
- ☐ Caribbean
- ☐ Any other Black /African / Caribbean background, write in

[write-in boxes]

E Other ethnic group
- ☐ Arab
- ☐ Any other ethnic group, write in

[write-in boxes]

Source: Office for National Statistics licensed under the Open Government Licence v.3.0.
© Crown copyright 2015

Box A.1	Research Problem(s): Categories and Categorisation

- *Think about how you might employ racial, ethnic or even faith-based classifications in your own research.*
- *What steps will you take to avoid imposing false categories on your research subjects and informants?*
- *How will you classify yourself, and what impact will this have on your work?*

Resource 3: Allport's (1954) Scale of Prejudice and Discrimination

Extermination

Physical attack

Discrimination

Avoidance

Antilocution

Box A.2	Research Problem(s): Allport's Continuum

- *How might you incorporate the continuum and the types of questions it prompts into your research?*
- *Even though racism which operates at the lower end may not at first appear serious, the impact of repeated low level racism can be as profound for the victim as a one off violent encounter.*

Resource 4: Ways in Which Majority Groups Keep Control and Hold Power Over Minority Groups

Restrict entry (to main group)

Attach labels

Hold power

Stereotype

Make rules

Exaggerate difference

Define what's normal

Impose values

Impose traditions

(Derived from Clements and Spinks, 2009: 48)

Box A.3

- *In what ways can you think about identifying these techniques and methods which suppress minorities in your own project?*

- *Can you develop interview questions and themes for your research which address these techniques?*

Resource 5: Ethical Guidelines

Ethical Guidelines in Research

British Society of Criminology: Code of Ethics for Researchers:* an edited version is presented below since it is this guide and previous forms of it which guided all three of the case studies in this text. See:

http://www.britsoccrim.org/docs/CodeofEthics.pdf

British Educational Research Association (BERA) Ethical Guidelines

http://www.bera.ac.uk/publications/guidelines/

Statement of Ethical Practice for the British Sociological Association

http://www.britsoc.co.uk/equality/Statement+Ethical+Practice.htm

American Sociological Association Code of Ethics

http://www.asanet.org/about/ethics.cfm

British Psychological Society Code of Ethics and Conduct

http://www.bps.org.uk/system/files/documents/code_of_ethics_and_conduct.pdf
http://www.bps.org.uk/the-society/code-of-conduct/code-of-conduct_home.cfm

---

*Code of Ethics for Researchers in the Field of Criminology

(© British Society of Criminology, February 2006)

The purpose of this Code is to offer some guidance to researchers in the field of criminology in keeping with the aims of the Society to value and promote the highest ethical standards in criminological research. The Code of Practice is intended to promote and support good practice. Members should read the Code in the light of any other Professional Ethical Guidelines or Codes of Practice to which they are subject, including those issued by individual academic institutions and by the ESRC. The guidelines do not provide a prescription for the resolution of choices or dilemmas surrounding professional conduct in specific circumstances. They provide a framework of principles to assist the choices and decisions which have to be made also with regard to the principles, values and interests of all those involved in a particular situation. Membership of the British Society of Criminology is taken to imply acceptance of these general principles and the need to be aware of ethical issues and issues regarding professional conduct that may arise in people's work.

The British Society of Criminology's general principle is that researchers should ensure that research is undertaken to the highest possible methodological standard and the highest quality in order that maximum possible knowledge and benefits accrue to society.

1. General Responsibilities

Researchers in the field of criminology should endeavour to:

i) advance knowledge about criminological issues;
ii) identify and seek to ameliorate factors which restrict the development of their professional competence and integrity;
iii) seek appropriate experience or training to improve their professional competence, and identify and deal with any factors which threaten to restrict their professional integrity;
iv) refrain from laying claim, directly or indirectly, to expertise in areas of criminology which they do not have;
v) take all reasonable steps to ensure that their qualifications, capabilities or views are not misrepresented by others;
vi) correct any misrepresentations and adopt the highest standards in all their professional relationships with institutions and colleagues whatever their status;
vii) respect their various responsibilities as outlined in the rest of this document;
viii) keep up to date with ethical and methodological issues in the field, for example by reading research monographs and participating in training events (see Further Information section below);
ix) check the reliability of their sources of information, in particular when using the internet.

2. Responsibilities of Researchers towards the Discipline of Criminology

Researchers have a general duty to promote the advancement and dissemination of knowledge, to protect intellectual and professional freedom, and therefore to promote a working environment and professional relationships conducive to these. More specifically, researchers should promote free and independent inquiry into criminological matters and unrestricted dissemination of criminological knowledge. As part of this, researchers should endeavour to avoid contractual conditions that limit academic integrity or freedom. Researchers should endeavour to ensure that the methodology employed and the research findings are open for discussion and peer review.

3. Researchers' Responsibilities to Colleagues

Researchers should:

i) recognise fully the contribution to the research of junior colleagues and avoid exploitation of them. (For example, reports and publications emanating from research should follow the convention of listing contributors in alphabetical order unless one has contributed more than the other(s));

ii) actively promote the professional development of research staff by ensuring that staff receive the appropriate training and support and protection in research environments which may jeopardise their physical and/or emotional well-being;

iii) not claim work of others as their own; the use of others' ideas and research materials should be cited at all times, whatever their status and regardless of the status of the ideas or materials (e.g. even if in draft form);

iv) promote equal opportunity in all aspects of their professional work and actively seek to avoid discriminatory behaviour. This includes a moral obligation to challenge stereotypes and negative attitudes based on prejudice. It also includes an obligation to avoid over-generalising on the basis of limited data, and to beware of the dangers of failing to reflect the experience of certain groups, or contributing to the over-researching of certain groups within the population.

4. Researchers' Responsibilities Towards Research Participants

Researchers should:

i) recognise that they have a responsibility to ensure that the physical, social and psychological well-being of an individual participating in research is not adversely affected by participation in the research. Researchers should strive to protect the rights of those they study, their interests, sensitivities and privacy. Researchers should consider carefully the possibility that the research experience may be a disturbing one, particularly for those who are vulnerable by virtue of factors such as age, social status, or powerlessness and should seek to minimise such disturbances. Researchers should also consider whether or not it is appropriate to offer information about support services (e.g. leaflets about relevant self-help groups);

ii) be sympathetic to the constraints on organisations participating in research and not inhibit their functioning by imposing any unnecessary burdens on them;

iii) base research on the freely given informed consent of those studied in all but exceptional circumstances. (Exceptional in this context relates to exceptional importance of the topic rather than difficulty of gaining access.) Informed consent implies a responsibility on the part of the researchers to explain as fully as possible, and in terms meaningful to participants, what the research is about, who is undertaking and financing it, why it is being undertaken, and how any research findings are to be disseminated.

Researchers should also make clear that participants have the right to refuse permission or withdraw from involvement in research whenever and for whatever reason they wish. Participants' consent should be informed, voluntary and continuing, and researchers need to check that this is the case. Research participants have the right to withdraw from the research at any time and for any reason without adverse consequences.

Research participants should be informed about how far they will be afforded anonymity and confidentiality. Researchers should pay special attention to these matters when participation is sought from children, young, or vulnerable people, including consideration of the need for additional consent from an adult responsible for the child at the time participation is sought. It is not considered appropriate to assume that penal and care institutions can give informed consent on research on young people's behalf. The young people themselves must be consulted.

Furthermore, researchers should give regard for issues of child protection and make provision for the disclosure of abuse. Researchers should consider the possibility of discussing research findings with participants and those who are the subject of the research;

iv) where there is a likelihood that identifiable data may be shared with other researchers, the potential uses to which the data might be put should be discussed with research participants. Research participants should be informed if data are likely to be placed in archives, including computer archives. Researchers should not breach the 'duty of confidentiality' and not pass on identifiable data to third parties without participants' consent. Researchers should also note that they should work within the confines of current legislation over such matters as intellectual property (including copyright, trademark, patents), privacy and confidentiality, data protection and human rights. Offers of confidentiality may sometimes be overridden by law: researchers should therefore consider the circumstances in which they might be required to divulge information to legal or other authorities, and make such circumstances clear to participants when seeking their informed consent;

v) researchers should be aware, when conducting research via the Internet, of the particular problems that may arise when engaging in this medium. Researchers should not only be aware of the relevant areas of law in the jurisdictions that they cover but they should also be aware of the rules of conduct of their Internet Service Provider (including JANET – Joint Academic Network). When conducting Internet research, the researcher should be aware of the boundaries between the public and the private domains, and also any legal and cultural differences across jurisdictions. Where research might prejudice the legitimate rights of respondents, researchers should obtain informed consent from them, honour assurances of confidentiality, and ensure the security of data transmission. They should exercise particular care and consideration when engaging with children and vulnerable people in Internet research;

vi) researchers should be aware of the additional difficulties that can occur when undertaking comparative or cross-national research, involving different jurisdictions where codes of practice are likely to differ.

5. Relationships with Sponsors

Researchers should:

i) seek to maintain good relationships with all funding and professional agencies in order to achieve the aim of advancing knowledge about criminological issues and to avoid bringing the wider criminological community into disrepute with these agencies. In particular, researchers should seek to avoid damaging confrontations with funding agencies and the participants of research which may reduce research possibilities for other researchers;

ii) seek to clarify in advance the respective obligations of funders and researchers and their institutions and encourage written agreements wherever possible. They should recognise their obligations to funders whether contractually defined or only the subject of informal or unwritten agreements. They should attempt to complete research projects to the best of their ability within contractual or unwritten agreements. Researchers have a responsibility to notify the sponsor/funder of any proposed departure from the terms of reference;

iii) seek to avoid contractual/financial arrangements which emphasise speed and economy at the expense of good quality research and they should seek to avoid restrictions on their freedom to disseminate research findings. In turn, it is hoped that funding bodies/sponsors will recognise that intellectual and professional freedom is of paramount importance and that they will seek to ensure that the dissemination of research findings is not unnecessarily delayed or obstructed because of considerations unrelated to the quality of the research.

Box A.4	Research Problem(s): Ethical Guides

- There will always be specific ethical issues which your individual project prompts but there are also generic ethical dimensions to social science research as reflected in the professional guidelines outlined above.

- Think about how your project conforms to these ethical standards as well as a consideration of whether you need to undertake an additional risk assessment to protect respondents, organisations and yourself.

- If you are conducting your research in a religious community and suspect that your research activities may cause offence, how would you go about assuaging the fears of members of that community?

- In order to appreciate the experiences of an ethnic minority group you choose to participate in their daily rounds. What potential ethical issues do you see in relation to your own well-being or even safety, and how would you cater for these?

- How would you ensure that your informants did not feel pressurised to consent to take part in your research?

Resource 6: Data Protection Act (1998)

2. THE DATA PROTECTION ACT *1998*

2.4 Special Exemptions covering Research

The new Act provides for various exemptions in respect of the processing of personal data for research purposes, including statistical or historical purposes (see Section 33 of the 1998 Act for full details):

- Personal data collected for research can be re-processed., provided that this is not incompatible with the purpose for which the data was collected (i.e. the purpose described to respondent);
- Personal data can be kept indefinitely, but this should not conflict with the fifth principle of the Act. The MRS Code requires: primary data records to be kept for one year, but this may not be sufficient for certain types of projects, such as panels as de-personalised data is exempt from the Act, survey data which has been anonymised can be kept indefinitely with no restrictions
- The rights of data subjects to request access to the persona data held about them does not apply once any personal identifiers (e.g.name and address, telephone numbers, e mail addresses, reference numbers etc) have been removed from the data. This means that respondents can request a copy of the primary data record (e.g. questionnaire) as long as it contains an identifier, or, any data held by the data controller in other forms (e.g. a database of panel numbers etc). Hence, it is advisable to remove any personal identifiers from the data collected in a survey as soon as is practical.

The processing of the data must be exclusively for research purposes, and the following conditions need to be met:

- The data are not processed to support measures with respect to the particular individuals, and
- The data are not processed in such a way that substantial damage or substantial distress is, or likely to be, caused to any data subject

Where the exemption applies :

- The further processing of personal data will not be incompatible with the purpose(s) for which it was obtained.

Personal data may be kept indefinitely despite the stipulations to: the Fifth Principle (see *2.1* above).

This: exemption will not be lost if the data is disclosed to any person for research purposes only, or to the data subject (or someone acting legitimately on their behalf).

There are other categories of exemption within the 1998 Act and these could apply to certain specific clients or projects. These are in areas such as national security, crime, taxation, health, education, social work, regulatory activity, journalism etc. Full details are listed in the Act.

These exemptions are not a substitute for openness and transparency

Resource 7: Consent Form, Draft Interview Guide and Sample Invitation to Participate

Racist Attacks in Greater Manchester

Draft Interview Guide

The racist attack
- What happened – where, when, moments before?
- Type of attack?
- Your perception of it being a racist attack?

The immediate aftermath
- What happened?
- Support?
- Your perception of the attack?
- Telling (seeking advice or help) – what made you want to tell/report?
- Experiences of telling/reporting?

A little while later
- How often did you think about the attack?
- Did it change your views or behaviour in anyway?
- Telling (seeking advice or help) – what made you want to tell/report?
- Experiences of telling/reporting?

Victim
- What does the term 'victim' mean to you?
- Intersectional factors in relation to 'victim'/'victimhood' status and experience of attack, reporting and recovery, i.e. class, age, faith, gender?
- Did you see yourself as a 'victim' of a racist attack – why and when?

Consent Form

Rationalising Racist Attacks: A Case Study of Greater Manchester

Please tick the appropriate boxes	Yes	No
Taking part		
I have read and understood the project information sheet dated 03.12.2013.	☐	☐
I have been given the opportunity to ask questions about the project.	☐	☐
I agree to take part in the project. Taking part in the project will include being interviewed and audio recorded.	☐	☐
I understand that my taking part is voluntary. I can withdraw from the study at any time and I do not have to give any reasons for why I no longer want to take part.	☐	☐
Use of the information I provide for this project only		
I understand my real name will be anonymised in the research and in any subsequent publications, reports, web pages, and other research outputs. I understand my personal details such as phone number and address will not be revealed to people outside the project.	☐	☐
I understand that my words may be quoted in publications, reports, web pages, and other research outputs.	☐	☐
Use of the information I provide beyond this project		
I understand that other genuine researchers will have access to this data only if they agree to preserve the confidentiality of the information as requested in this form.	☐	☐
I understand that other genuine researchers may use my words in publications, reports, web pages, and other research outputs, only if they agree to preserve the confidentiality of the information as requested in this form.	☐	☐
So we can use the information you provide legally		
I agree to assign the copyright I hold in any materials related to this project to Dr XXXX and Dr XXXX.	☐	☐

_____   _____   _____

Name of participant [printed]   Signature   Date

_____   _____   _____

Researcher [printed]   Signature   Date

Project contact details for further information

Racist Attacks in Greater Manchester

An invitation to take part in a research project

Who we are and what we are doing …
Hello. We are two criminologists from the University of Salford. We are doing a research project which looks at experiences of racist attacks in the Greater Manchester area. In particular, we are interested in whether people decide to report the attack – if so, why, and if not, why not. We would like to interview people about their experiences. This would be in an interview (lasting no longer than 30 minutes), where we would like you to talk about your experience; if you saw yourself as a victim of a racist attack; and, if you went on to report the attack or get some kind of other support.

Do I need to answer all your questions?
No. You do not need to answer every question if you do not want to. In fact, if you change your mind at any time, just let us know and you don't need to carry on with the interview.

Will anyone recognise me or know that I took part?
No. Everything is kept confidential. Your identity will be protected at all times. For example, we will use pseudonyms (i.e. a fake name) for you in all the work. Although for reasons of accuracy, the interviews will be tape-recorded, the recordings will only be used by the researchers and held long enough for transcriptions and detailed notes to be made. After this, all recordings will be destroyed. In the meantime, all material and recordings will be password protected and locked away at a secure location, only known to and accessible by the researchers.

When and where will the interviews take place?
All interviews will be held at a time convenient for yourself, and in places that are comfortable, secure and accessible by us both, maybe a local library or a café – you can even come to the university of you wish.

Contact
If you'd like to take part or for more information, please feel free to contact us:
(details removed in this sample)

Resource 8: Explanatory Letter and Consent Form

A. Explanatory Text

University of Salford

Consent Form:

Religion as Social Control: The Case of Muslim Ex-Offenders

I am conducting research on Muslim ex-offenders. I am investigating how Muslim ex-offenders experience life after prison; whether they experience racism, discrimination or difficulties in finding assistance from organizations. I am also interested in how Muslim ex-offenders practise their religion and how it informs their life. The project is an independent academic study. It is funded by XXXXXXX in XXXXXXX which is a charity interested in research regarding Muslim populations in the UK.

If you decide to take part you will be interviewed by the researcher about your life experiences. The interviews will be audio-recorded with your constent. If you do not wish to be audio recorded the researcher will make notes of the interview which will be shown to you at the end. You will have an opportunity to read what questions will be asked of you before the interview is conducted.

The interview will be confidential and your name will not be revealed to any third party providing you do not divulge any information which reveals participation in a criminal offence or preparation for undertaking a criminal offence. The data will be anonymous in the final report. No personal data will be linked to quotes or audio extracts used.

If you take part in this project your experiences may assist policy makers in providing facilities, programmes and support tailored to the needs of Muslim ex-offenders. Taking part in this project is entirely up to you, and no one will hold it against you if you decide not to do it. If you do take part, you may stop at any time without penalty. In addition, you may˙ ask to have your data withdrawn from the study after the research has been conducted.

If you want to know more about this research project please contact me at:

(Researcher contact details)

This project has been approved by the Ethics Committee at The University of XXXXXXX. Upon request you will get a copy of this consent form.

Sincerely,

(Project manager name.)

ID number _____

B. Consent Statement

I agree to take part in this project. I know what I have to do and that I can stop at any time.

_____   _____

Signature   Date

C. Interview Notes Consent

I have refused audio recording of the interview but consent to note taking of the interview. I have read these notes and confirm they are an accurate record of the interview and consent to them being used in this study.

_____   _____

Signature   Date

D. Audio Recording Consent Addition

I agree to audio recording at _____ on _____.

_____   _____

Signature   Date

I have been told that I have the right to hear the audio record before they are used. I have decided that I:

_____ want to hear the record

_____ do not wart to hear the record

_____   _____

Signature   Date

Box A.5

- *The explanatory letter, consent forms and draft interview guide in Resources 7 and 8 are the very ones used in Case Studies 1 and 2 in Chapter 6 of this text.*

- *They are provided here for you to have an example of the wording and nature of communications to potential research participants.*

- *The consent forms are staged to enable you to obtain informed consent for the project as a whole, consent for interview notes and for audio-recording where appropriate.*

- *Each project will have specific consent needs and if you are intending on using photography or video-recording then you need to amend and make provision accordingly.*

Resource 9: Example of Questions for Qualitative Interview Schedules Relevant to Race Research

- Could you please describe to me incidents where you feel you have been the subject of racial discrimination?
- Have you ever formally reported being the victim of racism? If so, could you tell me about how you went about doing this and what reaction you received from whomever you reported it to?
- Have you ever reported being the victim of racism to the police? If so, could you please describe this experience to me?
- If you have experienced racism but not formally reported it, could you please explain to me the reasons and factors which influenced your decision not to report?
- Please describe what you understand by the term 'racism'? (or could substitute 'Islamophobia' 'Anti-Semitism' 'Xenophobia', etc.)
- Please describe what you understand by the term 'institutional racism'?
- Do you think you have been treated fairly and without racial prejudice by your employer/fellow employees/clients/customers?
- Please describe to me the ways in which you feel others have acted in a racially discriminatory manner towards you?
- What strategies and behaviours have you adopted to avoid becoming a victim of racism?
- How important is racial identity to you?
- In what ways does your faith identity impact upon your day-to-day life?
- Please describe to me what you understand by the term 'racial hatred'?
- In what ways do you think that the intersection of your gender/faith/class/age and ethnicity have contributed to any racial discrimination you have experienced?
- How effective do you feel formal anti-racist policies are when it comes to preventing racism?

Box A.6	Research Problem: Qualitative Interview Encounters

- *The questions above should serve as a very basic guide since your own project will have very specific aims and objectives which will be reflected in your interview questions.*

- It is also important to stress that by adopting the qualitative lens that we have advocated throughout this text there is an emphasis upon allowing the respondent's own voice to be captured. Hence the questions are merely indicators or a path down which your conversations may travel. You should develop an approach which permits respondents to give as full a response as possible without feeling a need that you must follow all of the questions in any given schedule chronologically.

- Rapport: you need to develop phrases and techniques which will enable a respondent to talk freely and openly to you.

- Leading questions: avoid indicating your opinion or position on a topic.

- Flooding out and off-topic: having good rapport with the respondent may provide you with a whole flood of information, you need to enable this but also be aware of bringing the discussions back on track.

- Gaffes and faux pas: we may well misunderstand any social situation, particularly if it is unfamiliar, part of the role of the reflexive researcher is to learn when this has happened and to try to prevent it in future exchanges.

Resource 10: Fieldnote Extract

'There was a heavy police presence, there were four TAG units parked on **** Avenue and numerous police motorcycles and officers on foot. Barriers were in place on the side roads but traffic was being allowed to travel along **** Road. Police cones marked out 'no-parking' zones all along the main road and in the adjoining side streets. There was a vast volume of cars clogging the street and pedestrians clogging the pavements. We arrived at the restaurant and it was extremely busy. I was eventually seated with my friends (personal friends mainly from ****) and I sat next to the window and observed what was going on outside. There was a continuous flow of people, predominantly Asian males, but a significant percentage of Asian females walking past the window. I recognised a group of lads from my hometown; they walked past the window three times in a matter of minutes. There was a continuous passage of cars, music was blaring out from many of them. There were numerous police officers on foot mingling with the crowds. Cars were getting tickets for being illegally parked. I saw a white limousine drive slowly past, Asian males rolled the windows down and waved and shouted to the crowds. A white Ford Escort cabriolet drove past, with two Asian females, they had the roof down despite the cold weather. Numerous vehicles has the Bangladeshi or Pakistani flag draped over the bonnet or on poles attached to various parts of the car. Other cars also had 'Eid Mubarak' sprayed in fake snow on the side. Many drove recklessly or quickly with horns blaring'

(Fieldnotes, 1998: Adapted from Quraishi, 2005: 79)

Box A.7

- *The above example is a raw extract, taken from handwritten notes in the field.*
- *The note forms part of a larger research diary which helped the researcher locate the fieldwork within time-frames and to contextualise the interviews and social environment in which the research was undertaken.*
- *The note is not drafted in eloquent English or perfect grammar, this is missing the point and function of the note.*
- *The note was written immediately after the event was witnessed so that the incidents were captured as they appeared to the researcher.*
- *In your own project, think about how and when it would be appropriate to commit your observations and experiences to fieldnotes.*
- *Think about supplementing these notes with audio or visual records from the field.*

Resource 11: Hate Crime Operational Guidance (College of Policing, 2014)

Title	Definition	Included Subjects
Hate Motivation	Hate crimes and incidents are taken to mean any crime or incident where the perpetrator's hostility or prejudice against an identifiable group of people is a factor in determining who is victimised.	This is a broad and inclusive definition. A victim does not have to be a member of the group. In fact, anyone could be a victim of a hate crime.
Hate Incident	Any non-crime incident which is perceived, by the victim or any other person, to be motivated by a hostility or prejudice based on a person's race or perceived race, or	Any racial group or ethnic background or national origin, including countries within the UK, and Gypsy and Traveller groups.
	Any non-crime incident which is perceived, by the victim or any other person, to be motivated by a hostility or prejudice based on a person's religion or perceived religion, or	Any religious group, including those who have no faith.
	Any non-crime incident which is perceived, by the victim or any other person, to be motivated by a hostility or prejudice based on a person's sexual orientation or perceived sexual orientation, or	Any person's sexual orientation.
	Any non-crime incident which is perceived, by the victim or any other person, to be motivated by a hostility or prejudice based on a person's disability or perceived disability, or	Any disability including physical disability, learning disability and mental health.
	Any non-crime incident which is perceived, by the victim or any other person, to be motivated by a hostility or prejudice against a person who is transgender or perceived to be transgender.	People who are transsexual, transgender, transvestite and those who hold a gender recognition certificate under the Gender Recognition Act 2004.

(Continued)

Title	Definition	Included Subjects
Hate Crimes	A hate crime is any criminal offence which is perceived, by the victim or any other person, to be motivated by a hostility or prejudice based on a person's race or perceived race, or Any criminal offence which is perceived, by the victim or any other person, to be motivated by a hostility or prejudice based on a person's religion or perceived religion, or Any criminal offence which is perceived, by the victim or any other person, to be motivated by a hostility or prejudice based on a person's sexual orientation or perceived sexual orientation, or Any criminal offence which is perceived, by the victim or any other person, to be motivated by a hostility or prejudice based on a person's disability or perceived disability, or Any criminal offence which is perceived, by the victim or any other person, to be motivated by a hostility or prejudice against a person who is transgender or perceived to be transgender.	Any racial group or ethnic background or national origin, including countries within the UK, and Gypsy and Traveller groups. Any religious group, including those who have no faith. Any person's sexual orientation. Any disability, including physical disability, learning disability and mental health. People who are transsexual, transgender, transvestite and those who hold a gender recognition certificate under the Gender Recognition Act 2004.
Hate Crime Prosecution	A hate crime prosecution is any hate crime which has been charged in the aggravated form or where the prosecutor has assessed that there is sufficient evidence of the hostility element to be put before the court when the offender is sentenced.	

REFERENCES

Afshar, H., Franks, M., Maynard, M.A. and Wray, S. (2002) 'Issues of ethnicity in researching older women', *ESRC Growing Older Programme Newsletter*, 4: 8–9.

Alexander, C. (2000) *The Asian Gang: Ethnicity, Identity, Masculinity*. Oxford: Berg.

All Faiths for One Race (1978) *Talking Blues*. London: AFFOR.

Allen, C. and Nielsen, J.S. (2002) *Summary Report on Islamophobia in the EU after 11 September 2001*. Vienna: European Monitoring Centre on Racism and Xenophobia.

Allport, G. (1954) *The Nature of Prejudice*. New York: Addison-Wesley.

Ansari, H. and Farid, H. (2012) *From the Far Right to the Mainstream: Islamophobia in Party Politics and the Media*. Chicago: University of Chicago Press.

Anthias, F. and Lloyd, C. (eds) (2002) *Rethinking Anti-racisms: From Theory to Practice*. London: Routledge.

Ashworth, A. (2004) 'Social control and anti-social behaviour: The subversion of human rights', *Law Quarterly Review*, 120: 263–91.

Athwal, H., Bourne, J. and Wood, R. (2010) *Racial Violence: The Buried Issue*. Institute of Race Relations Briefing Paper No. 6, June. London: Institute of Race Relations.

Atkinson, J.M. (1978) *Discovering Suicide: Studies in the Social Organisation of Sudden Death*. London: Macmillan.

Atkinson, P. (1992) *Understanding Ethnographic Texts*. London: Sage.

Augoustinos, M. and Every, D. (2007) 'The language of race and prejudice: A discussion of denial, reason and liberal practical politics', *Journal of Language and Social Psychology*, 26 (2): 123–41.

Aye Maung, N. and Mirrlees-Black, C. (1994) *Racially Motivated Crime: A British Crime Survey Analysis*. Home Office Research and Planning Unit Paper 82. London: HMSO.

Back, L. (1996) *New Ethnicities and Urban Culture*. New York: UCLP and St. Martin's Press.

Back, L. (2000) 'Voices of hate, sounds of hybridity: Black music and the complexities of racism', *Black Music Research Journal*, 20 (2): 127–49.

Back, L. and Solomos, J. (eds) (2000) *Theories of Race and Racism: A Reader*. London and New York: Routledge.

Back, L., Crabbe, T. and Solomos, J. (2001) *The Changing Face of Football: Racism, Identity and Multiculture in the English Game*. Oxford and New York: Berg.

Bainbridge, P. and Thompson, D. (2010) ' "Racist" powder attacks closed hospital A&E and police station', *Manchester Evening News*, 3 August. http://menmedia.co.uk/manchestereveningnews/news/crime/s/1312819_racist_powder_attacks_closed_hospital_ae_and_police_station.

Ballard, R. (2002) 'The South Asian presence in Britain and its transnational connections', in Singh, H. and Vertovec, S. (eds) *Culture and Economy in the Indian Diaspora*. London: Routledge.

Banaji, D.R. (1933) *Slavery in British India*, 2nd edn. Bombay: Taraporevala, Sons and Co.

Banton, M. (1977) *The Idea of Race*. London: Tavistock Press.

Barry, B. (2011) *Culture and Equality: An Egalitarian Critique of Multi-culturalism*. Cambridge: Polity.

Becker, H.S. (1963) *Outsiders: Studies in the Sociology of Deviance*. New York: The Free Press.

Becker, H.S. (1967) 'Whose side are we on?', *Social Problems*, 14 (3): 239–47.

Beckford, J.A., Joly, D. and Khosrokhavar, F. (2005) *Muslims in Prison: Challenge and Change in Britain and France*. Basingstoke and New York: Palgrave Macmillan.

Bell, K., Jarman, N. and Lefebvre, T. (2004) *Migrant Workers in Northern Ireland*. Belfast: Institute for Conflict Research.

Bell, M. (2008) *Racism and Equality in the European Union*. Oxford: Oxford University Press.

Berger, P.L. and Luckmann, T. (1966) *The Social Construction of Reality*. Garden City, NY: Anchor Books.

Bhavnani, K.-K. and Davis, A.Y. (2000) 'Women in prison: A three nation study', in Twine, F.W. and Warren, J. (eds) *Racing Research, Researching Race: Methodological and Ethical Dilemmas in Critical Race Studies*. London: Routledge.

Bhopal, R. (2007) 'The beautiful skull and Blumenbach's errors: The birth of the scientific concept of race', *British Medical Journal*, 335: 1308–309.

Bignell, J. (2002) *Media Semiotics: An Introduction*. Manchester: Manchester University Press.

Bjorgo, T. (1993) 'Terrorist violence against immigrants and refugees in Scandinavia: Patterns and motives', in Bjorgo, T. and Witte, R. (eds) *Racist Violence in Europe*. London: St. Martin's Press.

Blee, K.M. (2000) 'White on white: Interviewing women in U.S. white supremacists groups', in Twine, F.W. and Warren, J.W. (eds) *Racing Research, Researching Race: Methodological Dilemmas in Critical Race Studies*. New York: New York University Press.

Blumenbach, J.F. (1969 [1775, 1795]) *On the Natural Varieties of Mankind*. New York: Bergman.

Blumer, H. (1954) 'What is wrong with social theory?', *American Sociological Review*, 19: 146–58.

Blumer, H. (1969) *Symbolic Interactionism: Perspective and Method*. Englewood Cliffs, NJ: Prentice-Hall.

Bolton, Jr., K. and Feagin, J.R. (2004) *Black in Blue: African-American Police Officers and Racism*. New York: Routledge.

Bolton News (2010) 'Racist yob jailed for attack on bus driver', 8 October. http://www.theboltonnews.co.uk/news/4670336.Racist_yob_jailed_for_attack_on_bus_driver/.

Bolton News (2011) 'Racist abuse drunks confronted students', 16 July. http://www.theboltonnews.co.uk/news/9143866.Racist_abuse_drunks_confronted_students/.

Bonnett, A. (2000) *Anti-racism*. London: Routledge.

Bottoms, A.E. and Wiles, P. (2002) 'Environmental criminology', in Maguire, M., Morgan, R. and Reiner, R. (eds) *The Oxford Handbook of Criminology*. Oxford: Oxford University Press.

Bourne, S. (2005) *Black in the British Frame: The Black Experience in British Film and Television*. London: Bloomsbury and Continuum Studies in Film.

Bowling, B. (1996) 'The emergence of violent racism as a public issue in Britain, 1945–81', in Panayi, P. (ed.) *Racial Violence in Britain in the 19th and 20th Century*. Leicester: Leicester University Press.

Bowling, B. (1999) *Violent Racism: Victimisation, Policing and Social Context*, rev. edn. Oxford: Oxford University Press.

Bowling, B. and Phillips, C. (2002) *Racism, Crime and Justice*. Harlow: Longman.

Brah, A. and Phoenix, A. (2004) 'Ain't I a woman? Revisiting intersectionality', *Journal of International Women's Studies*, 5 (3): 75–86.

British Society of Criminology (2003) 'Code of research ethics'. http://www.britsoccrim. org/codeofethics.htm. Accessed 29 November 2010.

British Sociological Association (1998) 'Statement of ethical practice'. http://www.britsoc. org.uk/ethgu2.html. Accessed 10 September 2010.

Brown, M.K. (2001) *Mama Lola: A Vodou Priestess in Brooklyn*. Berkeley, Los Angeles and London: University of California Press.

Bryman, A. (2004) *Social Research Methods*, 2nd edn. Oxford: Oxford University Press.

Bryman, A. (2012) *Social Research Methods*. Oxford: Oxford University Press.

Bulmer, M. (1984) *The Chicago School of Sociology: Institutionalization, Diversity, and the Rise of Sociological Research*. Chicago: University of Chicago Press.

Bulmer, M. and Solomos, J. (eds) (2004) *Researching Race and Racism*. London: Routledge.

Burleigh, M. and Wipperman, W. (2008) 'The racial state', in Bulmer, M. and Solomos, J. (eds) *Racism*. Oxford: Oxford University Press.

Burman, M. (2012) 'Immigrant women facing male partner violence: Gender race and power in Swedish alien and criminal law', *feminists@law*, 2 (1).

Butt, J. and O'Neil, A. (2004) ' "Let's move on" ', *Black and Minority Ethnic Older People's Views on Research Findings*. York: Joseph Rowntree Foundation.

Byron, J. (2003) *Slavery Metaphors in Early Judaism and Pauline Christianity*. Tübingen: Mohr Siebeck.

Calverly, A., Bankole, C., Kaur, G., Lewis, S., Raynor, P., Sadeghi, S., Smith, D., Vanstone, M. and Wardak, A. (2004) *Black and Asian Offenders on Probation*. Home Office Research Study 277, Home Office. London: Crown.

Campbell, B. (1993) *Goliath: Britain's Dangerous Places*. London: Methuen.

Cann, R.L., Stoneking, M. and Wilson, A.C. (1987) 'Mitochondrial DNA and human evolution', *Nature*, 325 (6099): 31–6.

Carlile, A. (2012) 'An ethnography of permanent exclusion from school: Revealing and untangling the threads of institutionalised racism', *Race, Ethnicity and Education*, 15 (2): 175–94.

Carmichael, S. and Hamilton, C. (1968) *Black Power: The Politics of Liberation*. Harmondsworth: Penguin.

Cashmore, E. (1996) *Dictionary of Race and Ethnic Relations*, 4th edn. London: Routledge.

Cashmore, E. (2001) 'The experiences of ethnic minority police officers in Britain: Under-recruitment and racial profiling in a performance culture', *Ethnic and Racial Studies*, 24 (4): 642–59.

Castles, S. (2003) 'Towards a sociology of forced migration', *Sociology*, 37 (1): 13–34.

Cavalli-Sforza, L. (2001) *Genes, Peoples and Languages*. London: Penguin.

Chahal, K. (1999) 'The Stephen Lawrence Enquiry report, racist harassment and racist incidents: Changing definitions, clarifying meanings?', *Sociological Research Online*, 4 (1). http://www. socresonline.org.uk/socresonline/4/lawrence/chahal.html. Accessed 2 May 2006.

Chahal, K. (2003) *Racist Harassment Support Projects: Their Role, Impact and Potential*. York: Joseph Rowntree Foundation.

Chahal, K. and Julienne, L. (1999) *We Can't All be White: Racist Victimisation in the UK*. York: Joseph Rowntree Foundation.

Cheliotis, L.K. and Liebling, A. (2006) 'Race matters in British prisons: Towards a research agenda', *British Journal of Criminology*, 46 (2): 286–317.

Christian, H., Hindmarsh, J. and Luff, P. (2010) *Video in Qualitative Research*. London: Sage.

Christmann, K. and Wong, K. (2010) 'Hate crimes victims and hate crime reporting: Some impertinent questions', in Chakrobarti, N. (ed.) *Hate Crime: Concepts, Policy, Future Directions*. Cullompton: Willan, pp. 194–208.

Clancy, A., Hough, M., Aust, R. and Kershaw, C. (2001) *Crime, Policing and Justice: The Experience of Ethnic Minorities: Findings from the 2000 British Crime Survey*. Home Office Research Study 223. London: HMSO.

Clark, T. (2008) ' "We're over-researched here!": Exploring accounts of research fatigue within qualitative research engagements', *Sociology*, 42 (5) : 953–70.

Clayman, S.E. and Gill, V.T. (2004) 'Conversation analysis', in Hardy, M. and Bryman, A. (eds) *Handbook of Data Analysis*. London: Sage.

Clements, P. and Spinks, T. (2009) *The Equal Opportunities Handbook: How to Recognise Diversity, Encourage Fairness and Promote Anti-discriminatory Practice*, 4th edn. London and Philadelphia: Kogan Page.

Cohen, S.P. (1971) *The Indian Army: Its Contribution to the Development of a Nation*. Berkeley: University of California Press.

Cohen, S. (2011) *Folk Devils and Moral Panics: The Creation of the Mods and Rockers*, 3rd edn. London: Routledge.

Cohen, S. and Taylor, L. (1992) *Escape Attempts*. London: Routledge.

Cole, J. (2005) *The New Racism in Europe: A Sicilian Ethnography*. Cambridge: Cambridge University Press.

College of Policing (2014) *Hate Crime Operational Guidance 2014*. Coventry: College of Policing.

Connolly, P. (2002) *'Race' and Racism in Northern Ireland: A Review of the Research Evidence*. Belfast: Office of the First Minister and Deputy First Minister Research Branch.

Connolly, P. and Keenan, M. (2001) *The Hidden Truth: Racist Incident in Northern Ireland*. Belfast: Northern Ireland Statistics Agency.

Cooley, G.H. (1902) *Human Nature and the Social Order*. New York: Scribner's Sons.

Cooper, H. (2014) 'Army's Ban on Some Popular Hairstyles Raises Ire of Black Female Soldiers', April 20, *The New York Times*. www.nytimes.com.

Corbey, R. (1995) 'Ethnographic showcases, 1870–1930', in Pieterse, J. and Parekh, B. (eds) *The Decolonization of Imagination*. London: Zed Books.

Crenshaw, K.W. (1991) 'Mapping the margins: Intersectionality, identity politics and violence against women of color', *Stanford Law Review*, 43 (6): 1241–99.

Crenshaw, K., Gotanda, N., Peller, G. and Thomas, K. (eds) (1995) *Critical Race Theory: The Key Writings that Formed the Movement*. New York: The New Press.

Cripps, T. (1977) *Slow Fade to Black: The Negro in American Film, 1900–1942*. New York: Oxford University Press.

Cuff, E.C. (1994) *Problems of Versions in Everyday Situations*. Washington, DC: University Press of America.

Dadzie, S. (2005) *A Toolkit for Tackling Racism in Schools*. Stoke-on-Trent: Trentham Books.

Daniels, J. and Houghton, V. (1972) 'Jensen, Eysenck and the eclipse of the Galton paradigm', in Richardson, K. and Spears, D. (eds) *Race, Culture and Intelligence*. Harmondsworth: Penguin.

Davis, K. (1951) *The Population of India and Pakistan*. Princeton, NJ: Princeton University Press.

Delgado, R. (2011) 'Rodrigo's reconsideration: Intersectionality and the future of critical race theory', *Iowa Law Review*, 96: 1247–88.

Dennis, A., Philburn, R. and Smith, G. (2013) *Sociologies of Interaction*. Cambridge: Polity.

Desai, P. (1998) 'Spaces of identity, cultures of conflict: The development of new Asian Identities'. PhD dissertation, Goldsmiths' College, University of London, in Bowling, B. and Phillips, C. (eds) *Racism, Crime and Justice*. London: Longman/Pearson.

Dominelli, L. (1997) *Anti-racist Social Work*, 2nd edn. Basingstoke: Macmillan.

Donnan, H. and O'Brien, M. (1998) ' "Because you stick out, you stand out": Perceptions of prejudice among Northern Ireland's Pakistanis', in Hainsworth, P. (ed.) *Divided Society: Ethnic Minorities and Racism in Northern Ireland*. London: Pluto Press.

Doward, J. (2008) 'Muslim gangs are taking control of prison', *The Guardian*, 25 May.

Drake, S.-C. and Cayton, H. (1945) *Black Metropolis: A Study of Negro Life in a Northern City*. Chicago: University of Chicago Press.

DuBois, W.E.B. (1996 [1899]) *The Philadelphia Negro: A Social Study. With a New Introduction by Elijah Anderson. Together with a Special Report on Domestic Service by Isabel Eaton*. Philadelphia: University of Pennsylvania Press.

Duneier, M. (1999) *Sidewalk*. New York: Farrar, Straus and Giroux.

Duneier, M. (2004) 'Three rules I go by in my ethnographic research on race and racism', in Bulmer, M. and Solomos, J. (eds) *Researching Race and Racism*. London: Routledge.

Duneier, M. (2006) 'Voices from the sidewalk: Ethnography and writing race', *Ethnic and Racial Studies*, 29 (3): 543–65.

ECHR (1950) *European Convention on Human Rights*. Strasbourg: Council of Europe.

Egharevba, I. (2001) 'Researching an "other" minority ethnic community: Reflections of a black female researcher on the intersections of race, gender and other power positions on the research process', *International Journal of Social Research Methodology*, 4 (3): 225–41.

El-Hamel, C. (2002) 'Race, slavery and Islam in Maghribi Mediterranean thought: The question of the Hamitic in Morocco', *Journal of North African Studies*, 7 (3): 29–52.

Ellis, M., Wright, R. and Parks, V. (2004) 'Work together, live apart? Geographies of racial and ethnic segregation at home and at work', *Annals of the Association of American Geographers*, 94 (3): 620–37.

Essed, P. (1991) *Understanding Everyday Racism: An Interdisciplinary Theory*. Newbury Park, CA: Sage.

Essed, P. (2004) 'Naming the unnameable: Sense and sensibilities in researching racism', in Bulmer, M. and Solomos, J. (eds) *Researching Race and Racism*. London: Routledge.

EUMC (2001) *Anti-Islamic Reactions within the European Union after the Recent Acts of Terror against the USA: A Collection of the EUMC Country Reports from RAXEN National Focus Points*. 3 October. Vienna: European Monitoring Centre on Racism and Xenophobia.

Eze, E.C. (1997) *Race and the Enlightenment: A Reader*. Oxford: Blackwell.

Fanon, F. (1967) *Black Skin, White Masks*. New York: Grove Press.

Farrington, N., Kilvington, D., Price, J. and Saeed, A. (2012) *Race, Racism and Sports Journalism*. Abingdon: Routledge.

FBI (2008) *Uniform Crime Reporting: Hate Crime Statistics for 2008*. Table 1. Washington, DC: Federal Bureau of Investigation, Department of Justice.

Fekete, L. (2009) *A Suitable Enemy: Racism, Migration and Islamophobia in Europe*. London: Pluto Press.

Fenton, S. (1999) *Ethnicity: Racism, Class and Culture*. London: Macmillan.

Fernandes, N. and Fernandes, K. (1994) *Volunteer Contributions to Social Integration at the Grassroots: An Urban or Pavement Dimension*. Karachi: Urban Resource Centre,

United Nations Volunteer Programme, United Nations Research Institute for Social Development (UNRISD).

Fielding, N. (1982) 'Observational research on the national front', in Bulmer, M. (ed.) *Social Research Ethics*. London: Macmillan.

FitzGerald, M. (1993) *Ethnic Minorities in the Criminal Justice System*. Research Study 20, Royal Commission on Criminal Justice. London: Home Office.

FitzGerald, M. (1997) 'Minorities, crime and criminal justice in Britain', in Marshall, I.H. (ed.) *Minorities, Migrants and Crime: Diversity and Similarity Across Europe and the United States*. London and Thousand Oaks, CA: Sage.

FitzGerald, M. (2001) 'Ethnic minorities & community safety' in Matthews R. and Pitts J. (eds) *Crime Disorder and Community Safety*. London: Routledge.

FitzGerald, M. and Hale, C. (1996) *Ethnic Minorities: Victimisation and Racist Incident: Findings from the 1988 and 1992 British Crime Surveys*. Home Office Research Study 152. London: HMSO.

Ford, R. (2008) 'Prisons watchdog says Belmarsh risks making Muslims more extreme', *The Times*, 15 April.

Frazier, E.F. (1932) *The Negro Family in Chicago*. Chicago: University of Chicago Press.

Fryer, P. (1984) *Staying Power: The History of Black People in Britain*. London: Pluto.

Fuchs, S. (2001) *Against Essentialism: A Theory of Culture and Society*. Cambridge, MA: Harvard University Press.

Gallagher, C.A. (2000) 'White like me? Methods, meaning and manipulation in the field of white studies', in Twine, F.W. and Warren, J.W. (eds) *Racing Research, Researching Race: Methodological Dilemmas in Critical Race Studies*. New York: New York University Press.

Galton, F. (1869) *Hereditary Genius: An Inquiry into its Laws and Consequences*. London: Macmillan.

Garfinkel, H. (1967) *Studies in Ethnomethodology*. Cambridge: Polity.

Garner, S. (2010) *Racisms: An Introduction*. London and Thousand Oaks, CA: Sage.

Garrard, J. (1993) 'The English dilemma: Political custom and latent prejudice', in Strauss, H. and Bergmann, W. (eds) *Hostages of Modernization: Studies on Modern Anti-semitism 1870–1933/39*. Berlin and New York: Walter de Gruyter.

Geertz, C. (1973) *The Interpretation of Cultures*. New York: Basic Books.

Genders, E. and Player, E. (1989) *Race Relations in Prison*. Oxford: Clarendon Press.

Gillborn, D. (1995) *Racism and Anti-racism in Real Schools*. Buckingham: Open University Press.

Gilman, S.L. (2010) 'The racial nose', in Moore, L.J. and Kosut, M. (eds) *The Body Reader: Essential Social and Cultural Readings*. New York and London: New York University Press.

Gilroy, P. (1993) *Small Acts: Thoughts on the Politics of Black Cultures*. London and New York: Serpent's Tail.

Gilroy, P. (2002) *There Ain't No Black in the Union Jack*. London: Routledge.

Glaser, B. and Strauss, A. (1967) *The Discovery of Grounded Theory: Strategies for Qualitative Research*. New York: Aldine de Gruyter.

Glesnec, C. and Peshkin, A. (1992) *Becoming Qualitative Researchers: An Introduction*. White Plains, NY: Longman.

Glover, J. (2009) *Every Night You Cry: The Realities of Having a Parent in Prison*. London: Barnado's.

Gobineau, A. de (1853) *The Inequlity of Human Races* (translation 1915). New York: Howard Fertig.

Godazgar, H. (2007) 'Islamophobia and British terrestrial broadcasting: The case of documentaries on Islam', *Nordic Journal of Religion and Society*, 20 (2): 149–66.

Goffman, E. (1959) *The Presentation of Self in Everyday Life*. London: Anchor Books.

Goffman, E. (1961) *Asylums: Essays on the Social Situation of Mental Patients and Other Inmates*. London: Anchor Books/Doubleday and Co.

Goffman, E. (1963) *Stigma: Notes on the Management of Spoiled Identity*. Englewood Cliffs, NJ: Prentice-Hall.

Goffman, E. (1967) *Interaction Ritual: Essays in Face-to-face Behaviour*. Chicago: Aldine.

Gold, R.L. (1958) 'Roles in sociological field observations', *Social Forces*, 36: 217–23.

Goldberg, D.T. (1993) *Racist Culture*. Oxford: Blackwell.

Goldenberg, S. (2006) 'Islamophobia worse in America now than after 9/11', *The Guardian*, 10 March.

Goldhagen, D.J. (1996) *Hitler's Willing Executioners: Ordinary Germans and the Holocaust*. London: Little Brown.

Goodey, J. (2005) *Victims and Victimology: Research, Policy and Practice*. Harlow: Pearson.

Goodhall, K. (2007) 'Incitement to religious hatred: All talk and no substance?', *Modern Law Review*, 70 (1): 89–113.

Gordon, P. (1990) *Racial Violence and Harassment*. London: Runnymede Trust.

Gordon, P. (1994) 'Racist harassment and violence', in Stanko, E.A. (ed.) *Perspectives on Violence*. London: Howard League.

Gott, C. and Johnston, K. (2002) *The Migrant Population in the UK: Fiscal Effects*. London: Home Office, The Research, Development and Statistics Directorate.

Government Equalities Office (2010) *Equality Act 2010: What Do I Need To Know? A Summary Guide for Public Sector Organisations*. London: Crown.

Grattet, R. and Jenness, V. (2014) 'The reconstitution of law in local settings: Agency, discretion, ambiguity, and a surplus of law in the policing of hate crime', in Larson, E. and Schmidt, P. (eds) *The Law and Society Reader II*. New York and London: New York University Press.

Gray, L. (2011) 'Refugee who fled Pakistan violence is beaten up by young thugs', *Rochdale Observer*, 16 November. http://menmedia.co.uk/rochdaleobserver/news/s/1465126_refugee-who-fled-pakistan-violence-is-beaten-up-by-young-thugs?rss=yes.

Guessous, F., Hopper, N. and Moorthy, U. (2001) 'Religion in prisons 1999 and 2000', *National Statistics Bulletin*, 15/01. London: National Statistics.

Gunaratnam, Y. (2003) *Researching 'Race' and Ethnicity: Methods, Knowledge and Power*. London: Sage.

Gutzmore, C. (1983) 'Capital, "black youth" and crime', *Race and Class*, 2 (2): 13–21.

Halfpenny, P. (1979) 'The analysis of qualitative data', *Sociological Review*, 27: 799–825.

Hall, N. (2013) *Hate Crime*. Abingdon and New York: Routledge.

Hall, S. (2000) *Media Studies: A Reader*. New York: New York University Press.

Hall, S., Critcher, C., Jefferson, T., Clarke, J. and Roberts, B. (1978) *Policing the Crisis: Mugging, the State, and Law and Order*. Basingstoke: Palgrave Macmillan.

Halliday, F. (1999) 'Islamophobia reconsidered', *Ethnic and Racial Studies*, 2 (5): 892–902.

Hammersley, M. and Atkinson, P. (1983) *Ethnography: Principles in Practice*. London: Tavistock.

Hancock, A-M. (2007) 'Intersectionality as a normative and empirical paradigm', *Politics & Gender*, pp. 248–54. doi:10.1017/S1743923X07000062.

Haney Lopez, I. (2006) *White by Law: The Legal Construction of Race*. New York: New York University Press.

Harris, A. (1990) 'Race and essentialism in feminist legal theory', *Stanford Law Review*, 42: 581–616.

Heathcote, T.A. (1974) *The Indian Army: The Garrison of British Imperial India 1822–1922*. Newton Abbot: David and Charles.

Helbling, M.(ed.) (2012) *Islamophobia in the West: Measuring and Explaining Individual Attitudes*. London: Routledge.

Herf, J. (2006) *The Jewish Enemy: Nazi Propaganda During World War II and the Holocaust*. Cambridge, MA: Harvard University Press.

Hesse, B., Rai, D.K., Bennett, C. and McGilchrist, P. (1992) *Beneath the Surface: Racial Harassment*. Aldershot: Avebury.

Hester, S. and Eglin, P. (1997) *Culture in Action: Studies in Membership Categorization Analysis*. Washington, DC: University Press of America.

Hirschi, T. and Stark, R. (1969) 'Hellfire and delinquency', *Social Problems*, 17: 202–13.

HM Government (2008) *Preventing Violent Extremism: A Strategy for Delivery*. HC Deb 3 June 2008, c54-5WS.

Holdaway, S. (1996) *The Racialisation of British Policing*. London: Macmillan.

Home Office (1991) *Census 1991: Small Area Statistics, Greenfield Ward*. Rossendale Collection. London: Crown.

Home Office (2005) *Preventing Extremism Together Working Groups August–October 2005*. London: HMSO.

Home Office (2006) *Home Office Statistical Bulletin 18/06. Offender Management Caseload Statistics 2005*. Reasearch Development and Statistics Directorate (RDS) of the National Offender Management Service (NOMS). London: Crown.

Home Office (2013) *Racist Incidents in England and Wales 2011/12*. London: Home Office.

Hood, R. (1992) *Race and Sentencing*. Oxford: Clarendon Press.

Hughes, D.L. and Dumont, K. (2002) 'Using focus groups to facilitate culturally anchored research', in Revenson, T.A., D'Augelli, A.R., French, S.E., Hughes, D.L., Livert, D., Seidman, E. and Yoshikawa, H. (eds) *Ecological Research to Promote Social Change*. New York: Springer.

Hughes, E.C. (1945) 'Dilemmas and contradictions of status', *American Journal of Sociology*, 50: 353–9.

Human Rights Commission of Pakistan (1997) *Annual Human Rights Report*. Karachi: HRCP Pakistan.

Hunte, J. (1966) *Nigger Hunting in England?* London; West Indian Standing Conference.

Hussain, A. (1996) 'The Karachi riots of December 1986: Crisis of state and civil society in Pakistan', in Das, V. (ed.) *Mirrors of Violence: Communities, Riots and Survivors in South Asia*. Delhi: Oxford University Press.

Hutchby, I. and Wooffitt, R. (2008) *Conversation Analysis*, 2nd edn. Cambridge: Polity.

ICAR (2004) *Media Image, Community Impact: Assessing the Impact of Media and Political Images of Refugees and Asylum Seekers on Community Relations in London*. The Information Centre about Asylum Seekers and Refugees in the UK. http://www.icar.org.uk/pdf/micifullreport.pdf. Accessed 18 September 2014.

Ignatieff, M. (2002) 'Intervention and state failure', *Dissent*, 49 (1): 114–23.

Institute of Race Relations (1987) *Policing Against Black People*. London: Institute of Race Relations.

Ireland, S. (2011) 'Not moving beyond the ASBO', *Justice Journal*, 8 (1): 73–81.

Islam, N. (2000) 'Research as an act of betrayal: Researching race in an Asian community in Los Angeles', in Twine, F.W. and Warren, J.W. (eds) *Racing Research, Researching Race: Methodological Dilemmas in Critical Race Studies.* New York: New York University Press.

IHRC (Islamic Human Rights Commission) (2001) *The Oldham Riots: Discrimination Deprivation and Communal Tension in the United Kingdom.* London: IHRC.

Jarman, N. and Monaghan, R. (2003a) *Racist Harassment in Northern Ireland.* Belfast: Institute for Conflict Research.

Jarman, N. and Monaghan, R. (2003b) *Analysis of Incidents of Racist Incident Recorded by the Police in Northern Ireland.* Belfast: Institute for Conflict Research.

Jay, M. (2009) 'Race-ing through the school day: African American educator's experiences with race and racism in schools', *International Journal of Qualitative Studies in Education,* 22 (6): 671–85.

Jefferson, A.M. and Jensen, S. (eds) (2009) *State Violence and Human Rights: State Officials in the South.* Abingdon and New York: Routledge-Cavendish.

Jenkins, R. (1997) *Rethinking Ethnicity: Arguments and Explorations.* London: Sage.

Katz, J.H. and Moore, K.R. (2013) 'Racism in the workplace: OD practitioner's role in change', in Vogelsang, J., Townsend, M. and Minahan, M. (eds) *Handbook for Strategic HR: Best Practices in Organisational Development from the OD Network.* New York: American Management Association.

Keith, M. (2004) 'Identity and the spaces of authenticity', in Back, L. and Solomos, J. (eds) *Theories of Race and Racism.* London: Routledge.

Kenny, L.D. (2000) 'Doing my homework: The autoethnography of a white teenage girl', in Twine, F.W. and Warren, J.W. (eds) *Racing Research, Researching Race, Methodological Dilemmas in Critical Race Studies.* New York: New York University Press.

Khan, O. (2002) *Perpetrators of Racist Violence and Harassment.* Runnymede Research Report. London: Runnymede Trust.

Klug, B. (2012) 'Islamophobia: a concept comes of age', *Ethnicities,* 12 (5): 665–681.

Knudsen, S.V. (2006) 'Intersectionality: A theoretical inspiration in the analysis of minority cultures and identities in textbooks', in Bruilland, E., Aamotsbakken, B., Knudsen, S.V. and Horsley. M (eds). *Caught in the Web or Lost in the Textbook,* Caen: IARTE. http//www.caen.iufm.fr/colloque_iartem (pdf)/knusden.pdf.

Kool, M., Verboom, D. and Linden, J. (1988) *Squatter Settlements in Pakistan.* Karachi: Vanguard.

Krippendorff, K. (2004) *Content Analysis: An Introduction to its Methodology.* London: Sage.

Kumar, D. (2012) *Islamophobia and the Politics of Empire.* New York: Haymarket Books.

Kundnani, A. (2007) *The End of Tolerance: Racism in the 21st Century.* London: Pluto Press.

Kvale, S. (1996) *Interviews: An Introduction to Qualitative Research Interviewing.* London: Sage.

Lacey, R. (1983) *Aristocrats.* Boston: Little Brown and Company.

Lambropoulos, V. (1993) *The Rise of Eurocentrism: Anatomy of Interpretation.* Princeton, NJ: Princeton University Press.

Law, I. (2010) *Racism and Ethnicity: Global Debates, Dilemmas, Directions.* Harlow: Pearson.

Lawrence, B. (2004) *Real Indians and Others: Mixed-blood Urban Native People and Indigenous Nationhood.* Lincoln: University of Nebraska Press.

Lea, J. (1987) 'Police racism: Some theories and their policy implications', in Mathews, R. and Young, J. (eds) *Confronting Crime.* London: Sage.

Lee-Treweek, G. and Linkogle, S. (2000) *Danger in the Field.* London: Routledge.

Levitt, P. (2003) 'You know that Abraham was really the first immigrant: Religion and transnational migration', *International Migration Review,* 37 (3): 847–73.

Lewis, B. (2003) 'From race and slavery in the Middle East: An historical enquiry', in Reilly, K., Kaufman, S. and Bodino, A. (eds) *Racism a Global Reader*. New York: M.E. Sharpe.

Liamputtong, P. (2010) *Performing Qualitative Cross-cultural Research*. Cambridge: Cambridge University Press.

Liebow, E. (1967) *Tally's Corner: A Study of Negro Streetcorner Men*. Boston: Little, Brown and Co.

Lincoln, Y.S. and Guba, E.G. (1985) *Naturalistic Inquiry*. London: Sage.

Lofland, J., Lofland, L.H., Snow, D.A. and Anderson, L. (2006) *Analyzing Social Settings: A Guide to Qualitative Observation and Analysis*, 4th edn. New York: Wadsworth.

Luhrmann, T.M. (1996) *The Good Parsi: The Fate of a Colonial Elite in a Postcolonial Society*. Cambridge, MA: Harvard University Press.

Macpherson, W. (1999) *The Stephen Lawrence Inquiry, Report of an Inquiry by Sir William Macpherson of Cluny. Advised by Tom Cook, The Right Reverend Dr John Sentamu and Dr Richard Stone*. Cm 4262-1. London: Home Office.

Mahmud, T. (1997) 'Migration, identity and the colonial encounter', *Oregon Law Review*, 76 (3): 633–90.

Mahmud, T. (1999) 'Colonialism and modern constructions of race: A preliminary enquiry', *University of Miami Law Review*, 53 (4): 1219–46.

Malik, K. (1996) *The Meaning of Race*. London: Macmillan.

Malik, S. (2002) *Representing Black Britain: Black and Asian Images on Television*. London: Sage.

Mandel, D. (2001) 'Muslims on the silver screen', *Middle East Quarterly*, Spring: 19–30.

Maney, J.R. Jr (2011) 'Burning', *American University Criminal Law Brief*, 7 (1): 48–56.

Mann, C. and Stewart, F. (2000) *Internet Communication and Qualitative Research: A Handbook for Researchers Online*. London: Sage.

Marranci, G. (2007) 'Living Islam in prison: Faith, ideology and fear'. University of Aberdeen Media Releases, 12 April. http://www.abdn.ac.uk/mediareleases/release.php?id=889. Accessed 3 June 2008.

Marranci, G. (2009) *Faith, Ideology and Fear: Muslim Identities Beyond the Prison Walls*. London and New York: Continuum.

Mason, D. (2000) *Race and Ethnicity in Modern Britain*. Oxford: Oxford University Press.

Massey, D. (1998) 'The spatial construction of youth subcultures', in Skelton, T. and Valentine, G. (eds) *Cool Places: Geographies of Youth Cultures*. London: Routledge.

Mawby, B. and Batta, R. (1980) *Asians and Crime: The Bradford Experience*. Southall: Scope Publications.

May, T., Gyateng, T. and Bateman, T. (2010) *Exploring the Needs of Young Black and Minority Ethnic Offenders and the Provision of Targeted Interventions*. London: Youth Justice Board for England and Wales.

McDermott, K. (1990) 'We have no problem: The experiences of racism in prison', *New Community*, 16 (2): 213–28.

McHall, L. (2005) 'The complexity of intersectionality', *Signs*, 30 (3): 1771–800.

McMaster, N. (2001) *Racism in Europe: 1870–2000*. Basingstoke: Palgrave.

McVeigh, R. (2006) *The Next Stephen Lawrence? Racial Violence and Criminal Justice in Northern Ireland*. Belfast: Northern Ireland Council for Ethnic Minorities.

Meeks, K. (2010) *Driving Whilst Black: Highways, Shopping Malls, Taxi Cabs, Sidewalks: How to Fight Back if You Are a Victim of Racial Profiling*. New York: Broadway Books.

Metropolitan Police Authority (2007) *Counter Terrorism: The London Debate*. London: MPA.

Miles, M.B. and Huberman, A. (1984) *Qualitative Data Analysis: An Expanded Sourcebook*. Thousand Oaks, CA: Sage.

Miles, R. (1982) *Racism and Migrant Labour: A Critical Text*. London: Routledge and Kegan Paul.

Miles, R. (1989) *Racism*. London: Routledge.

Miles, R. and Brown, M. (2003) *Racism*, 2nd edn. London: Routledge.

Mills, C.W. (1997) *The Racial Contract*. Ithaca, NY: Cornell University Press.

Milner, J. (2010) 'Equality law: From protecting "groups" to protection of "all" ', in Wetzel, J. (ed.) *The EU as a Global Player in the Field of Human Rights*. Abingdon: Routledge.

Ministry of Justice (2007) *Children of Offenders Review*. Department for Children, Schools and Families. London: Crown.

Ministry of Justice (2009) *Offender Management Caseload Statistics*. Table 7.25. London: Crown.

Ministry of Justice (2011) 'Population in prison establishment by religious group, June 2012', Table A1.23. *Offender Management Caseload Statistics Annual Tables*. London: Ministry of Justice.

Ministry of Justice (2012) 'Defendants proceeded against in magistrates' courts and found guilty at all courts for acts intended to stir up religious hatred, by police force area, England and Wales, 2007–2011', Table 53112. 26 July. London: Home Office. (Freedom of Information Request: 706693 by Mr R.D. Grillo.)

Ministry of Justice (2013a) *Statistics on Race and the Criminal Justice System*. November. London: Crown.

Ministry of Justice (2013b) *Transforming the CJS: A Strategy and Action Plan to Reform the Criminal Justice System*. Cm 8658. London: Crown/HMSO.

Modood, T. (1998) 'Anti-essentialism, multi-culturalism and the "recognition" of religious groups', *The Journal of Political Philosophy*, 6 (2): 378–99.

Modood, T. (2013) *Multiculturalism*. Cambridge: Polity.

Modood, T., Berthoud, R. with the assistance of Lakey, J., Nazroo, J., Smith, P., Virdee, S. and Beishon, S. (1997) *Ethnic Minorities in Britain: Diversity and Disadvantage*. London: Policy Studies Institute.

Moore, K., Mason, P. and Lewis, J. (2008) *Images of Islam in the UK: The Representation of British Muslims in the National Print News Media 2000–2008*. Cardiff: School of Journalism, University of Cardiff.

Moorhouse, G. (1983) *India Britannica*. London: Paladin.

Morey, P. and Amina, Y. (2011) *Framing Muslims: Stereotyping and Representation after 9/11*. Cambridge, MA and London: Harvard University Press.

Morgan, G. and Poynting, S. (eds) (2012) *Global Islamophobia: Muslims and Moral Panic in the West*. Farnham and Burlington, VT: Ashgate.

Morris, A. (1999) 'Race relations and racism in a racially diverse inner city neighbourhood: A case study of Hillbrow, Johannesburg', *Journal of South African Studies*, 25 (4): 667–94.

Morris, N. (2014) 'Number of Muslims in prison doubles in decade to 12,000', *The Independent*, 28 March.

Mosse, G.L. (1978) *Toward a Final Solution: A History of European Racism*. London: J.M. Dent and Son.

Mosse, G.L. (2000) 'The Jews: Myth and counter-myth', in Back, L. and Solomos, J. (eds) *Theories of Race and Racism: A Reader*. London and New York: Routledge.

Murji, K. and Solomos, J. (eds) (2005) *Racialization: Studies in Theory and Practice*. Oxford: Oxford University Press.

Nash, J. (2008) 'Rethinking intersectionality', *Feminist Review*, 89: 1–1.5.

Nelken, D. (ed.) (1997) *Issues in Comparative Criminology*. Aldershot: Ashgate/Dartmouth.

New Statesman (2011) 'The Prime Minister says that the "Doctrine of State Multiculturalism" has failed', 5 February. http://www.newstatesman.com/blogs/the-staggers/2011/02/terrorism-islam-ideology.

Nigam, S. (1990) 'Disciplining and policing the "criminals by birth", Part 1: The making of a colonial stereotype – the criminal tribes and castes of North India', *The Indian Economic and Social History Review*, 27: 131–64.

Nigosian, S. (1987) *Islam the Way of Submission*. Leighton Buzzard: Crucible Publishing.

Noaks, L. and Wincup, E. (2004) *Criminological Research: Understanding Qualitative Methods*. London: Sage.

Nott, J.C. and Gliddon, G.R. (1854) *Types of Mankind*. Philadelphia: Lippincott

O'Callaghan, R. (2014) *Neoliberal Racism 2: The Rise of UKIP. Post-structural and Critical Thought Research Cluster*. www.politicalhorizons.wordpress.com/2014/05/24/neoliberal-racism-2-the-rise-of-ukip/.

Office for National Statistics (2003a) 'Census April 2001'. London: Crown.

Office for National Statistics (2003b) 'Census April dataset 2001: Religion by ethnicity'. London: Crown.

Omi, M. and Winant, H. (1994) *Racial Formation in the United States: From the 1960s to the 1990s*. New York and London: Routledge.

Owens, A. and Randhawa, G. (2004) ' "It's different from my culture; they're very different": Providing community-based "culturally competent" palliative care for South Asian people in the UK', *Health and Social Care in the Community*, 12 (5): 414–21.

Panayi, P. (1996) *Racial Violence in Britain*, 2nd edn. Leicester/London: Leicester University Press/Pinter.

Park, R.E. (2004 [1950]) 'The nature of race relations', in Back, L. and Solomos, J. (eds) *Theories of Race and Racism*. London: Routledge.

Park, R.E. and Burgess, E.W. (1925) *The City: Suggestions for the Study of Human Nature in the Urban Environment*. Chicago: University of Chicago Press.

Patel, T. (2013) 'Ethnic deviant labels within the 'War on Terror' context: Absolving White deviance', *Ethnicity and Race in a Changing World*, 4 (1): 34–50.

Patel, T.G. and Tyrer, D. (2011) *Race, Crime and Resistance*. London: Sage.

Pathak, S. (2000) *Race Research for the Future: Ethnicity in Education, Training and the Labour Market*. Research Topic Paper 01. London: Department for Education and Employment.

Patrick, J. (1973) *A Glasgow Gang Observed*. London: Eyre Methuen.

Pearson, G. (1983) *Hooligan: A History of Respectable Fears*. London: Palgrave Macmillan.

Peirce, C. (1992) *The Essential Peirce: Selected Philosophical Writings, Vol. 1 (1867–1893)*. Bloomington: Indiana University Press.

Percy, A. (1998) *Ethnicity and Victimisation: Findings from the 1996 British Crime Survey*. Home Office Statistical Bulletin 6/98. London: HMSO.

Perry, B. (2001) *In the Name of Hate: Understanding Hate Crime*. London and New York: Routledge.

Petley, J. and Richardson, R. (eds) (2011) *Pointing the Finger: Islam and Muslims in the UK Media*. Oxford: Oneworld Publications.

Phillips, C. (2005) 'Facing inwards and outwards? Institutional racism, race equality and the role of Black and Asian professional associations', *Criminology and Criminal Justice*, 5 (4): 357–77.

Phillips, C. and Bowling, B. (2003) 'Racism, ethnicity and criminology: Developing minority perspectives', *The British Journal of Criminology*, 43 (2): 269–90.

Pidd, H. (2008) 'Staff unable to handle prison's Muslim gangs says report', *The Guardian*, 26 May.

Pilkington, A. (2003) *Racial Disadvantage and Ethnic Diversity in Britain*. Basingstoke: Palgrave.

Pink, S. (2007) *Doing Visual Ethnography: Images, Media and Representation in Research*. London: Sage.

Pink, S. (2009) *Doing Sensory Ethnography*. London: Sage.

Pittaway, E., Bartolomei, L. and Hugman, R. (2010) 'Stop stealing our stories: The ethics of research with vulnerable groups', *Journal of Human Rights Practice*, 2 (2): 229–51.

Plummer, K. (2001) *Documents of Life 2*. London: Sage.

Poole, E. (2002) *Reporting Islam: Media Representations of British Muslims*. London: I.B. Tauris.

Poole, E. and Richardson, R. (eds) (2006) *Muslims and the News Media*. London: I.B. Tauris.

Puar, J. (2011) *Intersectionality, Assemblage and Affective Politics. June 4, 2014. Katie W. Higgins. A Blog about my research in human geography*.http://katiewrighthiggins.wordpress.com/2014/06/04/puar-j-2011-intersectionality-assemblage-and-affective-politics/.

Quraishi, M. (2005) *Muslims and Crime: A Comparative Study*. Aldershot: Ashgate.

Quraishi, M. (2006) 'Muslims in prison: A barometer for British criminal justice and race relations', in Kühleand, L. and Lomholt, C. (eds) *Straffens Menneskelige Ansigt?: En Antologiom Etik, Retog Religioni Fængslet*. Copenhagen: Forlaget Anis.

Quraishi, M. (2008a) 'The racial construction of urban spaces in Britain and Pakistan', *Asian Journal of Criminology*, 3 (2): 159–71.

Quraishi, M. (2008b) 'Researching Muslim prisoners', *International Journal of Social Research Methodology*, 11 (5): 453–67.

Quraishi, M. (2010a) 'Transnational lives: Experiences of Muslim ex-offenders in the UK'. Paper at International Conference, University of Hokkaido, Slavic Research Centre, Japan, 3–5 December 2010.

Quraishi, M. (2010b) *Religion as Social Control: The Case of Muslim Ex-Offenders*. Final Report to the Islamic Foundation. Markfield: Islamic Foundation.

Quraishi, M. (2013) 'Race, religion and human rights: Valuable lessons from prison', in Cowburn, M., Duggan, M., Robinson, A. and Senior, P. (eds) *Values in Criminology and Community Justice*. Bristol: Policy Press.

Qureshi, Y. (2011) 'Police quiz pupils after boy injured in "race attack" outside Bramhall High School', *Manchester Evening News*, 17 October. http://menmedia.co.uk/manchesterreveningnews/news/s/1461982_police-quiz-pupils-after-boy-injured-in-race-attack-outside-bramhall-high-school.

Ramachandran, G. (2006) 'Intersectionality as Catch 22: Why identity performance demands are neither harmless nor reasonable', *Albany Law Review*, 69: 299–342.

Ratcliffe, P. (2004) *'Race', Ethnicity and Difference: Imagining the Inclusive Society*. Maidenhead: Open University Press.

Ray, B.K., Halseth, G. and Johnson, B. (1997) 'The changing "face" of the suburbs: Issues of ethnicity and residential change in suburban Vancouver', *International Journal of Urban and Regional Research*, 21 (1): 75–99.

Ray, L. and Reed, K. (2005) 'Community, mobility and racism in a semi-rural area: Comparing minority experience in East Kent', *Ethnic and Racial Studies*, 28 (2): 212–34.

Ray, L. and Smith, D. (2004) 'Racist offending, policing and community conflict', *Sociology*, 38 (4): 681–99.

Ray, L., Smith, D. and Wastell, L. (2004) 'Shame, rage and racist violence', *British Journal of Criminology*, 44: 350–368.

Rochdale Observer (2011) 'CCTV stills released following racist attack', 7 June. http://www.rochdaleonline.co.uk/news-features/2/news-headlines/57208/cctv-stills-released-following-racist-attack.

Rogers, S. (2010) 'General Election 2010: What's really happening to immigration?', *The Guardian*, 12 April. http://www.guardian.co.uk/news/datablog/2010/apr/12/general-election-immigration-data.

Runnymede (1997) 'Report on British Muslims and Islamophobia', Professor Gordon Conway, Chair, Runnymede Trust, London.

Runnymede (2012) *Criminal Justice v Racial Justice: Minority Ethnic Overrepresentation in the Criminal Justice System*. London: Runnymede Trust.

Sacks, H. (1992) *Lectures on Conversation, Volumes I and II*. Ed. G. Jefferson with an introduction by E. Schegloff. Oxford: Basil Blackwell.

Saeed, A. (2007) 'Media, racism and Islamophobia: The representation of Islam and Muslims in the media', *Sociology Compass*, 1 (2): 443–62.

Said, E. (1978) *Orientalism*. London: Routledge and Kegan Paul.

Saldana, J. (2000) *The Coding Manual for Qualitative Researchers*, 2nd edn. London: Sage.

Sales, R. (2002) 'The deserving and the undeserving: Refugees, asylum seekers and welfare in Britain', *Critical Social Policy*, 22: 456–78.

Sardar, Z. (1999) 'Development and the locating of Eurocentrism', in Munck, R. and O'Hearne, D. (eds) *Critical Development Theory: Contributions to a New Paradigm*. London: Zed Books.

Sayyid, B. and Abdoolkarim, V. (2010) *Thinking Through Islamophobia: Global Perspectives*. London: Hurst.

Sayyid, S. (2004) 'Slippery people: The immigrant imaginary and the grammar of colours', in Law, I., Phillips, D. and Turney, L. (eds) *Institutional Racism in Higher Education*. Stoke-on-Trent: Trentham Books, pp. 149–60.

Scarman, L. (1981) *The Scarman Report*. London: Home Office.

Scarman, L. (1986) *The Scarman Report*, rev. edn. Harmondsworth: Penguin.

Scheurich, J.J. and Young, M.D. (1997) 'Coloring epistemologies: Are our research epistemologies racially biased?', *Educational Researcher*, 26 (4): 4–16.

Schutz, A. (1945) 'On multiple realities', *Philosophy and Phenomenological Research*, 5 (4): 533–76.

Schutz, A. (1964) *Collected Papers II: Studies in Social Theory*. The Hague: Martinus Nijhoff.

Schutz, A. (1973) *Collected Papers. 1: The Problem of Social Reality*. The Hague: Martinus Nijhoff.

Schwartz, R.M. (1997) *The Curse of Cain: The Violent Legacy of Monotheism*. Chicago: University of Chicago Press.

Seddon, M., Hussain, D. and Malik, N. (2003) *British Muslims: Loyalty and Belonging*. London and Nairobi: The Islamic Foundation and the Citizen Organising Foundation.

Shaheed, F. (1996) 'The Pathan–Muhajir Conflicts, 1985–6: A national perspective', in Das, V. (ed.) *Mirrors of Violence: Communities, Riots and Survivors in South Asia*. Delhi: Oxford University Press.

Shaik, F. (2011) *The New Folk Devils: Muslim Boys and Education in England*. Stoke-on-Trent: Trentham Books.

Shaw, C.R. (1966) *The Jack-Roller: A Delinquent Boy's Own Story*. Chicago: University of Chicago Press.

Shaw, C.R. and McKay, H.D. (1942) *Juvenile Delinquency and Urban Areas*. Chicago: University of Chicago Press.

Sian, K., Law, I. and Sayyid, S. (2012) *The Media and Muslims in the UK*. Leeds: Centre for Ethnicity and Racism Studies, University of Leeds.

Sibbitt, R. (1997) *The Perpetrators of Racial Harassment and Racial Violence*. Home Office Research Study 176. London: Home Office.

Sibley, D. (1995) *Geographies of Exclusion: Society and Difference in the West*. London: Routledge.

Silk, C. and Silk, J. (1990) *Racism and Anti-racism in American Popular Culture: Portrayal of African-Americans in Fiction*. Manchester: Manchester University Press.

Silverman, D. (2001) *Interpreting Qualitative Data: Methods for Analysing Talk, Text and Interaction*. London: Sage.

Silverman, D. (2006) *Interpreting Qualitative Data*, 3rd edn. London: Sage.

Silverman, D. (2010) *Doing Qualitative Research*, 3rd edn. London: Sage.

Sivanandan, A. (1992) 'Racism, 1992', *Race and Class*, 30 (3): 85–90.

Sivanandan, A. (2006) 'Race, terror and civil society', *Race and Class*, 47 (1): 1–8.

Skellington, R. (1996) *Race in Britain Today*. London: Sage.

Smith, D.J. and Gray, J. (1985) *Police and People in London*. London: Gower.

Smith, S.J. (1989) *The Politics of 'Race' and Residence: Citizenship, Segregation and White Supremacy in Britain*. Cambridge: Polity.

Social Exclusion Unit (2002) *Reducing Re-offending by Ex-prisoners*. London: Cabinet Office.

Sophie Lancaster Foundation (2014) 'Hate crimes'. http://www.sophielancaster foundation.com.

Spalek, B. (2002) *Islam, Crime and Criminal Justice*. Cullompton: Willan.

Spalek, B. (2004) 'Muslims in the UK and the criminal justice system', in *Muslims in the UK: Policies for Engaged Citizens*. OSI/EU Monitoring Programme. Hungary, Budapest and New York: Open Society Institute.

Spalek, B. (2005) 'Muslims and the Criminal Justice System', *Muslims in the UK: Policies for Engaged Citizens*. Budapest: Open Society Institute, pp. 253–340.

Spalek, B. (2006) *Crime Victims: Theory, Policy and Practice*. Basingstoke: Palgrave Macmillan.

Spalek, B. (2010) 'Community policing, trust, and Muslim communities in relation to a new terrorism', *Politics & Policy*, 38 (4): 789–815.

Spalek, B. and El-Hassan, S. (2007) 'Muslim converts in prison', *The Howard Journal of Criminal Justice*, 46 (2): 99–114.

Spalek, B. and Imtoual, A. (eds) (2008) *Religion, Spirituality and the Social Sciences: Challenging Marginalisation*. Bristol: Policy Press.

Spalek, B. and Lambert, R. (2007) 'Terrorism, counter-terrorism and Muslim community engagement post 9/11', in Roberts, R. and McMahon, W. (eds) *Social Justice and Criminal Justice*. London: Centre for Crime and Criminal Justice Studies, Kings College.

Spradley, J. (1979) *The Ethnographic Interview*. Belmont, CA: Wadsworth.

Stam, R. and Spence, L. (1983) 'Colonialism, racism and representation', *Screen*, 24 (2): 2–20.

Stanko, E. (1990) *Everyday Violence: How Women and Men Experience Everyday Sexual and Physical Danger*. London: Pandora.

Strauss, A. (1978) *Negotiations: Varieties, Contexts, Processes and Social Order*. London: Jossey-Bass.

Strauss, A. and Corbin, J. (1998) *Basics of Qualitative Research: Techniques and Procedures for Developing Grounded Theory*, 2nd edn. Thousand Oaks, CA: Sage.

Sutherland, E. (1947) *Principles of Criminology*, 4th edn. Philadelphia: J.B. Lippincott.

Suttles, G.D. (1968) *The Social Order of the Slum: Ethnicity and Territory in the Inner City*. Chicago: University of Chicago Press.

Sztompka, P. (1990) 'Conceptual frameworks in comparative enquiry: Divergent or convergent', in Albrow, M. and King, E. (eds) *Globalisation, Knowledge and Society*. London: Sage.

Taylor, S., Singh, M. and Booth, D. (2007) 'Migration, development and inequality: Eastern Punjabi transnationalism', *Global Networks*, 7 (3): 328–47.

The Guardian (2013) 'Ex-EDL leader Tommy Robinson says sorry for causing fear to Muslims', 11 October.

This Is Lancashire (2010) 'Somali driver attacked in cab', 10 January. http://www.thisislancashire.co.uk/news/4829624.Somali_driver_attacked_in_cab/.

Thomas, W.I. and Thomas, D.S. (1928) *The Child in America: Behavior, Problems and Programs*. New York: Knopf.

Thomas, W.I. and Znaniecki, F. (1918) *The Polish Peasant in Europe and America: Monograph of an Immigrant Group*. Chicago: University of Chicago Press.

Thompson, E.T. (ed.) (1939) *Race Relations and the Race Problem: A Definition and an Analysis*. Durham, NC: Duke University Press.

Thompson, K. (1998) *Moral Panics*. London: Routledge.

Thompson, N. (1997) *Anti-discriminatory Practice*, 2nd edn. Basingstoke: Macmillan.

Travis, A. (2007) 'Tenfold rise in terrorism prisoners forecast', *The Guardian*, 8 November.

Travis, A. (2008a) 'Jail staff ailing to counter extremism warns inspector', *The Guardian*, 15 April.

Travis, A. (2008b) 'New plan to tackle violent extremism', *The Guardian*, 3 June.

Twine, F.W. (2000) 'Racial ideologies and racial methodologies', in F.W Twine and J.W. Warren (eds), *Racing Research, Researching Race: Methodological Dilemmas in Critical Race Studies*. New York: New York University Press. pp. 1–34.

Twine, F.W. and Warren, J.W. (eds) (2000) *Racing Research, Researching Race: Methodological Dilemmas in Critical Race Studies*. New York: New York University Press.

United Nations (1948) *Universal Declaration of Human Rights. Adopted and Proclaimed by General Assembly Resolution 217 A (III) of 10 December 1948*. New York: UN.

United Nations (1951) *UN General Assembly, Convention Relating to the Status of Refugees*, 28 July, United Nation, Treaty Series, vol 189, p. 137.

United Nations (2010) *Charter of the United Nations*. New York: UN.

Vanderstaay, S.L. (2005) 'One hundred dollars and a dead man: Ethical decision making in ethnographic fieldwork', *Journal of Contemporary Ethnography*, 34 (4): 371–409.

Van Dijk, T.A. (1991) *Racism and the Press*. London and New York: Routledge.

Vera, H. and Feagin, J.R. (2004) 'The study of racist events', in Bulmer, M. and Solomos, J. (eds) *Researching Race and Racism*. London: Routledge.

Vertovec, S. (1999) 'Conceiving and researching: Transnationalism', *Ethnic and Racial Studies*, 22 (2): 445–62.

Virdee, S. (1995) *Racial Violence and Harassment*. London: Policy Studies Institute.

Voyer, A.M. (2013) *Strangers and Neighbours: Multiculturalism, Conflict and Community in America*. New York: Cambridge University Press.

Wardak, A. (2000) *Social Control and Deviance: A South Asian Community in Scotland*. Aldershot: Ashgate.

Watkinson, D. (2010) '500 protest in Accrington over Koran burn threat', *The Citizen*, 10 September.

Watson, R. (1997) 'The presentation of motive and victim in discourse: The case of murder interrogations', in Travers, M. and Manzo, J.F. (eds) *Law in Action: Ethnomethodological and Conversation Analytic Approaches to Law*. Aldershot: Ashgate.

Weaver, S. (2011) 'Jokes, rhetoric and embodied racism: A rhetorical discourse analysis of the logics of racist jokes on the internet', *Ethnicities*, 11 (4): 413–35.

Weber, M. (1949) *The Methodology of the Social Sciences*. New York: The Free Press.

Weber, M. (1979) *Economy and Society: An Outline of Interpretive Sociology*. Berkeley: University of California Press.

Webster, C. (1994) *Youth Crime, Victimization and Harassment: The Keighley Crime Survey*. Paper in Community Studies No. 7. Bradford: Centre for Research, Department of Applied and Community Studies, Bradford and Ilkley Community College.

Webster, C. (1997a) *Local Heroes: Racial Violence among Asian and White Young People*. Leicester: Leicester University Press.

Webster, C. (1997b) 'The construction of British Asian criminality', *International Journal of the Sociology of Law*, 25 (1): 65–86.

Webster, C. (2007) *Understanding Race and Crime*. Maidenhead: Open University Press.

Wieder, L. (1974) 'Telling the code', in Turner, R. (ed.) *Ethnomethodology*. Harmondsworth: Penguin.

Williams, D.R., Neighbors, H.W. and Jackson, J.S. (2002) 'Racial/ethnic discrimination and health: Findings from community studies', *American Journal of Public Health*, 93 (2): 200–8.

Wilson, A.C. and Cann, R.L. (1992) 'The recent African genesis of humans', *Scientific American*, April.

Witte, R. (1996) *Racist Violence and the State: A Comparative Analysis of Britain, France and the Netherlands*. London: Longman.

Wolfe, L. and Copeland, L. (1994) 'Violence against women as bias-motivated crime: Defining the issues in the USA' in M. Davies (ed.) *Women and Violence*. London: Zed Books.

Wolpe, H. (1990) *Race, Class and the Apartheid State*. Trenton, NJ: Africa World Press/UNESCO.

Yang, A.A. (ed.) (1985) *Crime and Criminality in British India*. Tucson: University of Arizona Press.

Young, A.A. (2004) 'Experiences in ethnographic interviewing about race: The inside and outside of it', in Bulmer, M. and Solomos, J. (eds) *Researching Race and Racism*. London: Routledge.

Yuval-Davis, N. (2006) 'Human/women's rights and feminist transversal politics', in M. M. Ferree and A. M. Tripp (eds) *Transnational Feminisms: Women's Global Activism and Human Rights*. New York: New York University Press.

Žižek, S. (1989) *The Sublime Object of Ideology*. London: Verso.

Zuni-Cruz, C. (2001) 'Tribal law as indigenous social reality and separate consciousness: [Re] incorporating tribal customs and traditions into tribal law', *Tribal Law Journal*, January. http://tlj.unm.edu/tribal-law-journal/articles/volume_1/zuni_cruz/index.php. Accessed 18 September 2014.

INDEX

Note: Page numbers in *italic* refer to case studies.